CRICKET
IN
MANY LANDS

CRICKET
IN
MANY LANDS

Tony Lewis

Hodder & Stoughton
LONDON SYDNEY AUCKLAND TORONTO

British Library Cataloguing-in-Publication Data

Lewis, Tony
    Cricket in many lands.
    I. Title
    796.35809

    ISBN 0-340-50889-2

First published in Great Britain in 1991

Published by Hodder and Stoughton,
a division of Hodder and Stoughton Ltd,
Mill Road, Dunton Green, Sevenoaks, Kent TN13 2YA.
Editorial Office: 47 Bedford Square, London WC1B 3DP.

Photoset by Rowland Phototypesetting Ltd, Bury St Edmunds, Suffolk

Printed in Great Britain by Butler and Tanner Ltd,
Frome and London

Dedicated to
WILFRED WOOLLER
Player, Captain, Secretary, President
of Glamorgan C.C.C., 1938 to the present

Author's acknowledgements

Most of the articles reproduced in this book were first published in the Sunday Telegraph who appointed me their cricket correspondent in April 1975. I am grateful to the Editor of that paper, and to the Editors of the other newspapers and journals who are credited in the text, for allowing me to reproduce them in this book.

I should add that, while most of the articles are reprinted as they were originally published, I have felt at liberty to make small changes – whether for emphasis or to clarify a point of information that may have become dimmed by the passing years, or even punctuation. In no case, however, have I made major changes to the sense or style of the original. What I hope is that, by reproducing the articles in the chronological order in which they were written, some feeling, some reminder will emerge of how first-class and international cricket has developed in these years.

June 1991   TONY LEWIS

Contents

Note on the endpapers: Larkins (facing Hamesh Anthony) and Gooch batting against the Windward Islands at Warner Park, Basseterre, the capital of St Kitts-Nevis. The island of Nevis is in the background. Original photograph by Patrick Eagar, taken 4 February 1990

Introduction

The English season of 1975 was the first for twenty years which did not involve me as a county player. I played first in 1955 – a couple of matches as a young amateur for Glamorgan against Leicestershire and Warwickshire. I own up to being lbw b Walsh first ball in first-class cricket; I was c Spooner b Hollies in Tom Dollery's last match – just a signpost or two so that you can assess my part in the tide of events.

Come springtime 1975, for the first time for twenty years or more, I was not to be found 'playing-in' a straight-grained bat in Glamorgan's indoor cricket school but, instead, was crouched over a typewriter, tapping away more urgently than I had ever done before. I had been appointed Cricket Correspondent to the Sunday Telegraph newspaper.

At thirty-six, I was weary of county cricket. There was too much of it, day after day, week after week. I was later put on record in a book of sporting quotations of the 1970s as saying – 'I've never been a good professional cricketer . . . I'm bloody marvellous for three days on the trot, very good for another day, but, in terms of concentration, not so hot for the next two or three.'

I could see how many professionals went about their business. Failure mattered little when there was always another innings or another bowl the next day. County cricket was too workaday as far as I was concerned. For all the days fought in shining armour for Glamorgan there were too many days in overalls – la vie en bleus, as the French say it.

In my first piece as the Sunday Telegraph's Cricket Correspondent, in April 1975, I signposted an alternative road for the great summer game:

Brave new world for cricket

The Test and County Cricket Board, which administers first-class cricket in this country, has stretched its pants to ripping point. One foot is cemented in the old order trying to preserve the game's pristine skills in the only full-time professional circuit in the world; the other has been edging forward into the less familiar world of hard entertainment ever since the first one-day competition was sponsored by Gillette in 1963. Lack of income from the game and rising costs is the repeating tale. So just as stately homes have been jazzed up with safari parks and adventure playgrounds which would torment old Capability Brown if he could see them, so county cricket is doing its best to keep smiling even though some fancy cosmetics have been slapped on its face.

Life for the counties is crammed with fund-raising schemes. Last year only three clubs – Leicestershire, Kent and Essex – made profits, and modest ones at that. At this moment the Test and County Cricket Board's chairman, Doug Insole, and its Finance Committee chairman, Edmund King, are completing a report on the financial state of every county club, and will reveal the grisly news during the summer. In 1975 the first-class game will cost £2 million to run, but hopefully, this being an Australian year with four lucrative Test matches ahead, income will exceed that by a little. Yet it is sponsorship which accounts for almost half of the game's income, and over-shadowing all the deliberations at Lord's must be the fear of losing some of the extensive television coverage. Unfortunately, the form of cricket devised for a result in one day is a bastard-ised version of the true art. It places much emphasis on defensive skills – keeping a batsman tied down and waiting for his mistakes. In Test matches played over five days the bowler has to muster the wit and talent to penetrate and take wickets. Only in the three-day County Championship can he work at those skills. Yet even that game has been fitted with a bonus points system to produce an instant climax at the conclusion of the first innings, which comes compulsorily after 100 overs. Experimental laws have been heaped on, many of them intelligently conceived and beneficial, but everyone in the game agrees that too much short-cut cricket is suicidal. Young batsmen develop chancy techniques, and spectators are often ignorant of the game's complexities. The symphonic structure of the old game played by Hobbs and Hammond long ago is disappearing. It has disintegrated into a series of crash-bang overtures. The true intent of cricket needs restating – that one side shall bowl out the other, then go in to bat and try to score more runs. Simplicity itself.

In 1966 a sub-committee was set up under the chairmanship of former MCC tour manager, David Clark. Its terms of reference were 'To examine the future of county cricket in the widest possible terms and, if thought fit, to recommend alternatives in the structure and playing condition of the County Championship'. The committee faced a choice. Either it was satisfied that a wholly professional game was best for British cricket, or it could turn back and seek salvation in the amateur game. It chose to strengthen the professional set-up, and who is to say it was wrong? Professionals nearly always beat part-timers. The exceptions I recall are Yorkshire and Glamorgan being beaten in Gillette Cup ties by Durham and Lincolnshire, and Northamptonshire losing a Benson & Hedges regional game to Oxford University. The Clark Committee concluded that too much cricket is played by full-timers, and that the game might be missing potentially good players. For career reasons some outstanding cricketers have retired prematurely to commit themselves to more lasting work. Edward Craig, the prolific Charterhouse schoolboy who scored more runs at school than Peter May, his famed predecessor, opted for the academic life at Churchill College, Cambridge, after only six matches for Lancashire. The remainder of his first-class cricket was as an undergraduate at Cambridge, 1961–63, and from 93 innings he scored 3,103 runs at an average of 36.08. The large amount of cricket played excludes the part-timer altogether.

In fact, if that committee was to report now, it would also draw attention to the virtual disappearance of players who are professional footballers in the winter and cricketers in the summer. There used always to be about thirty of them. Now the football season has spread, and first loyalties go to the larger pay-packet. The one man I know who has made a stand for cricket by declaring himself unavailable for football until the cricket season is finished is Chris Balderstone, who plays football for Carlisle and cricket for Leicestershire. The show plods on, sometimes with a limp, nine years after that report.

I could argue that there is humour in the game which does not change; if only it could be communicated to audiences on the boundary's edge! Not all players get the message over like Fred Trueman, who once yelled to me before a full Scarborough Festival crowd after I had mis-fielded off his bowling (Fred knowing that my wife and I ran a new-style boutique in those days): 'Ayup! Pick your bluddy feet up, Mary Quant!' But is there a perfect answer for cricket . . . a Utopia in which everyone can play first-class cricket, as indeed they do through a longer season in other countries, club and Test player shoulder to shoulder; where pitches are good; where money problems are under control? Did the 'Dave Clark Five', as the Clark Committee was cynically called by us professionals, take the right turning? What would happen if we turned to amateurism for a solution?

In the crystal ball I see *town* cricket being as important as *county* cricket. Each weekend, Saturday and Sunday, with a national inter-town league, say in three divisions, two of them on a North and South basis to cut down excessive travel. The professional cricketers would play for their town sides in these two-day matches, not more than four professionals to a club. The remainder would be amateurs. This would break down the exclusion of the part-timer, who would have a chance to prove, by bowling out Geoff Boycott, the Sheffield opener, that his standards could be raised by high-quality opposition. One innings per team over two days would be ideal for restoring proper techniques and nurturing further County and Test players. The County Championship I see as consisting of three-day or four-day matches, on Tuesdays, Wednesdays and Thursdays; 16 matches per team, one against each county. This would be much fairer than the current 20 games, which may afford you the luxury of playing against a weak county twice, or, if luck is against you, of facing Andy Roberts of Hampshire in two games instead of one! However, when I look more closely at my crystal, I see no-one playing the county game who would not be free to play for England if chosen! Less cricket, Mr Clark wanted. This way he would have it. Monday and Friday would become free days for the professional, so ending the present chaos of weekend travel. Chaos is hardly too strong a word. The ultimate absurdity was reached by Glamorgan in 1974 when we travelled from South Wales to Buxton, in Derbyshire, for the Sunday match. At two o'clock on the Sunday morning we roused the night porter in the chosen hotel. His first remark – 'You lot ain't booked in 'ere' – we put down to the tetchiness of the insomniac. But within a minute we found ourselves, surrounded by kit-bags and cases, on the public benches in the town centre. An hour later we found beds in another hotel; later that day we threw away a match we were winning. Lack of sleep was no excuse, but neither was it any great help. How the hotel had managed to lose our booking remains a mystery, but it was on that Buxton bench that I determined to campaign to win cricketers a breathing space from the motorway treadmill.

It is a brave revolution that puts one-day cricket in its place irrespective of sponsorship, but just consider the good of cricket and cricketers. If the town and county competitions take place over sixteen weeks, then four whole weeks (not in succession of course) are left for one-day sport. The quarter-finals, semi-finals and final could even be played on Saturdays.

What of the schools, where so much is changing? There is a crying need for better pitches. Former Test selector Jack Bond believes that 'future Test cricketers in this country will come only from public schools, because no-one else has the proper facilities these days and very few care enough'.

Two schools I have visited recently bear this out. Colin Cowdrey took me round his old school, Tonbridge, last summer. The wide expanse of mown grass was inviting; the pitch, plumb and carefully manicured, had the feel of runs and good strokes. Neath Grammar School, now (unpronounceable to most) Dwr-y-Felin Comprehensive School, was where I played my teenage cricket. The school field looked poorly tended. It had been opened up to join the local playing fields. The pitch itself was scarred with white blotches apparently from a wrong dressing administered by someone who did not quite understand. Most people I have met who are connected with comprehensive education agree that team sports decline in such schools if no master interests himself. Off the boys go to the nearest sports centre and practise their archery, table-tennis, swimming and so on. It is a soft option for pupils and staff. Without denigrating those sports, cricket administrators must see the problems clearly and shift the emphasis from schools to local clubs. So they have in part. Four hundred Under-13 teams from clubs have entered this summer's National Cricket Association Competiton. Money must go into the clubs and they must care for the schoolboys.

So let us dream that hard cash will rush into the new world of amateur cricket from sports councils, local sponsorship, club contributions and other schemes, and into the professional game from television, major commercial sponsorship, football pools and Test-match gates. (Let's dream, too, of Test-match cricketers bowling 18 overs an hour. I can hear Tony Greig splutter: 'Is this the Welsh wizard who pleaded with me to slow it down to 12 in Calcutta?')

The game of cricket makes so many people happy. If only those who followed it avidly in the newspapers paid their county club subscription; and if only those who never missed an action-replay on television tossed 10p through the screen, visionaries like I could sit back in deck-chairs and enjoy it all.

Sunday Telegraph, 27 April 1975

1975

Summer prospect

Reviewing the summer of 1975 the editor of the 113th edition of Wisden Cricketers' Almanack began his notes. 'Surely the season of 1975 will go down in the annals of English cricket as one of the best of all time. England did not regain the Ashes, but the presence of the Australians, coupled with the tremendous success of the Prudential World Cup during weeks of glorious sunshine, created new interest and brought back the crowds to the best of all games when the right conditions prevail.'

At home in the Vale of Glamorgan I prepared to write a book on the season. I called it simply A Summer of Cricket.

I have always thought that you get most out of watching cricket by not expecting too much from a match. Sit patiently at the boundary, immerse yourself in the struggle, nod at the good ball, curse the full toss, but most important of all, recognise the moments of excellence when they arrive. They are uplifting, and cannot be forced. Out of the day-long pattern of cricket come the brilliant and the banal in their turn, and like a fine game of chess they should not be contrived before their time.

I therefore viewed the summer of 1975 with suspicion, even quiet cynicism. A 'World' Cup was at hand; cricketers from eight countries flown into England, rushed on to various pitches, to smite seven shades of hell out of each others' bowling in one-day 60-over contests – it was too much of a circus act. Indeed, the whole competition would be all over in a fortnight. Where did that leave the lovers of the patient vigil like me?

Furthermore, it could not be a true World competition without South Africa, one of the most talented cricket nations. Not since objections to their racial policy of apartheid had undermined their cricketing contacts, for reasons of disapproval or impracticability, had they played international cricket. That was last in 1969–70 when the Australians toured.

Yet the cricket purists have had to bow their heads to economic necessity. Commercial sponsorship, not gate money, has preserved first-class cricket in England and the Prudential Assurance Company was the organisation brave enough to bite at the idea of this fortnight's jamboree. Immediately it requested the media to refer to it as The Prudential Cup, not the World Cup; perfectly fair under the terms of sponsorships and especially as the latter was a misnomer. Yet, in the minds and mouths of everyone, this was the first ever cricket 'World Cup' and that above every other prospect made cricket in 1975 a unique experience.

Follow that with a first sight of the Aussie terrors Dennis Lillee and Jeff Thomson, two genuinely fast bowlers who had extracted frightening bounce and speed out of Australian pitches. . . .

Fast bowlers, this small, select breed, are usually lethal when hunting in pairs like Wes Hall and Charlie Griffith, Frank Tyson and Fred Trueman or Brian Statham, Ray Lindwall and Keith Miller. These are among the wonderfully rare sights in cricket. Apart from their runs-up to the wicket, their actions have to be balanced if they are to last and yet they must also pour down the malice which goes to make world-class fast bowling. English cricket therefore had the further prospect of seeing batsmen mustering the last drain of courage to fight them off.

Wesley Hall, back in 1963, when he was a little too fast for any batsman's comfort, bowled out one of Glamorgan's openers with the third ball of the day. I put on my gloves, picked up my bat and just before leaving the dressing-room for the middle glanced around, I suppose, for a gesture of encouragement from one particular senior player, himself a fine player of the 'quicks'. He was due in after me, and there he was in a corner wrapping his false teeth in a handkerchief and sneaking them into his blazer pocket! Yes, every batsman would be all alone when his turn came to step out to face those famous Australian undertakers, Messrs Lillee and Thomson, and it was going to be a rare spectacle for every lover of the game.

What else was there to look forward to? The Australians would tour around many countries, although it must be the first time in their history that Yorkshire have been omitted. The County Championship would go on, the bread and butter of professional cricket in England if you like, fought out over twenty matches for each county, three days to a match. Then the sponsored one-day spectaculars, all linked with television coverage – the Benson & Hedges Cup Competition in the first half of the season, the Gillette Cup in the second, and Sunday after Sunday from April until September the John Player Sunday League, the short game played over 40 overs a side. It was estimated that first-class cricket in 1975 would cost £2 million. Without the sponsors it would perish.

Thus one-day cricket is devised to bring about instant thrills, big hits for those who often cannot comprehend the delicacies of defence, or the vagaries of wickets covered or uncovered, which shape techniques and make the most adaptable players the best. The maiden over bowled short of a length to a defensive field earns applause all round; the bowler who attacks the batsmen by bowling a fuller length to encourage shots and therefore mistakes, and places slip fielders for that very reason, finds his art unwanted in the brave new sponsored world. Bishan Bedi, India's master of slow, flighted spin, sits on the sidelines every Sunday for his county Northamptonshire.

Did not Alec Bedser, Chairman of the England Selectors, declare in a lighthearted way in a small village hall at Lower Hutt up the superb estuary from Wellington in New Zealand, that he did not believe one-day cricket produced the sort of cricketers England required in Test matches. With a pitcher and a striker and most others scattered around, he saw it more like baseball than cricket.

So whereas the media duly banged the drums of welcome to the eight countries who arrived to compete for this unique

Prudential Cup, there were still many lined up with me, who felt that apart from true British rain which could turn everything to farce, the whole contest was just a glossy overture to the four Test matches against Australia; high ideals expressed in the most flimsy romantic form, which would just whet the appetite for the million classical variations on the Aussie-Pommie things to follow.

Unprecedented meetings in London on Friday 6 June told me that I had been a little hasty with my prejudices. They included a royal overture. Briefly, at Buckingham Palace, Her Majesty the Queen, with Prince Philip, Prince Charles and Sir Alec Douglas-Home, welcomed those who were to play a part in this first ever World Cup. There was a massive 'team' photograph before the players and officials moved on to Lord's. Prince Philip was again there to greet them.

It is easy to be uplifted by the sheer romance of an occasion which brings together cricket teams of eight nations in the presence of His Royal Highness the Duke of Edinburgh, President of the MCC, in the famous Long Room at Lord's. And why not? It has never happened before that the very best players from Australia, India, East Africa, New Zealand, Sri Lanka, West Indies, Pakistan and England have congregated under one roof in the company of the members of the MCC Committee, county secretaries and their Presidents, as well as a few former Test players.

There was, back in 1912, a Triangular Tournament held in England, when England, South Africa and Australia played nine Test matches. Yet it was the failure of this ambitious undertaking which ensured that no-one attempted to repeat it. Let me just quote *Wisden*.

The fates fought against the Triangular Tournament. Such a combination of adverse conditions could hardly have been imagined. To begin with, the Australians, who had been allowed to have everything their own way in choosing the time for the first trial of Sir Abe Bailey's ambitious scheme, quarrelled so bitterly among themselves that half their best players were left at home. In the second place, the South

Africans, so far from improving, fell a good way below their form of 1907 and, to crown everything, we had one of the most appalling summers ever known even in England. The result is that the experiment is not likely to be repeated for many years to come – perhaps not in this generation.

Yet from the moment Prince Philip offered his welcome with typical good humour, everyone instinctively realised that this tournament could succeed handsomely if the fine weather held, and if the players honestly accepted the challenge. Their immediate response was encouraging.

Ian Chappell, Australia's captain, assured that his side would fight all the way to win the Cup even though their emotions were pinned more firmly to the retention of the Ashes later in the season. Majid Khan held no doubts that Pakistan, playing under the captaincy of Asif Iqbal this time, were looking forward to doing well. The two minor cricketing countries, East Africa and Sri Lanka, were obviously quiet and guarded. To them it was a moment of pride to be rubbing shoulders with the major Test-playing countries and, for the next fortnight, enjoying equal status. I thought of the lovely old lady who is the groundsman, or rather the groundswoman at Colombo in Sri Lanka. For years she has tended the square; poured on the early-morning water to persuade the baked earth to give a little, and then tugged the roller by a dirty fraying rope for hours into the heat of the morning. Good pitches make good players, and because of that the Sri Lankans will surely achieve full membership of the International Cricket Conference very soon. Yes, the old lady would give a nod of approval to see her 'boys', champagne cocktails in their hands, lording it with the best in the world.

The quality of the East Africans was rather more uncertain. Many people have given endless service to the game in Kenya, Uganda, Tanzania and Zambia though sadly contact with MCC, in a playing sense, was broken in 1970. In fact I was to lead an MCC touring party to East Africa and then on to the Far East but, because MCC had sought to fulfil their traditional commitments with South Africa, political forces leapt at the throats of those who believed sporting contact with a country practising apartheid was beneficial to all. The East Africans refused to entertain MCC and we set off for the Far East instead.

So both these junior teams asked eager questions about limited-over cricket. 'Do we bowl to one side of the stumps to six fielders on that side? Or do we try to bowl straight, wicket to wicket, with five fielders on one side and four on the other? Can we bowl our leg spinner? Would you bowl him early or late?'

Most of the other players had played Tests against each other. Incidentally, Test match cricketers usually have to be dragged to official receptions, like bulls to the market, by the ring through the nose. Yet, for example, even England's Geoff Arnold, who never responds kindly to the chore of sipping cocktails and talking trivia, was seen to be enjoying himself. No-one, however hardened to such occasions, ever lost the feeling that he was in on something new. It was a whirl of perpetual surprises. There was New Zealand's Brian Hastings discussing the runners and riders on the English turf with Lance Gibbs of West Indies, with Sunil Gavaskar looking on; Abid Ali, beaming widely, sporting a new beard, eyes shining with the anticipation of returning to green English wickets where the ball moves off the seam for the medium-pace bowlers. Not much joy for him in India. That was it; everyone popped up out of context. Exhilarating, exciting and, most important for my doubting mind, the sight of old enemies sharpened their taste for the battles renewed.

A Summer of Cricket, 1975

In the dark: Dennis Amiss

Dennis Amiss was awarded a Benefit by Warwickshire in 1975. Because I had been his captain in India, Pakistan and Ceylon in 1972–73 I was asked to contribute to his Benefit brochure. I recalled an incident during that tour.

I was ushered into a darkened room by MCC 'medico' Bernard Thomas. In the half light (because it is practically impossible to shut out the Pakistan sunshine) I picked out the profile of Dennis Amiss prostrate on the bed.

When he is well his pipe slopes out of his mouth at a firm angle of confidence. Now it was a thermometer, limply held between sad lips, which projected weakly. He stared up at the ceiling with fixed glazed eyes, like one of those Westminster Abbey heroes entombed.

'Hell, the Test match begins in a day and a half,' I said. 'How is his temperature, Bernard?'

'Well up,' he replied. 'I've had the doctor. Says "Den" has to stay put for three days. Seems to have picked up some Oriental virus, so he said. He is calling tomorrow.'

That sort of news is not calculated to cheer a touring captain. Out came the thermometer, just making way for an involuntary sigh from England's opening bat.

The eyes closed. 'I'll be all right, Skip,' the man so close to death's door croaks.

'O.K., fight it out, Dennis, but of course you will have to obey the doctor's orders and we shall select the side from fifteen.' These were my parting words.

I strolled down the corridor with Bernard Thomas to his room, saying how weak and ill Dennis looked. Would we leave him behind after the Test and come back for him later? Should we telephone his family who would read about his illness? Should we tell the Press at all?

'Tell no-one,' Bernard chirped firmly. 'Oh, and by the way, captain, choose your side from the whole sixteen.'

I exclaimed, 'So you are trying to sell me one of those "pick up your bed and walk" jobs are you?'

He was . . . and he did. Amiss plays was the decision. Amiss did. Thus, Amiss with iced neckerchief knotted around his throat, cap pulled well down, and sweat-band mopping away the perspiration all day, began his sequence of Pakistan plunder: two hundreds and a 99 on that tour and many more to come.

Dennis Amiss Benefit Brochure, 1975

Defying death: odds shorten

In February 1975 a frightening accident had taken place in New Zealand, during the first Test between New Zealand and England at Auckland. It concerned Ewen Chatfield, on his Test debut, facing the bowling of Peter Lever. (N.B. In the 1980 Code of the Laws of Cricket 'Unfair Play' is Law 42. See page 102ff.)

The last time death was cheated on a first-class cricket field, as Ewen Chatfield thankfully managed this week, I was there, just a few yards away, standing at gully.

In the summer of 1971 my Glamorgan team-mate Roger Davis was hit on the side of the head just behind the ear by a ball which Neil Abberley of Warwickshire had whipped off his toes right off the meat of the bat. Before we realised what had happened Roger's body was in violent convulsions; by the time I reached him his face was deep dark blue and contorted; when two doctors arrived he was motionless and within seconds declared lifeless. The next few seconds as mouth-to-mouth resuscitation brought him back to life remain indescribable. In New Zealand this week Peter Lever cried. That tells enough.

When Roger Davis fell everyone in the game all over the world who fielded close to the bat on the leg side fell with him for a moment in the imagination. So it was with Ewen Chatfield. Reverberations raced around the world to everyone who picks up a bat in first-class cricket. 'That could have been me. There but for the grace of God . . .'

Instinctively too, one's mind turns to the great fortune of the MCC side in that no-one was killed last winter facing Thomson or Lillee in Australia. History gives long odds against that happening on the cricket field, but the odds are shortening because these days many more bouncers are bowled.

Only once in twenty years was I hit in the face while batting. I tried to duck under an intended bouncer from Saleem Altaf in a Test match against Pakistan at Hyderabad. As soon as the ball was thumped into the ground I decided to duck under it, but I took my eye off the ball. The bowler did not get the bounce he was looking for and the ball cracked me on the jawbone just

[24]

below the ear. I cursed myself for not obeying the laws of survival. If the ball is going to hit you, watch it hit you, then instinct will ensure you escape. Colin Cowdrey always used to reason – 'If someone tries to kill you by throwing a stone at your head the best way of avoiding the stone is to watch it all the way from his hand. You are more likely to be hit if you duck and take your eye off the ball.'

Against Peter Lever, who is not genuinely fast in the Thomson or Tyson sense, this can reliably be put into action. Exceptional speed, however, can bring involuntary reactions: fear can freeze a batsman for that vital split second and leave him fending off danger in a bad position.

How high will it bounce? I must watch it. How late can I duck? I must be on the back foot, ready. Which way shall I duck? Or shall I hook? If these thoughts scurry through a top-class batsman's head, how much more confusing and dangerous it must be for a tailender who does not possess the skills and reactions.

As Peter Lever immediately lost his appetite for cricket, so the Glamorgan bowlers, after the Roger Davis accident, did not wish to bowl with anyone standing at short square-leg. They said their hands perspired at the thought and sometimes they struggled to grip the ball firmly. The fear passed, as Lever's will, but that is twice in five years that a cricketer has died and lived again on a pitch. I have no fancy remedies.

Captains should not place fielders too close to the bat. Physical courage is very much a part of cricket especially at top level and Test match cricket must be played uncompromisingly for the highest stakes, but a lifeless pitch and low bounce drags in fielders too close for safety.

As far as tail-end batsmen are concerned, like Chatfield, the umpire has a duty to enforce the experimental Law 46, Fair and Unfair Play, if the bowling of bouncers is persistent. The only other observation to make is that tail-enders are much better defenders of their wickets nowadays, no easy touch for the fast bowler. The days which Fred Trueman describes of cowering no. 11s are passing – 'One in t'Adam's apple, one in t'block-'ole an' it's good-day, soonshine'.

Sunday Telegraph, 2 March 1975

England Boycotted

Geoff Boycott ended his Test career in 1981 having scored 8,114 runs,
more than any other England player and challenged only by David Gower
of those still playing in the 1990s. Yet from 1974–77 he refused to play for
England though his selection would have been automatic.

Geoffrey Boycott has long been accepted as the best batsman in
England. His techniques have been built up by a single-
mindedness in pursuit of the craft which has taken him into net-
practice after net-practice in all corners of the cricket world. On
MCC tours, instead of asking about the sights, the profitable
merchandise or the nightlife, Boycott will ask simply for good
net wickets to be put at his disposal and as many bowlers who
care to wear themselves out in sunshine or snow. He has played
65 Test matches for England between 1964 and 1974. Before
this 1975 season he had scored 85 centuries. He is the only
English player ever to average a hundred in a home season.

On 24 May he declared himself unavailable to represent
England this summer, the important summer of World Cup
and Ashes. Yet he will play for Yorkshire. His motives one
minute appear simple and sound, then unsportingly selfish the
next. He issued a statement through Lord's, taking care to do it
before the England captaincy for the Prudential Cup matches
was announced, because his open wish is to lead his country
and he wanted to avoid the conclusion being reached that he
had opted out once Mike Denness had been chosen. His poor
regard for Denness, under whose captaincy he refused to tour
last winter, clouds the argument further, but as far as this day
in May is concerned, Boycott's refusal to wear an England
sweater starts with the following statement:

For the first time in eighteen months, I have basically found
peace and contentment in cricket. I am enjoying the game
and do not want anything to upset the present trend.

I regard my main task as that of leading Yorkshire back to
supremacy and the next two summers are going to be
important ones. There is more to cricket than batting all day

and getting plenty of runs. Now I want to concentrate on developing the future of the game in Yorkshire where I believe I am best appreciated.

Geoff Boycott's last Test match before this decision was against India, in the first home Test of the 1974 season. He withdrew from the remaining games, missed the subsequent series against Pakistan and then the winter tour in Australia. There was still a lingering hope that changes in the selection panel might restore his keenness to play. Ken Barrington, for example, spent a couple of hours talking over the issues with him. Charlie Elliot, an umpire whom Boycott would respect, and Sir Len Hutton, whose experience and skill is legend, were the others recently allied to the Chairman, Alec Bedser. Was it Bedser or Denness, or both, who had raised the hackles?

Boycott's attitude was no surprise; he was simply perpetuating the stalemate which grew up principally out of Denness's succession to Illingworth as England's captain. This came about after the season of 1973 when, first, England struggled to beat New Zealand and then suffered a crushing defeat from the West Indies. Denness had been selected for none of these six Tests, yet was chosen to take the MCC side to the West Indies the following winter, when Illingworth was discarded. To Boycott this was a stinging slap in the face because he had been Illingworth's deputy.

However, that winter Boycott soldiered dutifully under Denness, making no secret of his intolerance of the captain. There was not a glimmer of personal friendship to make the situation work. Denness had been thrust into the uneasy position of having to prove himself as a Test-class batsman as well as a captain. Boycott not only felt personal grievance but also frustration that England were relegating themselves to mediocrity by weak decisions at the top.

Not many would subscribe to the captaincy being handed down to Boycott on the basis of seniority alone, or by the favour of a retiring captain, for Illingworth believed Boycott to be the right man. Had Boycott the personal qualities to attract the players' loyalty? His career has been riddled with tales of selfishness and conceit, two qualities which can upset team-mates, or alternatively live under the roof of single-mindedness and not offend the more tolerant. It would depend on England players spotting the soft, sensitive side of Boycott, behind the front of strong self-opinion.

Back in 1962 when he was new to the game Boycott, the bespectacled civil servant, impressed everyone by his intent to master the art of batsmanship. Within two seasons he was in the England side. Over a period of ten years and 65 Tests he has been striding confidently through county grounds and club-houses, never slow to project himself (whether he realised it or not) as an insatiable run-hunter; and the best player in the country. There was a splendid honesty in this, all the more so because he actually achieved what he set out to do. He was much admired.

Yet perfectionists get hurt and are notoriously hard on those around them, whose standards fall below theirs. Geoff Boycott became a super-player, with an agent to exploit commercial ventures, and a life far less private than was perhaps good for the sensitive young man from Fitzwilliam, in Yorkshire. In a way, his retreat to Yorkshire 'where I believe I am best appreciated', is rather like the scared monkey who retreats to the branches of the tree he loves best. (I would not expect this point to be conceded by Geoff or his supporters.)

There are other theories which to my mind are mistaken. He would not shirk the speed of Dennis Lillee and Jeff Thomson, though he missed ten Tests against them. He is vulnerable against the fastest bowling only by his own high standards of performance. His confidence certainly was not broken by the little Indian left-arm seam bowler, Eknath Solkar, though some suggested that at the time.

Since 1971, Boycott's Yorkshire captaincy has survived dis-putes with committeemen and with senior players. He was on the verge of losing the job in many people's eyes at the close of 1974. That he fought back almost exclusively with young players says much for his leadership. Only a few weeks before the end of this 1975 season Yorkshire were being tipped for the title.

Yet there remains one matter of principle which shatters the playing fraternity. To turn your back on your country is, in the eye of every first-class player in the world, the ultimate treachery. Just consider players in English counties who have spent a career on the fringe of honours, who value the crown and lions and regarded Boycott so highly because he had done magnificently in that sweater. These are the players who now ask whether Geoffrey Boycott should be allowed to play for Yorkshire at all when England have a game and he has refused selection. They would stir the Yorkshire committee too and ask them to consider their responsibility in the matter. Yorkshire accept their share of Test match revenue, they support England – yet their best player does not. Loud voices and arguments echo around the committee rooms of the country.

I have tried to tell the opinions of many, but who knows the truth for certain? A fellow Yorkshireman, Michael Parkinson, put Boycott's case as positively as any, writing in the Sunday Times. He believes the basic premise is that Boycott does not want to play for England because he has no faith in those who run the national team, and no regard for Denness under whom he was asked to play:

Like all perfectionists he is obsessive about his own standards, meticulous in his assessment of other players and to ask him to serve under someone who falls short of his requirements is like asking Field Marshal Montgomery to be a lance-corporal in Fred Karno's army. The important question raised by Geoffrey Boycott's refusal to play for England is not about the man, but about the way the game is run.

The purblind mandarins at Lord's joined at the hip by the majority of cricket commentators, will tut-tut about the bounder Boycott while ignoring the basic fundamental question he has posed. Boycott has challenged the hypocrisy of English cricket and will no doubt pay the price, but unless the lesson is learned the game will be the final loser.

So there is the division and the sadness. Possibly the greatest sadness has reached Boycott himself, who realises that if he had continued as England's opener when fears of ill-health, because he has no spleen, persuaded him to cry off as my vice-captain in India and Pakistan in 1972–73, Mike Denness would not have been selected for that tour at all . . .

Who is to say that Geoff Boycott would have made a good England captain? Or will? Was Mike Denness as bad as the criticism heaped upon him suggested? Briefly, Denness led MCC to a drawn series in West Indies after Ray Illingworth had lost to them at home just months before. He defeated India who had beaten us in two successive series before that, and drew with Pakistan at home. Finally, he lost mainly to the shattering fast bowling of Lillee and Thomson in Australia before defeating New Zealand in a two-match series out there. His 188 in the sixth Test against Australia without Thomson, and virtually without Lillee, proved that speed was the crucial difference between winning and losing; but apart from that it was the highest innings by an England captain in a Test in Australia, exceeding A. E. Stoddart's 173, also in Melbourne, in 1894–95. Criticism of Denness's captaincy has often masked his ability as a batsman.

Whatever Geoff Boycott's initial upset, it has now become an illness; nothing will persuade the patient that he has not taken a blow, or that the cause will be better served on the international field rather than off it. There is a leaden finality about the situation which no-one appears to have the power to lift.

A Summer of Cricket, 1975

Australia v. West Indies

World Cup Final, Lord's, 21 June 1975

As a final this match was all one could ever have hoped for a brave new venture in sponsorship. Two hours before the start, spectators gushed out of the underground station at St John's Wood, queues snaked right around the walls and cars filtered slowly into the park at the Nursery End. A capacity crowd and another hot shirt-sleeved day, completing the meteorological miracle which has blessed every single moment of this competition with blue skies and sunshine.

Ian Chappell won the toss for Australia and sent the opposition in to bat though there was nothing in the air that remotely sniffed of Headingley. Chappell had in mind, more likely, Lloyd's habit of 'inserting' others.

It had been West Indies' formula for victory all through the tournament so now, before a ball had been bowled in anger, perhaps Chappell had snatched away their good luck charm.

Gilmour, scourge of England, was no-balled three times in the first over, making it clear where the strongest West Indian encampment was. Bells rang out alongside the Tavern and flags were waved. The hubbub died down as Fredericks and Greenidge prepared to take on Dennis Lillee.

Fredericks is a compulsive hooker, sometimes a little chancy, especially with the shot that goes down to the fine-leg region. With typical West Indian lavishness he is happy to gamble, just to see the ball sail for six, and will consider himself hard-done-by if a fielder hangs on to a skier on the boundary fence. Well, this time he responded to Lillee's bouncer (one of few in the match) with a mighty swing of the bat. The ball cleared the fielder this time; all eyes followed it, yet there was a trick to the eye which fooled almost everyone. As he spun around in the crease, Fredericks had lost his foothold and slipped against the stumps, dislodging both bails . . . hit wicket, bowled Lillee 7. West Indies 12 for 1. There was a certain amount of bad luck in this dismissal for the batsman, and good fortune for the bowler. It was a well-judged bouncer putting Fredericks under pressure but possibly the crucial factor was that Fredericks was wearing boots with rubber soles. Most professional players would not dream of going into a match which starts as early as eleven o'clock in the morning when some moisture may still be retained in the turf, without spiked footwear.

To a hero's acclaim, out strode Kallicharran to face bowlers who could not have felt too happy about his treatment of them a week before at The Oval. His innings began with the confident ring of the bat, but perhaps he was lured into the trap of over-confidence. To a ball from Gilmour outside the off stump he tried a square cut, a flicked shot, feet out of position, the ball too close and bouncing reasonably high off a smooth slow surface. Marsh accepted the snick behind the wicket. 27 for 2, bringing Kanhai to the crease to join Greenidge.

They were now edging from a defensive corner and there was obvious unevenness of bounce which the height of Max Walker emphasised when he came on to bowl. Frequently he struck the splice of Kanhai's bat. Kanhai got well and truly stuck in a defensive rut and even lost Greenidge, caught low down by Marsh from a slower ball by Thomson.

Then Clive Lloyd loped into the arena wearing cap, spectacles and a quizzical look on his face. How often has he contradicted his studious appearance with thoughts of violence! Lillee was immediately brought back, but in easy, destructive style, the West Indies captain hooked a colossal six; then off the back foot, coaxed Walker through the cover field. To this point Ian Chappell had persevered with two slips and a gully, but the time had come to dream up defensive patterns. Men were despatched to deep positions on the mid-wicket and square-cover boundaries. Edwards dropped him at 26. Meanwhile at the other end, poor Kanhai limped on, eleven overs passing without his scoring a run. Experience told him that as long as Lloyd was plundering on he must persevere. The partnership realised 149 in 36 overs and this was the record stand for the whole competition. Lloyd's hundred came in 82 balls, and if figures alone do not persuade the world that something very special was happening, the inhabitants of London NW8 will tell how the mere sound of his bat, hammering out the music sweet to West Indian ears, destroyed their afternoon sleep!

It was an innings of surpassing talent and power. When Lloyd is at the crease, mid-on and mid-off automatically withdraw ten yards or so. His defensive pushes roast the hands like a lesser man's drives. Although his back foot wanders involuntarily in a small circle as the faster bowlers rush at him, he quickly beds it down on or around middle-and-leg and then levers off it into his strong front-foot attack. There is no shot he cannot play but one or two are not played by any other with the same ease. At his most vicious he 'picked-up' balls from Walker, just a fraction short of good length in line with the middle-and-leg stumps. These he flipped to square-leg off the front foot, and set the ball with a few bounces into the rails, just like sending a flat pebble hopping over a calm sea. Of course his long reach upsets the bowler's length. Without doubt he is one of the most dangerous batsmen in the world because he can change the drift of a match within such a short space of time. Ideal for one-day cricket, and it was yet another stroke of fortune for all who watched that he reserved this great innings for the final.

Gilmour eventually came back with a tight spell of bowling which swung the game marginally back Australia's way. He got rid of Kanhai, Lloyd and Richards – 209 for 6 in the 46th over.

One sadness was that Lloyd's innings should end in argument and confusion. Marsh 'went up' with Gilmour for a catch down the leg side. Gilmour prolonged the appeal, stared expectantly at umpire Bird, even though the adjudicator had turned to stone; but then after conferring with umpire Spencer, Bird gave Lloyd out. Kanhai took off his hat for more than the heat; Lloyd left his verbal mark on the 'middle' and a few missiles entered the arena from the terraces.

However, Australia's grip was promptly cracked open. One of the more unpredictable West Indians decided that the moon was in his quarter that day, and straightaway the bowlers felt the lash of Keith Boyce. Julien supported with Murray and when you think of it, the strength of batting is limitless when you have Deryck Murray, who has opened in Tests, lurking away at number nine. 291 for 8 was the total. To have beaten that would have set a record for the competition.

Just think how close Australia came! They began securely enough even though there is nothing in the styles of either Turner or McCosker to excite the aesthetes. McCosker particularly got turned round to work the ball through mid-wicket and when the score was 25 Boyce produced just the ball to penetrate. It swung away, found the outside edge of the bat and landed safely in the eager fingers of Kallicharan at second slip. It was low and beautifully caught. Turner's authority increased while Ian Chappell quickly showed that he was at his belligerent best. Then came the first of the run-outs. A complete misunderstanding left Turner racing for safety. Only a direct hit would beat him and that is exactly what Richards produced in under-arm style.

The Chappell brothers then put on 34 with mounting certainty until the plague returned – Greg was run out. Ian ran the ball out square on the off side. Greenidge and Richards could not agree over who was to field it. Greenidge relaxed, Richards turned and recovered the ball, then on the pivot he threw down the only stump of three which he could possibly see. Luck was going with the West Indies.

The third run-out was beyond all comprehension, especially as it saw off the captain himself and – would you believe it – Richards again was the destroyer. He first fumbled the ball, persuading Australia to break the golden rule 'Never run for a misfield', then spun around and fired the ball just above the bails like a rifle shot. Lloyd, the bowler, clipped off the bails.

Australia were well in with a chance before this latest casualty because Walters had settled in to play handsomely. Perhaps they misread the situation; the outfield was as fast as glass, they could well win. Or possibly they wanted to hustle before Roberts came back.

Whatever the causes the slide was started. Walker was the fourth man to be run out and Thomson the fifth.

It is often agony at the end of the day to weigh up the mistakes. The turning points, camouflaged then, stand up and mock you. Will Ian Chappell recall his superb innings or the five run-outs when he remembers this day? His side required 130 runs off the last 22 overs – very possible in fine batting conditions; then 76 off 10 overs with four wickets standing. Gilmour skied, Edwards too, but the character of the side came through when Lillee and Thomson embarked on a last-wicket partnership of bravado, surprising judgement and humour too. They came in at 233 and 52.5 overs gone. Within minutes their cutting and carving had West Indian fielders perched on the boundaries conceding the singles. The score mounted; 21 wanted from two overs. It was possible and even more so when Thomson struck a no-ball in the air to Fredericks at cover. Fredericks threw at the bowler's wicket for a run-out; no-one backed up and Lillee and Thomson raced the overthrows. Suddenly the field was full of West Indian spectators who, not hearing the call for no-ball, believed Thomson caught and the match won. It was an incredible sight. Fielders were knocked flying in the avalanche, the ball disappeared altogether, but calmly in midfield Lillee and Thomson ran their runs. Could they run 21 off one ball if the ball was not returned?

'Dead ball' was called by the umpires, 3 runs given. Within a minute Thomson was properly out. He played and missed, the ball went through to Murray. Thomson believed Lillee was going to chance running to the wicket-keeper, but instead he was sent back, and it was a fitting summary of Australia's innings to see Murray throw down the wicket without any trouble at all, while Thomson lay covered in dust, a few inches out. This final gallop by the demon fast bowlers revealed that Australia knew how to lose with humour. A game which begins at 11am and ends at 8.42pm inevitably kills and rekindles hopes by the minute and by the hour; it chars the nerve-ends, bringing, eventually, the delirium of victory for one and that unwelcome stoicism to the other. To the Australians' credit, they charged to their defeat with style and without a single bleat about one-day cricket not being to their liking. Yet as Ian Chappell confessed when asked to comment on the competition, 'Enough is enough' – and I am sure he was right. Meanwhile, none could deny the West Indians the right to wear the first Prudential crown, nor could there be any argument that their captain, Clive Lloyd, was the Man of this unique Match.

A Summer of Cricket, 1975

'J.T.' retires

This summer, on 31 May to be exact, John Murray passed the world record for wicket-keeping dismissals when he caught Dudley Owen-Thomas of Surrey off the bowling of Tim Lamb. This was his 1,494th victim and the record he overtook was held by Herbert Strudwick. In September Murray retired.

As a young lad in North Kensington John Murray turned his hand to many sports and was pleased to have a trial at Lord's as a batsman-cum-bowler. Yet he was playing in the final of a Boys' Club competition when his wicket-keeper broke a finger and 'J.T.' took over. It was still as a batsman that he was taken on the Lord's ground staff in 1950, but Archie Fowler, the head coach, had him 'keeping straightaway, and progress was so fast that two years later he had deputised for the injured Leslie Compton at Leicester. There followed two years in a powerful Royal Air Force side, and at the end of 1955 he took over from Compton, the following year winning his cap. Since then he has been an automatic choice for Middlesex as well as an England Test cricketer twenty-one times.

In that long career, achievements have heaped up and there will be those who recall his century against the West Indies at The Oval in the fifth Test of 1966 with special relish. Never before in Test cricket had the last three wickets produced as much as 361 runs, nor had the last three men scored one hundred and two fifties. 'J.T.' was lbw bowled Sobers 112; Ken Higgs caught and bowled Holford 63; and John Snow not out 59. Though it was Murray's partnership with Graveney that I remember most. (I was twelfth man and pretty close to the action.)

The West Indies were three Tests up, one drawn, and there was nothing to salvage for England save some pride. Tom Graveney had played magnificently through the series and in this Test scored 165. Graveney and Murray at the crease together for hours made the most aesthetically pleasing sight imaginable.

Murray struck me as one of the rare people I had seen who

could make the hooking of a fast bouncer truly elegant. Wes Hall and Charlie Griffith thundered in, but he pivoted with the balance of an ice skater and wafted the ball powerfully away to leg. His drives off the front foot were taken out of the MCC coaching manual, sideways on, left foot right to the pitch of the ball, and the follow-through generous. His wicket-keeping has always been stylish, and there is no doubt that he makes a conscious effort to preserve that feeling in all his movements. As a bowler runs into bowl 'J.T.' is synchronised to touch finger-tips, and raise both hands to the peak of his cap. Then, as he adopts the crouching position, his gloves are meticulously placed together, open for inspection, just touching the floor, his balance like a gymnast's. He always claimed to model his art on the talents of Wally Grout. 'I felt as I watched him,' confessed Murray, 'that here was the perfect pair of hands. I felt I wanted to keep wicket like him. He read the game so well, positionally right, you know, never diving unless he was going for a catch.'

After collecting a ball there comes the daily chore of lobbing it back to the bowler or to a fielder. Murray makes of this one of the miniature delights of physical movement. The body bends slightly to make room for a long, languid swinging arm. He truly cares about such things.

There are very few batsmen who played over the last twenty years who were not, at some time or other, caught Murray bowled Titmus. They were complementary characters. Almost without a sign to each other, Fred could feed 'J.T.'s' stumping skills by firing a ball quickly down the leg side, at almost yorker length. Then there was the drifter, floating away to the slips. 'J.T.' was very much part of the success of Fred Titmus.

On tour he has been a marvellously cheerful companion in spite of the bad luck of being reserve more often than in the Test side. He was blocked mainly by the Selectors' preference for Jim Parks who could bat and also keep wicket, in that order. It is a policy easy to decry now, but 'J.T.' would be the first to point out that Jim did many fine things for England behind the stumps and in front of them.

I recall his humour as the Commonwealth side of 1968 battled with an odd-looking meal in our residence, the Public

Works Department Rest House, Sargodha, in Pakistan. Every waiter or bearer all over the world he called 'George'. Coming in to dinner he saw everyone struggling with the sight and the smell of an unusual looking chicken curry; everyone except John Hampshire that is, who insisted it was good stuff. One sniff was enough for 'J.T.'

'Don't worry, lads,' he said, marching into the kitchen. We could hear his voice slow, deliberate and very London saying, 'Now, George, look here. These are the eggs; you crack 'em open like this . . . and fry them . . . like that. Now don't go away, George, look here. These are the potatoes . . . peel 'em, slice 'em, fry 'em too . . . egg and chips, George. OK, jaldi, jaldi. Oh, and George, every meal the same.'

Johnny Hampshire left the field the next day in much haste, returning two days later about two stone lighter!

John Murray came up the hard way. Young lads on the Lord's ground staff in his day laboured at the very bottom of a strict hierarchy. They sold scorecards, swept stands, bowled to members or pulled the vast heavy roller. Could he have imagined then how his career would end? Lord's packed out, the Gillette Cup Final, Middlesex against Lancashire, and a standing ovation as he made his way for the last time from the Long Room to the middle. The cheers must have been heard in those dark recesses of Lord's where scorecards are churned out on clanking machines, where brooms are kept and boots repaired and, without seeing, all recognised the departure of one of their favourite sons.

Twenty years of endeavour, success and disappointment must have welled up inside him, but perfectly dressed, smartly walking, he raised his bat with certainty and, yes, style, and even as Lancashire were hammering home their victory later in the day, and the prize was lost, 'J.T.' was as ever fingertipping his peak, fingertipping his fingertips . . . crouching . . . waiting . . . his very soul ticking with the rhythm of the wicket-keeping art.

A Summer of Cricket, 1975

Malcolm Nash: mistaken identity

For a long time I have wanted to shout out the truth about Malcolm Nash and the Sobers affair. Six sixes in an over, brilliant hitting without a doubt. But how many people realise even now that Nash was not bowling his usual medium-paced seamers on that day?

During that summer of 1968 he had been keen to try the Underwood style of slow-to-medium-paced spin, which was proving devastating when pitches helped. So he ran in to bowl to Sobers with his fingers wrapped around the seam, not along it. Meantime, at the other end, the great man was thrashing out to set up a declaration. For once, by a miracle, two and two made 36!

How do you console someone who has suddenly leapt rather ignominiously into the record books. 'Don't worry, I'll write a book about it,' chirped Malcolm in the dressing-room. 'They'll even make this one into a film.'

'Yes,' the voice of the professional decreed. 'And call it *Gone with the Wind!*'

It was a spectacular event for cricket, but an unlucky one for Malcolm Nash because, season after season, this very fine seam and swing bowler has been wrongly identified as cricket's fall guy.* He has had to tolerate unfunny comments from the

---

* Nash has taken 993 first-class wickets in his career, 1966–83, at an average of 25.88. He also made 7,129 runs at 17.73, highest score 130.

public benches, yet not complaining nor dragging his feet around in search of cover. Often he will wave, jest, and generally bounce back his replies. He has worn the hair-shirt with immense bravado.

I mention this now because after ten years with Glamorgan there are definite indications that he has matured as an all-rounder who could so easily be considered for England. His two centuries this year were efforts of spectacular hitting, but between them he has applied himself with patience too. Tucked away down the order he could be the lash in the tail which, on good wickets, could help England to get into winning situations – quick runs creating time in which to bowl out the opposition.

Nash's batting was the part of his game which required most effort. Without being afraid of fast bowling he has always laboured with a technical problem which has made him vulnerable. His back foot moved away outside the leg stump involuntarily, making it especially difficult to line up the ball on or around the off stump. During the winter he has worked hard to correct this.

No-one disputes his ability with the new ball. 'One of the most dangerous new ball bowlers in the game,' Mike Denness confirmed when I put the question to him at Worcester last week. The late swing into the pads of the right-handed and, of course, away from the left-handed player, has trapped the world's best batsmen. His pace is little more than a hustle, but this in itself means that the ball is in the air long enough to curve late – the deadliest weapon, and one which Alec Bedser would not be slow to appreciate.

There are things that Nash would have to prove at Test trial level or in representative MCC matches. Is his bowling tight enough on good wickets when the shine and swing are gone? Can he play an innings of responsibility as well as daring? Perhaps more importantly, can a selector like Sir Len Hutton see someone as unlikely as a tall, lean, blond Welshman with a short, gentle run-up to the wicket tread the ground which the ghosts of Lindwall, Miller, Tyson, Statham and Trueman patrol in his mind.

Well, maybe Malcolm Nash will have to spend this summer

persuading those who decide that he has the proper qualities. He certainly merits close inspection. He may fall short, but then again he could be of enormous value against Indian spin next winter – left-handed and a clean striker of the ball. Will the shadow of Sobers move on? Time for the real Malcolm Nash to stand up.

Sunday Telegraph, 16 May 1976

Greig's realistic training

I was interested to hear from the England captain, Tony Greig, how he worked at his batting during the last Test series.

He was lucky perhaps, to be able to see himself bat on television videotape. That surely is the greatest help of all. He greatly respected the West Indian bowling, but based his self-criticism on a tendency to try to hit the ball too hard. Eager not to be dominated by fast bowling, he set his cap too ambitiously at attacking it with the full swing of the bat. Of course, it is always said that a batsman should try to play the ball as late as possible but against Wayne Daniel, Andy Roberts and Michael Holding there appeared from the safety of the Press box to be little choice! However, the England captain went off with his brother Ian to the nets before the Headingley Test, the game in which his form and fortune changed.

At a sharp fast-medium pace Greig junior bowled from 17 yards and dug the occasional one in short. Remember Graham Wiltshire, the Gloucestershire coach, expressed the opinion that the MCC team, before going to Australia in 1974–75, should have done exactly this with lacrosse balls. The Greigs opted for the real thing. 'I wanted to get the feeling of that ball banging on the bat,' said Tony. 'I could feel the pace.'

I asked him whether an England side going into Test matches would benefit from similar practice and he agreed they would. There is nothing new about the ideas of Wiltshire or Greig, but rarely have I seen the form of practice continued over any period of time. If you ally that theory to the one Ted

Dexter and some others used to employ of standing absolutely
still in a net until the fast bowler actually releases the ball, then
I reckon English batsmen will soon develop the sharpest
reflexes in the world, even if they are only faced with medium-
fast bowling in their own domestic game.

The Cricketer, September 1976

Greig has to grovel
Old Trafford, 10 July 1976

For England this was a day of few options. It did not matter
what roller the West Indians used on the wicket; whether
England bowled seam or spin; whether those entrusted with the
ball attacked leg or off. The West Indians were in the masterful
position of being 303 ahead with nine second innings wickets
standing and Greenidge and Richards at the crease.

Perhaps there were a few English prayers for rain, the only
possible saviour, though it would have taken a great worship-
per of cumulus nimbus formations like Geoff 'Noddy' Pullar,
the former Lancashire and England opener, to have spotted a
distant depression on such a sunny morning.

Lancashire lads always said that the prospect of a day's
fielding was enough to send 'Noddy' to his prayer mat or,
rather, rushing to his window at the back of the players' shower
room at Old Trafford. 'Noddy's window' is now part of the
folklore. 'Ay, there's a drop cummin' up,' he would enthuse.
'Wi' luck we'll be back in by half-three.'

Clearly nothing was going to stop Greenidge and Richards
from setting up the assault. Greenidge became only the second
man in England-West Indies Test history to score two centuries in one match. George Headley did it twice, at Georgetown in 1929–30 and at Lord's in 1939. No England player has
done it.

Hendrick and Selvey opened up with two slips; soon there
was only one. The batsmen matched each other for strokes of

[42]

beauty and power. Richards flashed Hendrick through square-cover for four. Had no-one told him that square-cutting is a risk on wickets of uneven bounce? Greenidge leaned far on to the front foot to square-drive Underwood; he thundered a cover-drive of pure Caribbean pedigree off a Hendrick half-volley, weight massively on the back foot.

Richards square-cut Underwood one ball, then late-cut the next of good length with instinctive touch. The ball flew off to the fine third-man boundary over the hard, dry earth.

What a triumph for Greenidge! His studied defence has sometimes made him look vulnerable and, indeed, he had a lean spell of lbw decisions last year. The sheer style of his innings both at Lord's and here at Manchester, however, will be recalled by many in years to come as the perfect West Indian blend of physical power and art. His century was acclaimed by all. He played the next ball on to his wicket; the score 224 for two.

Richards, by this time, was in full command, combining watchful dead bats against Underwood and Pocock with wristy drives through mid-wicket or vicious cuts.

Lloyd reckoned that the spinners needed close attention, too. He was dropped by Close at backward short-leg off Underwood, but to be fair to Close he was standing far too near the bat for the pace and elevation of the catch which might have been picked up in the deeper position made famous by Tony Lock.

In the session after lunch it became even more obvious that the pitch was turning and sometimes lifting. Of course, England were unable to bring up attacking fielders. Greig's hope could only be to buy as much time as possible and, by way of pleasant change, this was better achieved by spinners bowling tightly than faster men loitering over their run-ups.

Richards discarded the adage of not playing the ball against the spin. He turned his wrists to drive Underwood through mid-wicket; a deep mid-wicket had to be posted even though the odd ball spun wide past the off-stump. Underwood limped with an injured knee.

Richards, who knows his way to a century better than most – this was his sixth Test hundred in the calendar year – judged it perfectly. He called for his hundredth run when the ball was almost in Underwood's grasp. Underwood's throw was stump-high and straight but Richards sprinted in at surprising speed. He looked to be struggling a few yards out, but there was no doubt that he made it home. The running of Richards with both Greenidge and Lloyd was a model for all.

Greig laboured under the taunts of the West Indian crowd, 'We want Greig – we want Greig'. I had the feeling that they meant it. Having taken the verbal battle to the opposition, as he did demonstrably against Australia, he may find that this time he has built his own funeral pyre now that he cannot get runs or wickets. He pretended he was going to bowl at one point.

It is an unnecessary pressure for an England captain but there truly does come a time when the fighting talk has to stop and the fighting action begin. I hope the captain's fortunes change.

Clive Lloyd's problem was scarcely arithmetical. It was simply a question of when to halt the destruction of the English bowling and unleash his demons. As long as he was striking Pocock for six over the sight-screen and Richards was feathering late cuts past Close, or scorching straight drives past Pocock to the accompaniment of West Indian choruses – 'We shall not be moved' – it seemed a shame to end the Caribbean orgy.

Lloyd hoisted Selvey into the safe hands of Underwood at wide mid-on – 129 minutes at the crease for 43 – but expectations of a declaration before 3.45 which would have split up the remainder of the day's play into two sessions, disappeared as Kallicharran arrived in the middle. As it was, the West Indian innings meandered on pointlessly. It was surely in Lloyd's interest to accelerate, not slow down and get English wickets while the weather remained fine.

Ball by ball, over after over, the West Indians gave England the hope that a rainy two days on Monday and Tuesday would salvage a treacherous situation.

Should Greig have set more attacking fields? Certainly Underwood would have got among the wickets and the run-getting would have been less comfortable for the tourists. The argument is mainly academic because Lloyd was able to declare at five o'clock and leave England eighty minutes of batting.

Roberts and Daniel steamed in. Close drew back because the tantrums of the crowd were disturbing him. Lloyd, a few overs later, went to request a reasonable quiet from the musical section.

Dust rose from the wicket and the change in pace was obvious. Edrich watched one ball scream over his right shoulder and another creep low past of the off stump. Batting was now a different game; there was no respite from fast bowling.

Only the brave, the technically sound and the extremely lucky all rolled into one were going to survive. The senior citizens were all of these. Close chested off a rising ball from Holding. Roberts was rested after three overs, but Daniel looked even more dangerous. Possibly the three of them pressed too hard. Close was hit again, this time by Holding. Close's first move is towards off stump and they appeared to be able to catch him in that line with sharply rising balls. His legs crumbled for a moment. Another bouncer later and umpire Bill Alley warned Holding for excessive use of intimidation. The crowds were incensed, the tom-toms beat louder and a small fight broke out in the crowd.

The tension was only defused when a lad ran on to the field and offered Edrich a joke bat which was a foot and a half wide! There were laughs all round and Padmore, the off-spinner, was brought on bowling to just two slips with fifteen minutes to go.

Sunday Telegraph, 11 July 1976

Wooden elephants and banana skins

The MCC cricketers arrive in Bombay on Thursday and by Saturday they will know how cricketers, like film stars, are idolised there. Before long their incoming telephone calls will be jamming the hotel switchboard. 'I am your fan, uncle. I would like to meet you to wish you best of luck.' There is no need to feel deprived of some virility by the 'uncle' tag either; in India it means 'brother'.

Quite quickly the player's hotel room will be filled up with gifts large and small. If Tony Greig bats as well as he did last time, in 1972–73, he will have to carry around a full-sized silver-coated bat. In the end it was always worth asking the pilots of Indian Airlines to squeeze a few more revs out of their ancient Fokkers to get 'Greigy' and his gear off the ground in one piece.

Wooden elephants, large and small, arrive by parcel post, and paper twists of rice or coconut for good luck. 'I as a cricket lover wish Your Honour and all your giant, superb team-mates a most hearty welcome on Indian soil and expect from you sprightliest, scintillating and glorious achievements to be recorded in our hearts.' Bouquets of flowers arrive and that telephone never stops ringing. Outside the door, wrapped in a blanket, your bearer guards your precious self.

Mind you, with the presents come the people and now the hardships start. At Calcutta there will be 85,000 people inside the Eden Gardens ground every day. There will be 85,000 outside too, probably paying a rupee each for the discomfort of sitting on rough ground and seeing one of the many 'tic-tac' men chalk up the scores on a blackboard as his 'business' colleague reports the changing fortunes from a transistor radio. Five thousand will gather outside the hotel, 1,500 in the foyer, and 50 in the upstairs corridor, all wanting to shake your hand, touch you, praise you . . . and ask for a ticket.

Tony Greig's mail will read: 'I pray Almighty to render you inexhaustible will-power and strength to achieve mighty success in every Test match. May God bless you. I await with keen interest most valuable autographed photograph.'

Derek Underwood lay exhausted in his bath on the 1972–73 tour. Suddenly, in came a party of young people who announced: 'We take your photo, famous Underwood.' Derek, too tired to bawl them out, said, 'Cheese'.

'That's when they've really beaten you,' he admitted next day when they presented him with a print: taking a photograph of the presentation.

[46]

Crowds do not end there of course. There is the part of touring which should be relaxing but is not – a private shopping trip. Players will have to be rescued from stores by police. Even shopping together has its penalty.

In 1972–73 we lost Leicestershire's Jack Birkenshaw. We all waited for him outside the store in a private bus. Suddenly his red hair was spotted. He was pinned to the side of a bus by the wild crowd and also by an ox-cart. Two sets of bovine eyes stared inches away from his face. Our manager shouted from the window that his rescue was being organised. 'Sorry, manager, to 'old you up, but ah told these big 'uns 'alf an hour ago ah'm not signing.'

So quite quickly the instant fame becomes hard to wear. The team shrinks more and more from exposure and hardens its spirit of resistance to the vast colourful but demanding country. Expatriate British understand and offer an air-conditioned room, a stereo set-up and a cool whisky-soda. This, too, is a sadness because if it is only possible to sort out which of the many Indian hosts are prepared to shape their hospitality to suit the visitor then the isolationist act would be unnecessary.

England cricket teams are at their worst when they turn in on themselves. They complain about tight-lipped Maharajahs, the colour of curry, and address genuine helpers, liaison officers, as village idiots when, say, up-country, in the Lantern Hotel, Indore, they cannot lay on steak and chips, a peach melba and a cheddar.

Coping with people and believing it a privilege to be travelling in someone else's country is also very essential to cricket success.

Imagine walking into the white-hot oven of a Test stadium. The roar goes up inside and outside, the rice and flowers drop around you as you walk to the middle, but they want your life. As the bowler runs in the gongs bang, the mirrors flash, the crescendo grows until . . . silence, the ball whirs down. It hits your pad. The bowler and keeper appeal, 75,000 inside the ground appeal, 75,000 outside appeal too. Along the baked tunnel of a pitch one man holds your fate. He shakes his head. 'Not out.' Then the banana skins fly up and down the terraces, small fires burn, the firecrackers begin and fights break out. After that it is a sheer pleasure to pop down the malaria pills and clean one's teeth in Seven-Up.

I can only offer Tony Greig the words of Phiroze B. Palsetia, a self-styled cricketer, umpire and poet. His poem, *Opus 190*, on MCC 1973 concluded, 'Good wishes with love and bon voyage to you from entire ocean of Indian cricketing humanity of pious land'. Amen.

Sunday Telegraph, 21 November 1976

Bishan Bedi

When you have seen Bishan Singh Bedi twirl down his left-arm spinners after sixty overs with the same gentle rhythm and control as he first settled into the start of his spell, you understand why his is a great bowling action. Even more so in his own country, where the test of stamina is more severe in burning heat and on hard-baked grounds which tug on the muscle and jar all the joints.

I have always thought that a great clockmaker would have been proud to have set Bedi in motion – a mechanism finely balanced, cogs rolling silently and hands sweeping in smooth arcs across the face. Yet it would be wrong to portray him as something less than human – all hardware and no heart – because he bowls with an aggression which belies his gentle and genial nature. His rhythm too has only come after countless hours of practice in the nets.

His captains, who for most of his Test career have been 'Tiger' Pataudi and Ajit Wadekar, often introduced him to the attack within the first half-hour of a Test innings. Indeed when England fell prey to the pressures of spin and close catching out in India in 1972–73, the brightly turbaned, left-arm spinner was seen loosening up at third-man while Solkar was only in his second over.

That is not such crazy logic. On many overseas surfaces the shine is often gone within a quarter of an hour. So, without having genuine pace at their disposal, these Indian captains offered their high-class spinners a fairly new firm ball which settled easily into the hand and, most important of all, produced bounce at the batsman's end. Bedi thrived, with close fieldsmen leaping around the bat as batsmen attempted to fight through their first few overs.

Bishan Bedi was never formally taught the bowling skills. He confesses: 'As a young boy in Amritsar I just happened to get hold of a ball and roll it around as it left my hand'. So it is not surprising to learn that, as the instinct to spin grew quickly, his stamina developed alongside, and the young man who had taken up the game only at the late age of thirteen at St Francis High School was making his debut in first-class cricket two years later for Northern Punjab in the Ranji Trophy.

'I was lucky with my easy action,' he admits, inferring that it came naturally. 'It is smooth, I suppose, and I have spent hours developing the rhythm. So I am not like lots of other spinners who get sore fingers, you know, strains in the ankles and thighs. A good action spares you that. Do you know, I have never had finger trouble.'

The fine art of Bishan Bedi is based on his personal philosophy. He bowls to get wickets by deceiving batsmen, tricking them into false shots, crowding them initially, but carefully placing fielders to trap the one that looks like getting away. I once asked him if he bowled differently in attack and in defence. 'I have never bowled defensively,' he quickly came back at me. 'Some left arm spinners in English cricket set their fields straightaway, six on the off and three on the leg. I like a couple up close to start, especially with the new batsman – a slip, a gully and a square gully if I can, and then one on the leg side, because the batsman might fear the off trap and play outside the ball. I always bowl at the stumps. I have never bowled one side or the other just to contain.'

In an era when limited-overs cricket has pushed British spinners along the defensive road, blocking shots and waiting for the indiscriminate move by the batsman, Bedi's approach is becoming almost a treasure of the past. Or should we consider ourselves fortunate that the very best of the world's spinners like Bedi and Intikhab Alam are playing in county cricket, and have flare-lit the way for young spinners and their coaches?

The skills he has acquired therefore are attacking skills. Apart from the orthodox spin which leaves the right-handed batsman, he also grips the ball less firmly and slides the wrist under it, genuinely under-cutting it, so that it goes straight on at the other end, despite the appearance of genuine finger-spin. Another ball, seam up, with similar action, he floats down at rather quicker pace. It can dip into you through the air, though I must be honest, when I have faced him abroad, the ball that has intrigued me most is the seamer which appears to drift outwards towards the slips. It never seems to happen in England. Or is it just me?

We return again to the personal qualities which have made Bedi exceptional even by the highest standards, because he is surely the best left-arm spinner in the world.

Running hopefully in pursuit of a ball along the boundary line he bounces along, one-paced, without ever being able to summon the muscle strength to slip his solidly-made body into third gear. His head rolls from side to side and a large smile tells the crowd that here is a man prepared to joke at his own limitations. They love him in India.

When the moment comes to bowl, the smile vanishes. A frown joins the pleats of the turban (patka, strictly speaking), a serious concentration. Classically, the eyes of aggression appear over the right shoulder, behind the raised right arm as he bowls. He beats the bat and he groans, does it twice and he hates. Yet should the victim leap from the crease and crack a six, the first applause will come from the bowler. Stoically Bishan Bedi casts his bait, over after over, each ball looking like the last, until the victim is drawn forward where the ball no more is, and that is the dream for which he endlessly toils for Northamptonshire and for India.

The Cricketer's Companion, 1976

Sweet delights of singing for your supper

Half-time has come in the winter of a million cricket dinners. After-dinner speakers have flopped in quiet corners to build up strength for the second half which always feels as if it is played into the wind when the verve has long departed, left with the cold meat and spuds in a chilly November pavilion, or still twirling around some smart banqueting room with the piped music against which it fought and lost. . . .

If you speak at cricket dinners there are hazards, and you find yourself in some unusual places. Beware, for instance, the cricket dinner in a smart new hotel. Drink is the problem. Under the glare of the manager, waitresses top up your glass of house wine even before you have decently gargled the palateful before. Then, given the impression that you are making no impression on the glass, you rush it nervously, slurping faster and faster. Some speakers can handle this. By their own chemical miracle the wine turns to adrenalin and they are soon standing and delivering words of relaxed brilliance. Not me.

With alcohol my tongue grows twice as fat and dries like a felt duster on a school blackboard. Words slide into each other and I hurtle into the pitfalls of silence left by a confused audience, until they start to talk amongst themselves. You do this only once.

Alas I chose the Savoy in which to 'die'. I remember it was Vivian Jenkins, that marvellous all-round Glamorgan cricketer and Welsh rugby player, who was once unlucky enough to hit what Dorian Williams would have called the most testing triple of the lot – a long journey to the dinner, a free-pouring drinks waiter and a seat on the top table in front of a full-blast gas heater.

Viv's was the final speech. He got to his feet at eleven o'clock and gave 'em . . . 'Gentlemen, Wally Hammond was a bloody good player'. So saying he returned to his seat with a bump, a smile and a wave of the hand. The audience, seeing that he was not going to get off his stool for a second round gave him a standing ovation. Come to think of it, it was the finest eleven o'clock speech I ever heard.

Professional nightmares are different, without the fun or the charity. My own nightmare was in one of those subterranean banqueting suites in the City and I had been hired on this occasion to talk after dinner to the sports clubs within the Confectionery and Allied Trades, the night when the liquorice makers of Pontefract come south with the Quality Streeters of York and join with the Cadburys and Ovaltinies of other parts.

There were over five hundred out there, I was told. Apart from that no-one said much to me, but after the coffee came the announcement, 'Now gentlemen, the one you have been wait-ing for . . . Nadine'. A lady spun herself out of the darkness into the floor space in front of us. At first all you could see was her white face and laddered stockings. Fifteen minutes later with a little help from some 'juicy fruits' in the audience, I could see all of her!

Follow that, I thought. How is my story about facing Les Jackson at Chesterfield going to go down now? Shall I switch to that old, unsavoury one about Nurse Thomson, the Sydney abortionist, or what about 'Sorry, skipper, I should have kept my legs closed'. Answer: 'Not you, son, your mother'. Hell, I thought, have I come to the right place?

The chairman asked me to write out a few things about myself on a card so that I could be properly introduced. 'Sorry, don't know much about cricket,' he said. Next I was on my feet wooing the audience which Nadine had left in such a feverish state.

I used familiar tactics. I threw out as many cricketers' names as I could and waited for a response, holding back on F. S. Trueman of course, upon whom we all rely. 'Wot abart Fletcher?' a lovely Londoner shouted out. Trusting that he meant Keith not Cyril, I waded in with tales of Fletch and Essex cricket. Good response: encouraging audience, so I moved on to the next tactic. I gave them the Fred Trueman tales and sat down. The applause was kindly and I sat down to murmurs on my right of 'Oh, that's who he is'.

I was then just thinking how after-dinner speakers should go into the disposable shirt business when Colette made her entrance, walking along the top of the top table. She stopped in front of me, showed a leg and demanded my tie. Hypnotised, I gave it to her; nice tie, too, from Turnbull and Asser.

Colette never gave it back, though to be honest I never truly waited. My tie was last seen playing a minor role in a major strip. Poor Colette's tape broke. But she found a way of distracting the audience. Before anyone noticed, I was up and away, sweating in the mid-winter chill of Leadenhall Street. Whoever had thought that I would make an interesting filling for a sex sandwich? What was the confectionery trade coming to? Now, Fred Trueman? That is different.

Recently, at the fine hostelry known as the Tempest Arms at Earby, near Skipton in Yorkshire, the proprietor, Peter Parfitt of Middlesex and England, has built a magnificent dining-room out of a barn – a very large barn. It is purpose-built for the sporting dinner and, at the Jack Simmons benefit night, the batting order was Lewis, Parfitt and Trueman.

I offered a little southern Welsh plainsong. Parff followed with tales of Middlesex and Lord's, but both of us relied heavily on touches of Trueman to raise the northern smiles. F.S.'s reaction, when his turn came, was to give them an hour and a quarter, straight from the shoulder, opening with a blitz on the previous speakers. 'I've been retired for twelve years and these two little b . . . s are still making money off my back.' 'D'y'know,' said Sewards, 'that Parfitt: call himself a publican. He's done for the licensed trade what Colditz did for holiday camps.'

Laughter. 'And that Welsh b . . . Lewis. Ever seen his batting average? He's done less for cricket than Telly Savalas has done for Brylcreem.' I thought to myself, come back, Colette, all is forgiven.

So, to all those who turn out at the sports dinners and have to sing for their supper, I drink and urge you to relax and enjoy it. As the great Sewards himself would put it, 'Sip up, lad, and let some other sod do the talkin'.'

Sunday Telegraph, 19 February 1977

Rebellion or reform: a case of paradise lost

Tony Greig arrived at this season in a position of strength and popularity. He had studied the captaincy of England before it fell to him. That is not to say that he was overtly ambitious but he understood from the start how to provide exactly those qualities which were urgently required at the time – a captain who could be seen to battle to the dying death on the field, and off it perform with a shrewd articulacy to keep the cricket public well informed.

During the 1976–77 winter in India, Sri Lanka and Australia he had virtually perfected the role. The wider the stage the more eagerly he lengthened his stride and projected his voice. He even won a few matches and, before this week, had arrived at the point where his sceptics were forced to agree that everything was fine as long as Greig's ambition coincided with the health of English cricket.

It was good for English hopes that the captaincy was not in dispute. Greig had the satisfaction of knowing he would lead England in another series for the Ashes, that, in doing so, his earnings were assured (he was said to have earned about £100,000 last year), and that his world was as near a personal paradise as could be.

He has always been known to care about money and has keenly sought to commercialise his cricket talents in a game which pays very little money even to its best players. Last summer there were tales of him calling early morning meetings in the City, amassing contracts all over the world to the extent that many in Sussex believed he would be up and off to Australia as soon as he had finished with the English captaincy.

I have never met a single person in cricket administration who wants to deprive a cricketer of more money. Everyone wishes that the game produced a greater revenue in its present form, but there is clearly a limit to what counties especially can hand out in earnings when they are on the breadline year after year.

Sussex supporters were more concerned that their side would be submerged in this mass of commercial interest. Last season

Greig played 22 innings in the County Championship and averaged only 22.9 with the bat, including two not out innings. He bowled 339.5 overs taking 31 wickets at 31.29 apiece. A fistful of dollars is one thing; a few dollars more was what they feared. But then Sussex did not pay him enough to argue.

In fact Greig was immensely popular with his MCC side during the winter and he has that strong independent streak which enables him to cope with business as well as produce runs and wickets when he knows he needs them.

However, independent or not, last week his announcement that he was to join the Kerry Packer cricket circus in Australia next winter and that he wanted the cricket boards of the world to readjust their Test match dates for the planned series – MCC in Pakistan and New Zealand and Australia against India – shocked everyone.

Greig himself approached Underwood and Knott and they too accepted an offer they could not refuse. The Test and County Cricket Board were not asked for comment or observation. Naturally, all those who have worked to see cricket through some very lean financial years during the 1960s have been stunned by such a brazen act of piracy which simply takes advantage of the increasing television and therefore commercial interests in the game.

The TCCB were moving that way, too. Indeed £20,000 prize money was put up for this coming series which, when split up, could raise a player's match fee from the basic £210 to £350–£400. They were obviously not moving quickly enough for the world's best known players.

It is twice as painful when an adopted son defects because so much more attention has been given to him along the way to help him settle. So, let us turn to that hard caucus of patriots who never saw Greig as anything other than a South African imposter as England's captain.

Geoff Boycott and Johnny Hampshire up in Yorkshire are not alone but their voices are prominent. It was a sad day at Headingley during the last Australian tour when Hampshire said that he hardly enjoyed playing for England when the team was led by a Springbok. It was an opinion without malice towards Greig. It is just the way the majority of people see their country's cricket up there. There are a lot of people all over the country saying 'I told you so'.

Each player recruited by Mr Packer for his Rest of the World series, first against Australia, has been prepared to risk his country's wrath. Jeffrey Stollmeyer, the president of the West Indies Cricket Board of Control, did say that he had no quarrel with players who wanted the best possible financial rewards. Majid and Imran have been told by the Pakistan Board that they are barred from taking part so long as they work for Pakistan International Airlines and wish to play for Pakistan.

Yet Mr Packer has solved the major problem in the lives of these cricketers which is the meagre return they get for playing the game at Test level. Is Tony Greig the professional's martyr? Will everyone be indebted to him and to the whole of the side in seasons to come when cricket is perhaps offering handsome rewards at the top? It could happen that way.

The ordinary county professional player does not make much money from his cricket. A junior capped player in an average county gets a basic salary of £1,500 to £2,000. A senior player, £2,200 to £2,500. With appearance monies and a variety of bonuses paid a senior player could arrive at £3,500. Some receive more and Lancashire, for example, are able to pay higher basic wages.

The professional player's constant plea is for that higher basic wage which can accommodate regular domestic planning such as mortgage or hire purchase. Unfortunately, county committees are only able to offer substantial increases if linked to performance and therefore to gate money.

The thoroughly modern cricketer believes that he should be able to earn a reasonable living from cricket alone and the Test players of the moment, who have found themselves feted as personalities through considerable television exposure as well as cricketers pure and simple, see their lives travelling parallel to top golfers, jockeys, tennis players and the like.

Maybe they are mistaken to compare team games with individual pursuits, but they certainly have a point. Receiving a modest fee to play, say, in the Centenary Test when you are the chief protagonist and have filled the ground day after day by your efforts, can leave you resentful. Worse still, it can drive many cricketers into cheap money-grabbing such as the sale of players' complimentary tickets for Black Market prices, the refusal to talk to the Press unless paid, the selling of miniature bats among Indian crowds, and so on. I have witnessed the sale by one cricketer of his Test sweater.

When I captained England for five months through India, Sri Lanka and Pakistan in 1972–73 I was paid £1,300. Mike Denness, who led England winter and summer in 1973–74 claimed to have made £7,000 from all cricket sources in that year. Some players are lucky with their other jobs but these days are asked to play regular Test match series and so some struggle to find a job at all. Certainly those with jobs rarely stand a chance of promotion within that career.

Psychologically it can be a miserable business too. I can recall, as Glamorgan captain, ringing up hundreds of people asking if they could fit players into winter jobs on a part-time basis. In the summer England were wanting Jeff Jones, a successful Test fast bowler, to be confident and aggressive in his play, yet in the winter he was forced to read gas meters, house to house.

However, I do not see county players viewing Greig as their hero, though their lot has had prominence and, hopefully, it will lead to a deeper search for security. Nor do I see them acknowledging that such a self-styled group as 'Top players' playing 'Super Tests' is more than the delusion of the few.

The media has done more to separate Greig from the body of the game than his talents. Players like David Steele, Bob Woolmer, Derek Randall and others have recently shown that the very good county player does not find Test cricket full of insurmountable difficulties.

England's newest selector, John Murray, emphasised his opinions before he started the job. 'Let's not get excited,' he said. 'We did play well in [the Centenary Test at] Melbourne, but we lost. Unfortunately we have only two world-class players in the England side, Underwood and Knott.'

The conceit is unmistakable in the Packer set-up. Do the best surgeons go around calling themselves 'top surgeons'? I personally liked the statement from Clive Lloyd, a man who does have extraordinary talent, when he honestly agreed that the money was too much for him to refuse and that, for the first time, he stood to make his talents pay. Fair enough.

If the Rest of the World matches were not to coincide with prearranged Test cricket, there would be no argument. Good luck to them all. If, in England, a proper approach had been made to the Test and County Cricket Board, with the aid of the Players' Association, then much would have been understood. If Greig had decided to go it alone after his plans had been rejected, then we would be applauding a man with the courage to lay his England captaincy on the line. If the Players' Association now take the cue, or maybe they have already, to probe the administrators for higher Test-match fees linked to crowd attendance, then there will be sympathy for that, too.

What has polarised all the support towards the establishment is the undercover betrayal and the contentment with which England's captain would damage the game that has made him.

Tony Greig assured the TCCB that Mr Packer's door was open if the various Boards of Control wished to discuss the matter with him. It is a Wellsian situation – the television tail wagging the dog. Nor is the potential of television to be underestimated.

Independent Television in this country might well enjoy receiving packages of Test cricket from TV9 in Australia. At present it cannot compete with the BBC, but that particular series might be an interesting dart at the opposition's dominance, and the English cricket world might be glued to it. We might all be part of it yet.

What lies behind Mr Packer's door? For the players, surely, disillusionment with the chore of playing against each other all the time; barren cricket which ultimately becomes barren in appeal.

Might there not be a sick conscience awaiting Tony Greig in that he went behind the backs of those who spend their days and nights working for the good of cricket? Will he not regret the lack of dignity with which this operation has been launched? What can showbiz cricket mean to anyone, especially when they have played Test cricket with the country's honour at stake?

Or perhaps, so frustrated have our Test players become with the administration that they do genuinely equate a large handout of money with the quality of life. To my eyes, for Tony Greig it is a case of the perfect situation sacrificed, of paradise lost. Obviously to him as captain of the Rest of the World it is better to reign in hell than serve in heaven.

Sunday Telegraph, 15 May 1977

'Old Trafford the place to be'

Old Trafford was the place to be last week. It positively showed off as one of our richest homes of cricket. England won a mighty victory over Australia; record receipts of £96,000 were taken even without a fifth day; it produced one of the best cricket wickets for a long time on a square that was criticised even before the first ball had bounced on it; and most unforgettable of all, two men, Greg Chappell on Monday and Clive Lloyd on Wednesday in another match, played innings of the highest conception and class.

That massive Victorian pavilion, which so often appears to live on the breath of the past, was roared, clapped and shaken by the foundations into the present day.

There was no mistaking the skill or the style which these two batsmen showed. Had Old Trafford's best-loved chronicler, Sir Neville Cardus, lived to be a witness, even he who was rarely stirred by modern batting techniques would surely have recognised that the best of old and new had merged in both of these innings.

Greg Chappell, slender, straight in the back and sleeves buttoned down, went to the crease with the Australian second innings score 0 for 1. His neat appearance always suggests a neat mind, and by the time he had faced up to the raging Bob Willis and the new ball, he looked composed, deaf to the crucifying roars of the excited crowd and blind to the fielders who were coiled ready for the catch close to his bat. His side was 140 runs behind on the first innings and he must have been fearful of defeat.

Emotions are of no use on such occasions. Chappell simply obeyed the law of all fine players, relying on his known method, and played within the limitations he set himself.

Willis was fiery. Chappell got behind a lifting ball and dropped it from his chin to his feet with a straight but relaxed bat. Underwood, with flight and spin, penned him in between two fielders, Greig close on the off and Woolmer to leg, and varied his approach from around to over the wicket. Some balls spun and turned and others went straight on, but always Chappell let the ball come on to the bat patiently rather than stretching to meet it, and treated each one, as coaches will tell you, on merit.

The other Australians came and went. Badly played hooks from McCosker and Davis, a hoick from Marsh who was huffing and puffing to get hold of Underwood, all proved that hearts were ruling heads.

Greg Chappell's initial move at the crease is like Clive Lloyd's, a firm but small step across towards the middle stump. He does not throw his weight about at this stage as many of the more pronounced shufflers do. It is the initial build-up of rhythm before the launch into the stroke. He was very quick on to the front foot to straight-drive, cover-drive and to execute with flowing bat, but no flourish, his favourite on-drive.

His head is always still. It was an innings of all those skills and an almost imperceptible character – shunning excess, rarely faltering, full of continuity. When he had scored 112 Chappell attempted a risky cut off Derek Underwood and chopped the ball on to his stumps.

Fine bowling deserved the prize of ending a great innings. Old Trafford knew that they had seen something special. How lucky was I, then, to witness the other great innings on Wednesday. Clive Lloyd's 86 embodied all the extravagance of a West

Indian on stage. He hit the ball far more often in the air and far harder.

They were the moves of a bigger man with a wider arc of swing, with a faster bat speed, and indeed a heavier bat. Lloyd's bat is reputedly 3lb. 3oz. Can that be true? Surely railway sleepers do not come much heavier! Yet if Lloyd was in a hurry and Chappell had time, the essential matters were much in common, beginning with the mental approach.

Lloyd did not slog. He too faced a crisis. Lancashire had been reduced to 30 for 4 by the Surrey seam attack in this 60-over Gillette Cup match and the ball had moved about off the pitch under grey cool skies.

Lloyd loped down the steps in a long-sleeved sweater, peering through his spectacles which glinted under the dipped brim of a porky white sun-hat. He limped. His recent cartilage operation has made him lame and fluid had been taken off both knees before the match. He had jogged up and down on the practice ground before deciding to take the chance and the pain.

In spite of the mental problem of playing with injury and also the build-up of tension at the crease as Geoff Arnold, the menace in chief, was brought back to attack him Lloyd behaved with Chappell's detachment.

Arnold pitched up the ball, Lloyd took that move towards middle with the back foot as Chappell had done. And then springing on to the front foot he cracked a straight four. Arnold was angered and dug one in which Lloyd calmly hooked for six.

Lloyd miscued one but was dropped. He coldly but flamboyantly took the bowling apart. The ball no longer moved off the pitch; only off the bat. Roope's bowling disappeared twice in two successive pulls for six. Intikhab's leg-spin was bludgeoned, each ball according to merit, cuts, drives, hooks and glides and young Baker, the medium-pacer, must have been delighted not to have got his hand to a straight-drive which would have taken a couple of fingers with it to the sight screen.

It was pure Clive Lloyd playing very straight, exciting everyone but himself, always obeying his known techniques and looking like carrying on forever.

So Manchester saw two great innings in the modern style. But surely the game has not changed that much? It is the essence within the performer which decided whether natural talent can find its true expression. Watching television in my hotel room on Wednesday evening I heard one of the country's best-loved contraltos, Helen Watts, declare that four things mattered in performance – to see the romance but never let it take you over; to know your capabilities and how far to stretch yourself; to base all performances on technique and, lastly, to keep on as long as you feel the compelling need to do so.

Very much the gospel of Chappell and Lloyd. So you see, Sir Neville above all would not have mistaken the qualities of this Old Trafford week.

Sunday Telegraph, 17 July 1977

The first day of Packer

The moving message on the electronic scoreboard at the Victoria Football League Stadium in Melbourne yesterday, 25 November 1977, informed the 1,200 paying spectators that the World XI captain, Tony Greig, had won the toss and put the Australians in to bat.

From a long underground tunnel the light blue caps of the fielders emerged, and they doubtless experienced a gladiatorial feeling as they left the shadow of a massive five-tiered grandstand and ran, twirling their shoulders, into the dazzling sunshine.

McCosker and Davis followed and it was Mike Procter who bowled the first historic ball of World Series Cricket to McCosker. It went harmlessly down the leg side. Knott moved smartly to his left and took the ball low down.

The irony to many was that the so-called superstars, having hired a theatre for 77,000 entered only to a cheer and a chuckle. To my eye, there was a sadder twist. Whereas all the other players had been suitably transformed into mercenary outfits by their new colours, Alan Knott was too vivid a reminder of the past. An England team without him was unthinkable.

Meanwhile at Adelaide, the other historic first ball was being bowled by Andy Roberts to Dennis Amiss, armour and all, who padded away three balls and scored five off the remainder.

Back at Melbourne, the moving electronic message ran through the batting order, gave the umpire's names as Peter

Enright and Jack Collins, and the twelfth men. Then, later, when the crowd had edged to upwards of 2,000 by teatime, it was able to offer the advice that 250 had come up in 275 minutes and that R. Benuad (presumably Benaud) was required in the scorebox. You gather that the sale of scorecards is not part of Packer cricket.

The pitch, without reservation, was a triumph of groundsmanship. Lowered into the ground in two halves, it dried in the hot sun in quite different colours. Imran Khan did make one ball leap off the joining ridge to hit McCosker on the glove, but otherwise it played safely and slowly.

Greg Chappell afterwards said that the bounce had been a little uneven, but no more so than Melbourne Cricket Club on a first day and certainly nothing as erratic as Old Trafford has been of late. He even felt that the vast stadium was well suited to cricket. 'We did not feel at all remote out there,' he said. 'Somehow the response of the crowd sounded clearer than on many smaller grounds.'

The effort of the players was faultless. Ian Chappell, who has been out of top-class cricket for a long time, played a wonderfully proficient innings of 118 not out.

The rough, returfed fielding areas had been watered and the eccentricities of bounce were slowed down. Everyone coped well.

The moving message completed its active day's work by relating the news of Amiss's 81 at Adelaide. It was a day for novelties, but even by the close of the first act it was a struggle for the impartial viewer to sustain an interest in the cricket.

To Australians it is, obviously, a different deal. There were rapturous reactions from the boys with the beer cans in the sun as Richie Robinson, the local hero, went through his usual repertoire of bludgeoning drives and hooks. 'On you, Richie,' they yelled. They barracked Walters, too.

Finding it hard to identify with the Rest of the World, I was more interested in the knowledge that the overnight scoreboard was recorded in a cassette, ready to be fed in for the morning.

That is not meant to be over-harsh judgement. Clearly, the 'Super Test' between the WSC West Indies and WSC

Australia will attract greater interest. Even if most of the spectators are sitting in front of the television screen.

Sunday Telegraph, 27 November 1977

Why Packer's door must shut

'My door is wide open.' Thus spake Kerry Packer, and all the fifty-four disciples gathered round, rejoiced, and waited for a new Heaven and a new Earth.

I offer a pulpit text for my judgement of World Series Cricket because all those Packerites who have flouted the authorised version are now convinced that they are on a crusade which is as much spiritual as financial.

The players, who include some of the most pleasant men in cricket, have been coldly treated in Melbourne and, by being thrown together in one hotel, have strengthened the communal commitment to make this enterprise work. With the glazed eye of a latter-day Cromwell, Packer himself justifies putting the cricket world to the sword in the name of some divine justice for the players.

Religious wars do not end quickly. The Packer boys look amazed if you suggest failure. The solution to the problem, say they all, is to organise a get-together; for the control of the game to revert to the Boards; and for Mr Packer to withdraw to his television citadel, the door of which is 'wide open'.

I remember the morning of the High Court success, when Kerry Packer played the schoolboy bully with the English Press. I had never met him before but tracked him down in the Australians' dressing-room. It is a vast room and he and Dennis Lillee were playing a game of kick-and-catch with an Australian Rules football; just like kids except that they were thumping it from wall to wall with the venom of grown men.

'Yeh, we'll talk,' he said to me, in jovial mood I thought, as he took another thundering ball into the chest and crashed it back to the retreating Lillee. Packer was in shirt-sleeves and perched on his head was a sailer hat which carried the message

'Super Tests'. It was a confirmation that he loves to rub shoulders with successful sportsmen, but I had forgotten all that by the time he had kept me waiting around for fifteen minutes, deliberately prolonging his game. It was his privilege: he had what I wanted – himself.

'You are no friend of ours, are you,' he stated. 'And I know exactly who you are.' He brushed past, I trailed after him. 'A lot of you fellas are hopping over the fence today.'

Out in the sunshine in front of the cricket I eventually got in a word. 'Are we to chat or not?' The cat and mouse game was becoming painful. School bully then suddenly melted into a delicate advocate. 'We must put cricket first now. I realise they must be disappointed in England, but they are men who will accept the umpire's decision. But d'y'know, I went to England five or six times to hang around their door. It's not going to happen that way this time . . . But, my door is wide open.' There it was again.

He got up, told two other English correspondents of his intense disregard for them, and departed into the stadium's executive suite. School bully was back again.

The early assessment of World Series Cricket is tinged with some sadness on my part that such superb cricketers took to such a field in such a way before so few people in their first Super Test. What are the chances of the series surviving?

First of all, Mr Packer has hefty assets, and not just the dollars. The players are convinced they are playing the highest standard of cricket possible and they are loyal to a man, even more so now that Mr Justice Slade has made them honest traders. They have made light of their modest practice facilities and rather delight in the image of brightly track-suited experts, talented enough to overcome the public scepticism.

Their good works are accumulating too. Coaching clinics have been enthusiastically attended by children and 2,000 hours of super-star coaching culminate with live-in courses at Cranbrook School in Sydney, where five hundred specially selected children, a hundred a week for five weeks, will enjoy the tuition of a lifetime.

The International Country Cup matches are also working in

Mr Packer's favour, even though there are counter-campaigns launched like the one in Queensland which recommends 'Fair Dinkum Cricket' as the righteous alternative.

The manufactured pitches, the fresh television approach with eight cameras and ball-by-ball radio commentaries around the ground on local frequency, night cricket and electronic scoreboards are all brave inventions but, most urgently, World Series Cricket needs gate-money, advertising income and sponsorship.

There are four major sponsors so far – McDonald's Hamburgers; Samuel Taylor, manufacturers of pressure packs; Qantas; and Berger Paints. This weekend a 'secret' survey is being conducted by a Sydney agency as they monitor the respective viewing ratings of the three channels which are putting out sport: The India v. Australia Test; the Davis Cup; and, on Channel 9 of course, the World Series Cricket. Wavering sponsors may note the figures carefully.

I would not be surprised if Mr Packer's television arithmetic works out. People accept the constant jangle of advertisements so much more easily here than in Britain. I find the advertisements naively scripted, brash and mind-bending. The tempo of the game is destroyed by twelve minutes of ads to the hour. All this persuades me that the High Court decision did not take the World Series one millimetre closer to success and so it must be queried whether the TCCB was premature in applying its ban.

Packer cricket lacks identity and loyalties for the public, though not, I agree, for the players. Yet how can those players themselves maintain their zest in empty stadia, playing always against the same opponents in some shape or form? Will the feeling of being pawns in a commercial charade ever hit them?

Through this maelstrom of dollars come clearly the merits of the Boards of Control at home and the value of so many people who worked for the game without cost, of good wickets and facilities, and of the careful marriage of sponsorship with the natural tempo of the game. The BBC's sensitivity in their coverage is precious and the sponsors of English cricket earn credit for their modest demands.

Of course, television history is being made because this is the first time an independent commercial company has televised cricket of this standard. That is why the money has been available to the players, because the cost of their contract is linked to an estimate of advertising revenue.

The Boards of Control can never match these stakes, but nor need they be panicked into more hasty reactions. They may blame themselves for imposing the expensive ban, but they must also wonder whether they and the Cricketers' Association should not have thought up their own Super-Star tour, now that professional cricketers expect to make a twelve-month-a-year living from cricket. Is it too late to devise cricket competition for the months when Test players are idle?

I came with an open mind to see these World Series Cricket matches and have failed to be interested in the cricket. I can see how much the players love it and feel sorry for them that no-one wants to watch. Only time can help it, but time too might end it.

If Kerry Packer's door stays open long enough and no Board official arrives cap in hand, then I believe the winds will blow harder and he will freeze slowly to death. It may take three years, but then I am convinced that the first Heaven and the first Earth will refuse to pass away . . . well, not exactly.

They have been changed already, Packerised into thinking harder about the remuneration and the aspirations of players, and for that the game will always owe its debt to this amazing experiment in international cricket, whatever the outcome of private enterprise.

Sunday Telegraph, 4 December 1977

Voice in the wilderness

'As I have delved into the lockers of my memory to tell this story, one paradox has stood out. In 1967 no young man could have loved cricket more than B. A. Richards; ten years later there could be no more disenchanted player in the first-class game, with only the hope of "pirate" circus to breathe life into my dying enthusiasm.' (From The Barry Richards Story.*)*

I had sat with that Springbok voice of disillusionment among the pin-tables and hamburgers of a Hampstead restaurant this week, and a good night we had. There was no sign of the mournful script on his face.

This was getaway time and the neat teeth flashed the old Richards smile; his eyes darted everywhere. Barry has always been happy when casually dressed and anonymously merged with the world away from cricket.

As with Gary Sobers before, and many other players of independent spirit, non-stop county cricket has dragged his spirits low. 'The ritual totally numbs me, of hotel, to ground, to lunch, to tea, to steak bar, to hotel and back to the ground ever and a day.'

Of course the tale of disillusionment goes deeper than that. Here is one of a brilliant set of young South African schoolboy cricketers who caught our imagination back in 1963. For years he had kicked along the sands at the Surf Club in Durban, dreaming of batting for South Africa in Tests. Now, at the age of thirty-three, although he has broken records in Hampshire and made dazzling marks in English county cricket, he has no country to represent, no great cause to stretch his concentration or raise his ambitions. *Dulce Et Decorum Est Pro Patria Mori.*

The restaurant was a hubbub of music, machines and excitement, but with a sip of lager his eyes glazed to recall his four Test appearances. They were in 1969–70, South Africa's annihilation of Australia.

'I never attached the importance to them then. Always thought we would be back. No, the deprivation is deeper; it really hurts. This is why Packer's cricket was so essential to me recently. It was a chance to prove myself among Test players once again.' In fact, Richards struggled a bit out in Packerland by his own standards. A lot of people did. 'I saw great players sink to the bottom of the pool. In retrospect I was not fit enough. I shall make sure I am next time.'

The doubt exists in his mind about the future of World Series Cricket. 'Traditional Test matches will always be with us, and I still hope that a miracle can bring South Africa back – everyone is trying hard there – but I am not certain how Kerry

Packer sees the shape of his own game over the next ten years.'

Barry Richards freely acknowledges his debt to Hampshire and to English county cricket. 'I don't mean in money-making either, but in the sheer satisfaction of proving myself as a professional player. Occasionally, team-mates and other professionals have called me too mercenary, but I think I have been too honest.

'You see, in South Africa there is no socialist state with National Assistance. In business you have to be successful and so money is important. I had extra problems too. My father was made redundant at a difficult age. Our lifestyle, not an extravagant one, was very much in my keeping. So I wanted my job to work as well as possible for the family.

'Many English professional players used to be happy to touch their caps to the county club and step on the treadmill without question every spring. I was honest enough to disagree with that. I think it breeds lack of ambition, lack of flair and a levelling down to mediocrity. Trouble is I have been outspoken and sensitive and that is a painful combination.'

So whither Barry Richards and his magic wand? Realistically he sees no greener grass at present. His Hampshire contract runs for another season. 'Ethically maybe I should have refused it, but at least they knew what they were getting.'

Then it all comes back to the greatest cheat of all for him, for Mike Procter, Graeme Pollock, Eddie Barlow, and so many others. Will South Africa take the international field again soon enough to release him from the English circuit, his daily burden?

That, I think, is the only way by which his exceptional talent can be prolonged. He has always been something special. My own recollection will be of leading MCC against Hampshire in the first match of the 1974 season. I went home and recorded in my diary the most brilliant fanfare any season can have had. It reads like this:

'Swathed in many layers of Hampshire sweaters Barry Richards today defied the biting cold, swung his bat freely to score 189 unforgettable runs. A most reputable MCC attack of Hendrick, Jackman, Knight, Acfield and Edmonds appeared to be sending down half-volleys and long-hops all day. It was not so, but sadistic flashes by Richards even put third-man in danger. Then there were persuasions to fine-leg and lofted golf shots for six over long-on. The MCC captain tinkered with his field all day but concluded that he must have taken the field four or five men short!'

How did Richards produce such majesty on this first freezing day of the Lord's season? The winds howled through tunnels and empty stands. It was a chill, cheerless theatre. Shadowy faces peered from behind the pavilion windows, ground staff workers padded around hunched up in the cold. The scorers froze stoically in their loft and the barmaid at the Tavern went unusually short of good company.

Yet Richards gave them an unbelievable day if they knew their cricket. I remember thinking in the field that it was just as if Yehudi Menuhin had called into the Festival Hall of a morning, taken his fiddle on stage and reeled off faultless unaccompanied Bach all day – just for the pleasure of the cleaners, box-office clerks, odd electricians or a carpenter who chanced to be there – without central heating of course – without taking off his coat.

That is *the* Barry Richards story. Catch it while you can.

Sunday Telegraph, 14 May 1978

Anti-hero and young lion

I can imagine the chunterings in Urdu and a medley of many sub-Continental languages when the slender Sikander Bakht limped into the Pakistan dressing-room before play yesterday – the third day of the first Test at Edgbaston – and told his captain that he was unfit to bowl.

Sarfraz, the front-line seam bowler, was already injured and resigned to the spectator's role. How could the tourists possibly face the new day, 92 runs behind and seven English wickets standing, with a new ball attack (or defence) of Mudassar and Liaqat?

Sikander not only made it to the field, but eagerly grasped the new ball, taken immediately, and presented the England batsmen with enough movement and variable bounce from the City end to give his side respectability. More than that, he took the wickets of Radley and Roope and raced in for a lengthy, almost unbroken morning spell. Happily for Radley, it took just a couple of his own authentic nudges to take him to his second Test hundred in successive innings. The last was in Auckland.

A long innings by Radley pulsates with effort, which makes it compulsive and warm. It is heartening for anyone who cares about devotion to duty to see him wear even the embossed crown and lion of an England sweater with the unawareness of a workman grafting away in overalls. It would be possible to be clever and almost unkind about his style because there are few Compton genes coursing through his Middlesex blood, but if I was to write that eventually he is going to leave cricket with memories of a classical nudge, it is said with affection.

The innings of an anti-hero can never be a glamorous affair, but as young boys at Edgbaston waved their Union Jacks and chanted 'England, England' at his century, I was happy that the bat raised politely in acknowledgement was held by a fighting, die-on-the-splice authentic piece of England. He was lbw to a ball from Sikander which came back into his pad from the off.

Graham Roope was solid and sensible, threatening to expand his enterprise when he raised his eyes theatrically to appreciate his off-drive even before he had made contact with the ball. He was bowled when he would have wished to have gone on to a big innings.

If there was a moment of relative optimism for the tourists it was when they managed to get two batsmen to the crease, Miller and Botham, who had still to get the touch of the job in hand. They clearly had to consolidate first, but both made it a pleasant exercise because they are natural strokemakers.

Miller does unsteady himself before striking the ball by suddenly shifting his ground to the off stump, but he easily hooked away the projected fast-medium bouncers and tickled the ball finely to leg.

[72]

Sikander earned his sweater, a rest and applause. He had taken four wickets. Iqbal Qasim stood in, but for the briefest time. The skipper, Wasim Bari, was soon gesturing to the outfield that he wanted Sikander back again, remembering how Fred Trueman used to come back into the attack with a grunt and a groan and insist that he could only do it because God had given him a good firm backside. I realised that Sikander presented an alternative. It is obviously possible to be worn out and be blown into bowl down the breeze, that is if you are built as narrowly as Sikander and catch the wind in your wide flannels.

At lunch England were 330 for 5, Botham and Miller having taken the measure of the bowling. If they could then bat their way into the afternoon it was clear that Pakistan would fall apart.

At 3.20, when the drinks were brought out, Botham was in full flow with 64 on the board. Miller, untroubled but more the deflector than the driver, was two short of his fifty.

In the field Pakistan stuck manfully to their task. They tried their luck with Wasim Raja's spin-bowling, but the England players are familiar with his style and tend to treat all his wrist spin as top-spin or googly. Scarcely a ball leaves the bat in orthodox leg-spin fashion.

Botham gave warning of his power by square-cutting first Wasim Raja and then the medium-fast bowling of Liaqat, Mudassar and Sikander. He is strongly-built and his natural power is allied to an outstanding ball sense. He is a destructive player at his best. Sikander bowled him a ball which kept low, dangerous to some, but Botham despatched it with a thunderous flick through mid-wicket. A similar ball from Mudassar he hammered off the back foot through a cover field which was already deep-set.

Wasim Bari was forced to place a sweeper-up behind the covers. Liaqat dived out of the way after bowling a ball to Botham which the young man struck back at him around head-high. Understandably, the bowlers tired, the fielders retreated, runs were there for the taking. Eventually even the brave, toiling Sikander had to suffer first a pull of unhealthy disrespect, next an arrogant straight-drive over the top, followed by the most regal cover-drive. The Botham century was not long in coming. When he was out for exactly 100, Brearley declared England's innings closed at 451 for 8.

More threatening still to the tourists were the signs that the wicket played with mild irregularities. The odd ball tended to keep low and one or two, especially with the new ball, hopped up to jam the fingers on the handle. They would still be considered batting conditions, but the deficit of 287 looked a long way off in the circumstances.

Of course, the challenge from this point onwards for Pakistan is mainly one of confidence. They will play like beaten men if that is how they see themselves. Their senior players will have to be seen by the younger members to be working hard at their game. It is too easy to demonstrate that weakness stems from the absence of Zaheer, Majid, Asif and Mushtaq, the Kerry Packer players.

They are committed to rebuilding and rediscovering the skills which they demonstrated against England in Pakistan last winter.

Sadiq and Mudassar responded bravely against the new-ball bowling of Willis, Old and Botham. Mudassar found comfort on the front foot, watchful and in line. Sadiq picked up runs, as he always does, by angling the bat out towards the off side. In between balls he rehearsed the safer arcs, directing the full face of the bat towards mid-on and mid-off, but between them they enjoyed a happier and more profitable experience than many would have thought possible.

For the first time in three days there was the sniff of real Test-match warfare. Sadiq was dressed for it, gleaming crash helmet and bulging thigh pad. As he and Mudassar, his partner, profited from their own watchfulness and from Brearley's attacking field, analysing the game expanded to a deeper and more meaningful study. The spinners, Miller and Edmonds, bowled; sleight and guile arrived as long-lost strangers to the middle.

At first, there was not much evidence of turn, but both spinners kept up a good length, having the batsmen stretching to the front foot, bringing Roope into the action in the close-fielding positions in front of the bat. Then Edmonds spun one sharply to Mudassar and apprehension grew in the young Pakistani's plunging defence. Edmonds won the duel when he bowled Mudassar, in the last over before the close, with the score 94–1.

Sunday Telegraph, 5 June 1978

'England, dear England, the agonies you bring us!'

Sydney Cricket Ground no longer has the feel of being just a cricket ground. Six fat cigar-like towers enclose the green oval and the floodlighting they carry at the top tells the story of multi-purpose. This is the one Test ground which admitted Packer cricket. So the World Series stars come out at night.

Already the Australian Board has discussed moving the sixth and final Test of this series to Melbourne because the monster towers will cast shadows across the pitch as the sun dips earlier in the February afternoons.

Sentinels of tradition are dwarfed, such as the pavilion which is flanked by the ladies' and members' stands, delicately tiered with pencil-thin pillars, green corrugated roofs, wrought-iron balustrades. From the tiny towers flags fluttered in the welcome breeze. The reshaping of another old stand has deprived this particular match of larger crowds. They have the builders in here in a big way.

The field itself also displayed its scars, lines from football pitches and a trench which directs a cable to the middle for the benefit of Kerry Packer's actuality microphones. The square itself was thought before the start to have suffered from too much cricket this season. However, when England won the toss, Brearley happily settled for batting.

Boycott and Brearley are very much the men the Sydney Hillsiders love to hate, probably because they represent the twin Pommie lead of captain and most notorious batsman. They withstood the roars for Hogg and kept him out for three overs which, in these days, is considered a minor triumph. Dymock tested Brearley's judgement of left-arm in-swing and yelled twice in the first over for possible lbws.

Both the captain and his partner were then treated to the unexpected sight of Rodney Hogg going off the field. It was announced that he had gone to change his socks. He looked in some discomfort, but returned a few overs later after Hurst had taken up the attack.

Fifty-five minutes' play had gone and the wicket looked good with just enough bounce to encourage the quickies when Hurst unleashed a series of fine deliveries at Boycott. Two bouncers were followed by a ball well up on the off stump. Boycott obliged with an edge of the bat to Border who held a superb catch to his left at second slip.

Enter Randall, hopping about through a routine of defensive shots as he approached the crease. Brearley talked to him. Randall drove the first ball, then hooked the second straight down the throat of Wood at backward short-leg. Wood was standing deep and square in that position made famous by Tony Lock and he picked up the ball straight from the bat. Although he had two pecks at the cherry, he held it comfortably.

Brearley stared at Randall. Could this be the moment for the captain to address himself to the responsibilities of the day? To his merit he did just that for an hour and thirty-six minutes. Then Hogg returned to send down four short, sharp balls which flew either side of the captain's body. They were well avoided.

Hogg's next was a classic skidding breakback from off, through the 'gate' and crack against the stumps. Exit the desperate captain and there was not an England supporter on the ground who had not been willing him to succeed.

England are used to poor starts and recoveries lately have usually centred on David Gower or, at Melbourne, on Graham Gooch. On this occasion it was not to be Gower. Hurst threw his hefty frame into a last effort before lunch. He went around the wicket to Gower to bowl the final ball. It flashed steeply up from the turf, freezing Gower's mind for a split second, before flicking his glove en route to Maclean's safe hands – 51 for 4 at lunch.

The conditions for batting were so propitious there was always a feeling that the recovery would come, especially as Gooch was playing so well. He used his height to meet the shorter balls half-way up, played very straight off back and front foot and always had time. He then made a dreadful error. He hooked a long-hop from the leg-spinner Higgs in the air straight to Toohey on the deep mid-wicket fence. It was a major crime in the circumstances even though Toohey made ground brilliantly and scooped a wonderful catch low in front of him.

From there on Botham had least trouble of all in staying in the middle, but he lacked the specialist support which Gooch could have given him.

England's first innings was effectively crippled from then on. Botham struck handsome drives off Dymock, scythed Higgs through the covers and pulled the short ball through mid-wicket. There was a limit to what he could do for the pain in the England dressing-room, but he certainly demonstrated to the Australians that they need have no fears about the pitch itself.

Yesterday's play was a classic case of initiative stolen. The Test is far from over, but England had a lot of questions to be asking themselves overnight.

Sunday Telegraph, 7 January 1979

'Hoggy, Hoggy, Hoggy'

Every 36.22 balls Rodney Hogg sends another Englishman on his way to a quiet corner of the dressing-room, or to the practice nets, or even to leap into a series of forward defensive strokes in the hotel lift, as I saw Derek Randall demonstrate at the Melbourne Hilton.

However the departed batsmen choose to chastise themselves is their business. Mr Hogg has finished with them. He has taken 27 wickets in this series conceding only 11 runs for each one. The record books await him.

I was looking for a tearaway quickie like Lillee or Thomson when I got to Melbourne last week believing that great fast bowlers propagate in their own image. Just to get the batsman's view of Hogg's assault with the new ball I watched from the end to which the lean, blond South Australian was directing the fire.

I was mystified. I chewed quietly on the evidence of a lively approach: a good line which kept the batsmen playing all the time and some movement off the seam almost always into the right-handed batsman from the off. But bowlers have managed that before without leaping at Arthur Mailey's Ashes record of 36 wickets in a series and that in only four games. Why is Rodney Hogg so different?

Out on the cover-point boundary, taking a sideways look at Hogg's run-up, I felt pinpricks of panic for the English batsmen as the demon fast bowler set the terraces ablaze with chants of 'Hoggy, Hoggy, Hoggy'. From this angle he looked much faster, of course, leaning low into his approach, rather like Frank Tyson from the waist up, but prancing like Jeff Thomson from the waist down. Better forget the past, I said to myself, there was no violent coiling of the spring à la Tyson and nothing of Thommo's winding catapult of an arm action. This was pure 'Hoggy', very plain and simple.

The delivery is whippy, the follow-through classical. It is an action without the overdrive which was fitted into such models as Lindwall, Trueman, Tyson, Hall, Lillee and Thomson. Even though the rising blood on the terraces demanded the scalp of more Englishmen and Hogg's blond hair cast a romantic streamline, there was not the breathtaking crescendo of muscle and mind. In fact he is said to be short of stamina as the result of an asthmatic condition.

Yet, I had to be wrong. The evidence was before me. I was watching history in motion, rattling out figures, forever to be recorded in the 1978–79 Ashes series: 6–74 and 1–35, 5–65 and 5–57, 5–30 and 5–36.

It would help to talk to an England batsman on the subject. I chose David Gower because he was one of the comparative successes of the Melbourne defeat and it is kinder to tax the cool mind of a run-getter than someone who is still trying to find the middle of the bat in the lift, for example.

'The main threat, though maybe not to left-handers like me, is the way he cuts the ball back off the pitch,' revealed Gower. 'He bowls fast off-breaks. He uses the crease a lot; he makes you play and he is very, very sharp. What more do you want?'

I wanted more and help came from Bobby Simpson. 'Hogg is straight and always at you. He gets plenty of movement in off the pitch, but if you ask me for one reason why he is a wicket-taker in this series, I'll tell you – he uses the crease at his end and gets very close to the stumps especially when he is around the wicket.

'That's odd. Then your fellows play into his hands because mostly they move back and across the stumps before he bowls. Hogg's good, varying line, plus a bit of nip-back from outside off stump, has them all playing around their pads, in a hurry . . . that means across the line . . . and that's goodbye Brearley, Boycott, Randall, Gooch and Miller. That's most of your batting.'

So that was it. Hogg is much more the Statham than the Trueman, more the dripping water than the dynamite. Just think how long it took for Brian Statham or Les Jackson or Derek Shackleton to be recognised as masters. Hogg is not yet as good as any of them.

Sunday Telegraph, 7 January 1979

No escaping Packer fast guns

The most dangerous act in the entertainment business these days is not balancing on the high wire, nor even putting a head in the lion's mouth. It is, without doubt, batting in Kerry Packer's Flying Circus.

You can spot a World Series batsman anywhere in Australia by the feverish jokes he makes about his Rollerball lot in the cricket world. Anecdotes spill out about helmets, bouncers, uneven pitches, night cricket and all the razzmatazz projecting them on to Packer's TV Channel 9. It is the heady elation of war, humour underlaid with fear.

'Can you see the white ball after it has been used for, say, twenty overs?' I asked. 'Can't see Wayne Daniel, let alone the ball.'

Fast bowling and repeated bouncers are destroying some of the best batsmen we have ever seen. The week's worst casualty was Majid Khan, my old Glamorgan team-mate, one of the bravest and most talented of batsmen. He was hit in the face by a ball which reared up from not too short of a length. Andy Roberts was the bowler, so Majid had a mere split second to evade it. He managed to turn his head, but had to settle for a depressed fracture of the cheekbone, rather than a full frontal impact.

When I have suggested to WSC batsmen that they are shell-shocked, they have all nodded, and again offered the falsetto chuckle.

I have never seen so many bouncers bowled in a session as by the World Team against the West Indies in a one-day game last week. Garth Le Roux, who is fast and nasty, Imran Khan, Mike Procter and Clive Rice all extracted cheers from the crowd, most of whom have been drawn to cricket for the first time by the showbiz presentation on Channel 9.

Clive Lloyd was not applauding. The great man cringed hesitantly at the first bouncer; gone was the animal ferocity of his brilliant hook shot, and the ball flicked his glove on the way into first slip's hands for an easy catch.

Fast bowlers have always dominated cricket matches. Usually they are in short supply, so when pairings like Lindwall and Miller, Statham and Trueman, or Lillee and Thomson come along there are few escape routes for the batsmen. For World Series batsmen there is no escape at all, because after Roberts comes Holding, comes Daniel, comes Garner or Lillee, after Snow, Procter and Le Roux comes Pascoe. The world's collection of knuckle-breakers.

I offered the observation that playing against fast bowling every day must make them better players. This was discounted by the argument that players in poor form had no chance to repair their techniques. The natural apprehension at the bouncers and the sheer speed the ball arrived at their end of the pitch, often zipping in or out off the seam at ninety miles an hour, deprived them of slow and medium-fast bowling which might have got them into form. Even the medium-fast bowlers are some of the best in the world.

World Series Cricket has a huge following in parts of Australia. It suits a lot of Australians who see it as a television game and they turn out to watch those TV stars when the show is in the area.

I have met several World Series devotees among the public who all compliment Packer and Co on their television coverage. They are right. By comparison, ABC's treatment is light years behind. You can play a spot-the-ball game in the concurrently televised Ashes and not even three action replays can find it sometimes.

If I were running World Series Cricket, I would restrict bouncers in order to restore a little of the grace to the wonderful stroke-makers. World Series obviously argues that only the very best batsmen should apply. Read Tony Greig in the *Sun Herald*. 'The competition on WSC is so intense, teams can no longer afford to allow the opposition tailenders to hang around. Consequently the pace bowlers are dishing out an unprecedented amount of bouncers to the "rabbits". So it is pleasing to see that cricketers like Dennis Lillee and Garth Le Roux have got the message, swallowed their pride and are wearing helmets.'

The problems of batters and bowlers alike do not end on the field. WSC cricketers are performing amazing leaps across the continent by aeroplane. Hours of play are more akin to a stage life than a cricketer's with its accent on 1.30pm starts and 10.30pm finishes.

Everyone says that the final stage of a Super Test, after the dinner break to the close, is the most exhausting cricket they have ever played. By the time they have taken a beer and a rest to unwind the nerves it is close on midnight.

Wives and children are out here with many of the players, but the most they share with them is a brief chat mid-morning. When asked out for a meal by friends they have to suggest breakfast. It was Mushtaq who was last to board the World XI bus to go to a rare match which started in the morning. Everyone was slumped in a seat asleep. 'Wake up, you lazy lot,' he shouted. 'You've got to get used to this daytime cricket.'

The plea of the batsmen too is that constant air travel dulls the reactions and there must come a day when the fast bowlers catch up with you.

Barry Richards jokes and says that World Series Cricket will soon be played only by fast bowlers and batsmen in armour. No fielders will be necessary because the batsman will be unable to run in his protective gear. Circles around the square to the boundary will determine the runs scored by each blow.

That is the sort of humour which, to me, betrays the disillusionment of great players who have been unable to reproduce anything resembling their old style at the crease. They are still loyal to the Packer cause to a man, but everyone evades the question about signing a new contract after the third season; this is the second. I doubt if they will.

Members of ICC met WSC on Thursday this week. ICC were represented by chairman Charles Palmer (president of MCC), David Clark, immediate past chairman, and Jack Bailey, MCC secretary. The pressures may now be less on ICC to compete, perhaps their role is to await the agonised pleas of the Packer batsmen and only then decide whether to release them from their lavish doom.

Theirs is a sporting existence without the heroism of a national cause. I am left thinking of mercenaries facing the flak every day and the false standards of the tinsel television fame. But the show goes on:

'Last night's game ended dramatically when no. 11 batsman Joel Garner, playing with a broken left middle finger from an accident only nine days previously, was struck on the finger by a short ball from World XI all-rounder Clive Rice (3–16). Garner was in considerable pain and walked from the field giving the World XI a win by 35 runs.' (*The Australian*, Tuesday 9 January.)

Sunday Telegraph, 14 January 1979

Beware Boycott's revenge!

Although England are 3–1 ahead with a lot of help from their opponents, it has to be acknowledged that the team has played with a lot of purpose. It has retained the Ashes, and only at Perth did the most decisive single influence on modern Test cricket, Geoff Boycott, play an important role. That is a marvellous team effort. But why has Boycott become almost the least influence in this side?

He admits that he has been carrying all the Yorkshire troubles around the field with him. That is understandable. Because of that, or as well as it, he has lapsed into technical error at the crease. After Rodney Hogg had bowled him out at Melbourne in the third Test, some of the England senior players drew his attention to a strange movement of his front foot as the bowler brought his arm over. They said that it shifted back and outside the leg stump. Boycott disbelieved them. He wanted proof, and later got it on the television highlights that night.

After such an initial movement, he is not surprisingly late across to the off stump and even when he does get across, he has already lost the split second in which he can launch himself on to the front foot far enough to escape the Hogg lbw-danger area; the half-cock stage.

Boycott's dismissals prove that he is either keeping the slip fielders in practice or falling over across the line of the Hogg ball which cuts back sharply from outside off stump. Another result of the head falling over to the off-side is that the straight ball often feels as if it is coming along the line of leg stump or outside.

Geoff swore that he could not have been out lbw by Hurst in the last Test. Television replay again came to the aid of his advisers. Hurst delivered the ball from close to the stumps at his end and it was going along the middle-stump line all the way.

Another consequence is that he has been incapable of driving the ball anywhere. Happily, at Newcastle, the upright Boycott took over again, the fours flowed and Bob Taylor still clings to his bet that he will witness a Boycott double-century in a Test before the end of the series.

Sunday Telegraph, 21 January 1979

Give the people what they want

The big, black panthers in strawberry-mousse clothing closed in, patient but lethal around the Australians.

The lone figure in wattle yellow fidgeted, though he stood bravely upright. For him there could be no easy escape. He was stuck out there in the middle, trapped in the floodlights, relying on his skill and reflexes – no-one else's – to repel a flashing white ball.

'Come on, Aussie, come on,' blared the public address speakers and 45,000 of his fellow-countrymen joined the act. The sheer loneliness of a batsman was never so well illustrated when friend and foe alike dressed in white.

Again the panthers crouched, coiling the vertebral spring, ready to pounce on to the catch or leap into a loud appeal. Nobody doubted the loneliness of the umpire, either. The decision was torn out of him with yelling and jumping, arms raised to the sky. If he turned them down they kicked the dust, snarled and prowled. The lonely arbiter made off to square-leg.

Yes, the cricket at Sydney last week was vivid entertainment and so it should be because World Series Cricket is a brilliant marketing exercise of which the guiding principle is the public's pleasure. Give the people what they want, or, as I more often heard it put: 'It's bums on seats that count'.

Long-legged girls woo the crowd with promotional literature, including scorecards which carry the photographs of all the Packer players. No-one passes incognito in this set-up, though Kerry Packer himself is working hard at his personal retreat into the shadows. Drinks go out to the players by buggy and the public address system does even more addressing.

The yellow Australian hit a four. The finger went on the button and out came that war-cry again, 'Come on Aussie, come on'.

[84]

Incredibly, this World Series jingle is now in the Top Ten of the Sydney charts and last week climbed twenty-two places to no. 33 in the national ratings.

You've been training all the winter.
And there's not a team that's fitter,
And that's the way it's going to be;
'Cos you're up against the best, you know,
This is Super Test, you know.
You're up against the best the world has seen.
Come on, Aussie, come on, come on,
Come on, Aussie, come on.
Lillee's pounding down like a machine,
Pascoe's making divots in the green.
Marsh is taking wickets,
Hooksie's clearing pickets,
And the Chappells' eyes have got the killer gleam.
Come on, Aussie, come on, come on,
Come on, Aussie, come on.

Sunday Telegraph, 28 January 1979

Peace on the beach

Kerry Packer has won his war. The exclusive TV rights once denied him to cover Test and Sheffield Shield cricket on his Channel 9 are now in his pocket subject to the next six weeks or so of negotiations.

He was annoyed by his original rejection, all the more so because his offer was higher than that of the Australian Broadcasting Commission, who retained the franchise almost three years ago.

It was then, with the explosive mixture of the irate mogul and the hurt schoolboy, that he threw sand in the eyes of the establishment and set up his own stumps alongside theirs on the same beach.

In the summer of 1977 Packer knew he was attacking a game which was strong in spirit but legally and economically fragile.

He saw professional players receiving the thinnest pay packets in sport; in their county contracts he sensed elements of unfair restraint; at county grounds he was aware of spectators, or, in his language, customers, queuing for a tough sandwich and often freezing out a day's play on a splintering seat.

So last week, two and a half years since the first World Series ball was bowled in the VFL Stadium outside Melbourne, Mr Packer has been awarded his exclusive rights for a three-year spell. Mission accomplished.

Ultimate victory sprang from the nuisance value of WSC but, if Mr Packer had what the ICC wanted most – their best players – the Council itself was holding his coveted TV rights. Exchanging those for the death of WSC appears to be a reasonable equation.

It is likely that the WSC organisation will be sustained under another name and used to run the flagging Sheffield Shield matches. Even night cricket might go and the truth is that Packer cricket never paid its way.

The Australian Board clearly requires that Channel 9 pictures be available to the whole of Australia. To this end the Packer organisation has already talked of offering Test cricket packages to commercial country stations. Independent TV stations will account for 96 per cent of the population and, for the remainder, free coverage will be offered rather ironically to ABC.

It will always be a shame that the revolution happened as it did. Too many loyalists were hurt: too many old cricketing friends became enemies.

So Packer has got what he wanted. But it is an unusual victory because, looking around that beach again, there are few losers. I can see only the Australian Broadcasting Commission limping away, maimed and humbled by defeat.

The Australian Board has certainly not been defeated. Its members were first dazed and angered and, even now, I would guess, unforgiving, but they have turned Mr Packer's power to the good of the game they administer, and are likely to kill off WSC in the process.

The advantages accumulate. Mr Packer's television

coverage is superior to any other in Australia; his commercialism has put cricket on the level of big entertainment; night cricket has a lucrative following; the advertising on Channel 9 can promote cricket and individual cricketers to the game's advantage; Mr Packer's accommodation of the public's pleasure has been a lesson to all.

In these next weeks of negotiations, the Australian Board will surely try to restrict the number of jarring advertisements which appear between overs, and then again Mr Packer may not wish to relinquish his position of strength by handing over his whole cricket organisation. However, this is strictly for the lawyers and it must be recorded that both sides are winning at this stage.

Cricketers themselves have already benefited. In county cricket the move to a minimum wage of £4,000 has been accelerated. The financial rewards in traditional cricket may not match the World Series wages, but few Packer players will regret the passing of a charade of a game which committed them to an exhausting and unfulfilling lifestyle.

Most of all Test cricket will resume loftier standards than have recently been on view. Woolmer, Underwood, Knott and Amiss might again play Test cricket for England as soon as they can satisfy the patient and sensible Cricketers' Association that they are available for all English Tests and tours. Recrimination should be out.

Yes, if peace comes there will be few losers and the established game should recover from this hefty punch on the nose and continue undisturbed if it digests the giant lesson of the revolution that cricket's potential is large, it needs to be run as big business, and players have rights by law.

The value of the amateur committee man should now simply be as a representative of those who elected him, as a watchdog guarding high standards of behaviour and the game's deep roots. The day of the highly paid Chief Executive of a County Club is with us: it is now as much a matter of commerce as cricket.

Sunday Telegraph, 29 April 1979

1979–1980

Friendly Essex win the championship

From skipper H. G. Owen and all who pioneered from 1895, to Keith Fletcher's boys in 1979, over a century's cricketers have toiled, seamed and spun in the land of the three scimitars before the County Championship title finally came their way.

It was almost in Essex's character never to win it at all. They have always been a delightful road show whose charm was one day their brilliance, the next their vulnerability.

They were a 'natural' to be taken for 721 in a day by the 1948 Australians at Southend, but then, in 1957, with almighty Surrey on the rampage, who else could scramble past the follow-on, bowl out Surrey for 119, and then proceed to smash off the 256 runs to win in under four hours against Bedser, Loader, Lock and Laker to win by two wickets. Only Essex.

They played mostly at Leyton, which was rural in the early part of the century, but when London's eastern suburbs spread, engulfing the county ground, the Essex circus set out around the county to play its cricket on eight or nine grounds every season: Leyton, Southend, Westcliff, Romford, Brentwood, Ilford, Colchester, Clacton and Chelmsford.

On the road went every piece of equipment, hundreds of yards of seven-foot screening with poles, stands, chairs and benches, scoreboard printing machinery, boundary boards, a heavy roller, marquees and a portable office. And later went the famous double-decker buses which housed the scoreboard and the ladies' loo.

The modern Essex, set calmly into action by Tom Pearce after the Second World War, resumed the have-bat-will-travel spirit. From 1949 Trevor Bailey became, first, assistant secretary and later secretary.

'It was wonderfully impromptu stuff. I recall a game at Romford when there was a huge crowd and I had to ask the opposing captain if I could leave the field to put on my secretary's hat and attend to the latecomers. I did. I went off and helped shift some tables and found room for the extra people to sit on them right in front of the sightscreen. We were always impoverished. No-one ever got turned away.'

Unfortunately, as far as Championship hopes were concerned, the travelling circus act always hampered Essex. They had many fine sides playing well under the leadership of Pearce, Insole, Bailey, Taylor, but they were effectively playing all their matches away from home.

In 1965, Chelmsford went up for sale. Trevor Bailey attended a dinner to celebrate Worcestershire's Championship and told Warwickshire representatives whom he met there that Essex would like to buy the ground. Essex were short of cash, but Warwickshire came up with an interest-free loan. So at Chelmsford this weekend a quiet glass should be raised in the direction of Edgbaston because the home base has been an important factor in the advance to the top.

Keith Fletcher was groomed for captaincy. He used to stand at first slip, advising his old captain Brian Taylor. Mind you there was a time when I thought there was only one conversation.

'What d'y think, Fletch?'

'Slip'm Boycey from the other end, Tonker.' Fairly simple tactics, often effectively repeated.

Now Essex have their most talented team of all time and they are splendidly led by a thoughtful, modest man, whose shy prep-school walk out to bat belies a competitive spirit. His achievement is that he has managed to bring out the best cricket from his side without depressing their own personalities and their love of fun. Essex are entertainers.

Consider the most extrovert, Ray East. When he bowls, his Pinocchio legs and windmill arms conceal his skill. His love of comic mime sets everyone laughing. Yet the pathos of this particular clown is that his serious intent is often lost amid laughter. However, Ray East is good enough to play for England; most professionals will tell you that.

The batting has been speedy and talented with the classical McEwan, Gooch in full flow, lusty Pont, wisdom from Denness, Hardie and Fletcher himself. There is promise from Lilley, consistency with gloves and bat from Smith. With the ball, Lever has been a sheer sensation, backed by inspired effort from Philip and Turner, as well as by the two patient mature artists, Acfield and East.

In 1979, Essex have gloriously proved in days of increasing financial reward that money need not be the incentive. They have played at cricket, not manipulated it for cash, and have transmitted their own obvious enjoyment to their patient and loyal supporters; the prize all the more delightful because of the . . . well, er . . . brief 103-year wait.

Sunday Telegraph, 26 August 1979

Aggro on the Hill, but excellent cricket

Following the disbandment of World Series Cricket, the Australian Cricket Board of Control staged, in December–February 1979–80, a three-cornered contest, the Benson & Hedges World Series Cup, of one-day internationals between Australia, England and the West Indies. At the same time a short rubber of three Test matches each was played between Australia and West Indies, and between Australia and England in which the Ashes were not at stake.

I have reached the end of another week on the Australian cricket 'triangular' experiment much more confused than I was.

This is not to refer to Geoff Boycott's refusal in Perth to inspect the Test pitch with his captain. That is not in the least confusing. It was a conversation which might have happened a hundred times before. However, this time it was overheard and Mike Brearley had the option of shrugging his shoulders, laughing and defusing the comment in the public eye, or of exposing Boycott's attitude as a point of principle by taking it seriously. . . .

This England party is one of the happiest ever, a tribute to its leadership and management. The directness of Mike Brearley is very much appreciated and his open reaction to Boycott's jibe shows his own attitude, that Boycott is there to play cricket, not to be understood.

The West Indians have moved away from the television eye to nurse their wounds. Viv Richards' hip refuses to heal and Clive Lloyd faces a crucial week in his career as he tests the knee on which exploratory surgery was carried out a fortnight ago.

By comparison, Australia has the real problems. As the host it has to solve entirely new problems which are being thrown up almost daily, as well as to face up to old problems such as the belligerence on field of Ian Chappell. This week, too, their team has lost three one-day internationals in a row.

I suppose it is not so much that I myself am confused, but that I am confused watching Australia getting so confused, if you see what I mean. For instance, the Board of Control looked like being strong last week, making a lot of wise statements about the behaviour of players on the field. Yet Ian Chappell got away with a six-week suspended sentence after an incident in the South Australia/England game at Adelaide. Provoked or not by a pernickety umpire, the question is, did he or did he not throw his bat? The answer is that he did. Does not their lenience place Ian Chappell above the game, above the unwritten laws of personal conduct which cricket needs urgently to re-establish?

On Sunday I sat out in the members' stand at the Melbourne Cricket Ground to relax and watch the Australians play the West Indies in a one-day international. 43,369 others presumably arrived with the same idea, but 35 of them changed their minds late in the afternoon and ended up in the police van.

No alcohol was on sale inside the ground as per Sunday law, but spectators could bring their own liquor with them in the eskis (ice-boxes for picnics). It turned out that eminently sober members were able on one side of the ground to witness, through their binoculars, some of the most ferocious fighting I've ever seen anywhere at any time, let alone on a cricket ground. Beer cans were hurled in every direction. Empty they could cut or graze; full they could knock someone senseless.

There followed shameful sights of parents trying to shield their children from the storm, turning their eyes from the mass brawling and ultimately looking to escape. Others cheered fight after fight.

Again the Australian Board and other state ground authorities acted. There would be no liquor taken into the Sydney ground for England's one-day game on Tuesday, nor into the WACA ground in Perth during the Test. However, South Australia added their own confusion by saying they would allow alcohol through their gates because few would turn up to watch otherwise.

But was it simply the beer and the sun turning the crowd into animals? A clinical psychologist from Sydney, Dr Norman Rees, blamed PBL, the Board's new marketing company. 'Their television advertisements are aggressive,' he said. 'They show Lillee really tossing a heavy one and another player getting his cap knocked off. They represent a different image of a game that by tradition is dignified and, in doing so, they attract, not more devout cricket fans but a different type of spectator altogether.

'The result is a modelling of aggression – that is, you get a group of people watching something which involves aggression and it has a copying effect. They copy their peers and idols. The ads promise people they're going to see lots of action but when they roll up and find only a slow, quiet, game they start throwing beer cans to liven things up, to relieve the boredom.'

I sat on the Sydney Hill on Tuesday. Beer was on sale inside the ground. The cans flew about in outrageous barrages for completely unknown reasons. The targets were strictly personal choices, but when they turned their attention to the field, Graham Gooch and Derek Underwood did not escape the flying debris. Still it was relatively a calm night. The Hillsiders are younger than they used to be, less knowledgeable about cricket, and therefore less amusing than ever. 'Why do you come to the Hill to watch cricket?' I asked a typical loud-mouth. ''Cos it's great. I just come for the fight.'

The simplest affairs of the week have been the delights which the players have put before us. It is essential to balance the picture: it has not been all obscenity, hard-sell and wobbling authority. There has been excellent cricket.

I witnessed what I consider to have been the greatest innings ever in one-day cricket. Viv Richards went to the crease in the ninth over against Australia at Melbourne. He faced 131 balls and scored 153. Dennis Lillee, balding now and not as fast as he was once, raced in to bowl. Before he reached the delivery stride Richards was advancing down the pitch. Then, with a savage crack of the wrists, he flat-batted the ball over mid-off: a couple of bounces into the pickets for four.

Thommo's fast yorker he drove for four through the covers, having first stepped back outside the leg stump. (Keith Fletcher, Mike Denness, Dennis Amiss, David Lloyd, John Edrich, Colin Cowdrey and all England Aunt Sallies of the 1974–75 tour can come out from behind their sofas now.)

Greg Chappell proved that his classic style can triumph in the one-day game and Geoffrey Boycott turned the clock back to his famous Gillette Cup innings of 1965.

To see Peter Willey go for his shots, David Bairstow relishing the contest, Mike Brearley contributing good sense with the bat have all been warm moments for England followers.

I shall take one special moment back with me – of Rod Marsh being bowled by young Graham Dilley, played on, and looking up slowly from his shattered stumps only to find the bristling twenty-year-old towering above him having followed-through a good eighteen yards. Dilley did not curse. He said nothing: just stared, and Marsh padded away.

Sunday Telegraph, 16 December 1979

Examples which young people follow

My history master used to award penalty kicks for dull play on the rugby field. If a boy ever risked a punch or a tantrum, he would expect to be sent to 'the cooler', which really meant standing still on the touchline until recalled to play.

The schoolmaster's name is worth recalling because it came to mind in Australia a short while ago as I sat watching, first, Ian Chappell's bat-throwing argument with the umpire at Adelaide, then Dennis Lillee's aluminium equivalent at Perth [when for 9½ minutes he refused to change his aluminium bat for a wooden one until his captain insisted]. Sam Evans would have had them both on the sidelines. . . .

Although Ian Chappell and Dennis Lillee are a long way out of school jurisdiction, a million schoolmasters are still desperately interested in them. Theirs is the example which young people follow, even more so now that billions of viewers are watching cricket on television . . . What Lillee and Chappell demonstrated was an example which might make schoolmasters tear out their hair and youths throw beer cans on the Sydney Hill. . . .

It is obvious that the Packer Revolt was all about cricketers fighting for the status of their profession and for money which was a fair compensation for being among the best players in the world. Finally, Mr Justice Slade undid the cage which had trapped their aspirations.

The Australian Board gave them wings by setting up the triangular commercial experiment, and many sponsors came up with the hard cash.

Most players, I know, understand that with their new incomes from commerce comes a widening of their responsibilities. No longer does their involvement begin and end on the field. There are receptions to honour, prize-givings to attend, and many miles of video-taped promotion to act out.

At the reception which launched the Australian winter back in November, England turned up smartly in their uniforms, the West Indies took the trouble to don suits, even waistcoats, but there were those Australians who looked dog-eared in sweat shirts and thongs.

On another occasion, Clive Lloyd, so disgusted with the closing actions of one match, did not even appear for the presentation. Deryck Murray deputised. David Hookes threw his bat, causing about £25 worth of damage to a dressing-room. Viv Richards' bat bounced off a seat through a window.

I am certainly not the judge of any of these reported happenings, but it is worth the new regime of international cricketers standing back, while the guns are cooling, to consider the style, indeed the image, of their profession as a whole. Surely the right sponsors will only stay with a game of honourable behaviour?

No-one likes to see the schoolmaster-little-boy attitude adopted by administrators in cricket, though clearly, if you choose to earn a living in the game as run by the various Boards of Control, you must abide by the laws and playing conditions. But perhaps golf is a good example of how individuals, for slow play, bad sportsmanship and other blights on their game, are fined, suspended or banned by their fellow professionals.

Would a formally elected Cricketers' Disciplinary court work best? It would mean that the restraint comes from within the profession. Yet everyone knows that the discipline we are looking for must come from within a player himself. There is nothing like the trials of Test cricket to examine the habits you have acquired for life.

Sunday Telegraph, 16 December 1979

Golden Jubilee

a) A Family party

We all turned up to the fiftieth birthday party of the Indian Cricket Board of Control, shunning, on the way to Wankhede Stadium, offers to sell 'eclipse glasses', guaranteed to 'prevent your retina from falling out' on yesterday's amazing, sun-gazing day. Bombay awaits a total eclipse of the sun.

I was travelling with the former Indian Test cricketer, Abbas Ali Baig, who was hurrying to make the parade of old cricketers before the start. He was forced to brush aside the vendor with the words: 'Look, dear chap, my retina has fallen out so often while at the crease, it is far too late to worry now'.

And so India's old heroes formed a large circle in front of the stands, balloons floated skywards, the Indian and British National Anthems were sung twice – well, India is India. MCC president, Billy Griffith, stood with the British High Commissioner alongside the Indian Board's president on a raised platform. Minutes later, just to prove to the England team that India never changes in some respects, John Lever had what looked like a plumb lbw turned down.

Those who can remember that far back, will recall Arthur Gilligan, who led MCC's first tour out here in 1926–27, urging the Indians to form a controlling body. He, more than anyone, would have been aware of the Indian aptitude for cricket; the British legacy.

His Sussex county had been spellbound once upon a time by the great Ranjitsinhji and were soon to fall in love, however poignantly and briefly, with the wristy elegance of his nephew Duleepsinhji. These two played for England in the days when there was no India to represent. The bridge between those days and the new, organised India, which came with the Board's formation in 1929, was the Nawab of Pataudi. He played three times for England and three times for India.

It was at Lord's on 25 June 1932 that India first played official Test cricket. C. K. Nayudu was the captain and with splendid cricketers like Wazir Ali, Nazir Ali, Lall Singh, Jahangir Khan, Amar Singh and Mahomed Nissar pressed England hard over three days before collapsing and losing by 158 runs. The record books include one historic note: England debuts – W. E. Bowes; India debuts – All.

England cricketers who have played in India will recall it with a smile; not that it has ever been easy to perform with skill and consistency in extreme heat in front of a cricket-crazy crowd. When the Tests are on, the whole nation stops.

The transistor radio has, of course, compounded the effect. A fair example occurred only last week when I was among the horse-racing crowds watching the Indian Derby in Bombay. Seconds before the race, I worked my way down to the finishing post, which was also the start. Jockeys settled their horses before taking them around to the back of the stalls. Suddenly there was a surge of agitation among the spectators, horses became agitated too. One or two reared up and the jockeys strained their arm muscles, glaring with annoyance at the crowd.

'What happened?' I asked my friend. He turned and asked someone else, and came back. 'Disturbance was for appeal for lbw in Calcutta. It was badly turned down.'

Whereas in the 1930s England players will remember tiger shoots and palaces of Maharajahs, those of the 1950s always talk about travel, which was exclusively by train. Donald Carr, who was Nigel Howard's vice-captain in 1951–52, remembers how he and the skipper, the amateurs, emerged after long overnight trips from first-class compartments on to the railway platform to see the professionals clambering out from the second-class carriages with heavily barred windows. Blazers covered in red dust, cursing the country and their cricketing lot, they were players like Dick Spooner, Allan Watkins, Tom Graveney, Frank Lowson, Brian Statham and more.

Others will recount tales of lodging up-country in the familiar PWD (Public Works Department) rest-house. In my own experience of 1972–73 I recall a water shortage when one bucket of the stuff was provided for four players sharing for their morning ablutions.

Tales abound of life under mosquito nets. Fast bowlers almost in tears after hours of rushing in to bowl on hard-baked surfaces; drag-plates clanging out their own death knell.

The ball beats bat at last, the appeal is heaved out to pumping lungs and a dusty mouth. But the inscrutable Indian umpire is, by now, looking at the ground muttering: 'I'm terribly sorry, but that is not out'. Ah, well, another couple of hours and we might beat the bat again.

Jack Ikin once asked me if India had changed. 'What do you mean, Jack?' I said. 'Well,' he laughed, 'y'know, as the bowler

[97]

brings his arm over to bowl, the sight screen bursts into flames.'

Calcutta, more than Bombay, has the image of an inferno. If the ball hits an Englishman's pad, 85,000 inside the ground appeal for lbw – and so do 85,000 outside the ground. Very probably those outside have duplicated tickets. But also they pay a rupee to sit on the ground and follow the game's progress on a blackboard, manned by a gentleman who holds a transistor radio to his ear. 'Fletcher, c Engineer b Prasanna.'

I saw the blackboard in action last week during the Pakistan–India Test. This time it was in the splendour of one of the world's finest hotels, the Mougal Sheraton at Agra. Part of the hotel service was providing the latest Test scores.

One or two days later, England players Graham Gooch and David Bairstow arrived there for a look at the Taj Mahal at Agra. Seeing them relax at the poolside, accompanied by their wives, forced me into one or two comparisons between their lot and mine some eight years ago.

So times have changed, and who would be surprised at that? Indian cricketers, like those around the world, have enjoyed a surge of status and of income since the advent of Kerry Packer.

Two years ago an Indian Test player earned a fee of around £500; 4,000 rupees of which would be deposited by the Board of Control into a provident fund for each player's retirement.

However, the professional's cause is not the only one. The Indian Board of Control administers nationwide competitions and spreads its planning and its endeavour right through universities and schools. In every way it has come of age and probably for the only occasion since England and India first played Test cricket against each other, the England side are simply joining a huge family party to make up the numbers.

Sunday Telegraph, 17 February 1980

b) The Test

India had every right to feel confident that the Golden Jubilee would be celebrated in grand style. India had beaten both Australia and Pakistan and England had suffered humiliation in Australia. Moreover, after over a year of continuous Test cricket India had decided not to tour West Indies, a wise decision for which players were most thankful. Indeed, it was the non-availability of several leading players, especially Gavaskar and Kapil Dev, which made the cancellation inevitable. The only disturbing feature of the cancellation of the tour was that the decision came late from the Indian Board and appeared to have been made by the players rather than the Board. One must emphasise, however, that as the Jubilee Test would be India's seventeenth Test in eight months, the decision was the correct one. We are suffering from a surfeit of Test cricket. It took India sixteen years to play her first seventeen Tests. . . .

As prelude to the Test a double-wicket tournament was held, and a crowd of nearly 50,000, underlining that all cricket has charm for the Indians, saw Gooch and Botham win the tournament with Kapil Dev and Sandeep Patil in second place. Derek Randall's tale of woe continued when he was dismissed six times and he and John Lever ended with a score of minus one.

India omitted Chauhan from their Test side, Roger Binny moving up to open the innings with Gavaskar, which seemed to be asking a lot of the young Anglo-Indian. England's selection problems were not helped by illness and injury. When one reflects that Bairstow was considered in order to strengthen the batting and that his highest score in first-class cricket in Australia had been 12, it shows the dilemma which faced the England selectors, who chose Taylor.

The match itself provided cricket which was totally unexpected in character. Viswanath won the toss and India batted. Quick scoring is not usually a feature of Indian batting, but runs were rattling along at just under four an over. The crowd was less than expected, and with the wicket a little green and the atmosphere heavy, the ball swung and seamed in perfect English conditions.

Gavaskar survived a very close call for lbw in Lever's opening over and then hit the same bowler for 22 runs in the next two. After forty-five minutes India had reached 56 when Binny hesitated after playing firmly to leg and was run out by Larkins at the bowler's end. Gavaskar, who had scored 41 of

[99]

the runs in the opening stand, became more circumspect and finally fell to Botham when one short of his fifty. Bewilderingly, India were 108 for 2 at lunch.

They were 108 for 3 after the first ball of the afternoon which Vengsarkar touched to Taylor. Stevenson was the bowler and this gave him his first wicket in his first Test match. Viswanath was bowled by Lever off an inside edge and as Patil began to show a range of strokes which, coupled with his positive approach, has made him one of the most exciting of India's emerging cricketers, Botham returned to have him and Kapil Dev caught at the wicket in the same over by balls which lifted alarmingly by Indian standards.

Kirmani held the innings together but neither Botham nor Taylor was to be denied and India were all out before the close for 242, better than expected after five wickets had been lost while only 58 were added. Once more Ian Botham was a hero. His 6 for 58 meant that in twenty-five Tests he had taken five or more wickets in an innings thirteen times. In honours, however, he came second to Bob Taylor whose seven catches equalled the wicket-keepers' Test record set up by Wasim Bari in Auckland the previous year. Honours have come late in the game to Bob Taylor. He was not at his best in Australia, but there was nobody who would begrudge this nicest of men a place in the record books.

Acting like a portent in a Shakespearean tragedy, a total eclipse of the sun, the first in the Indian sub-continent this century, turned the second day into the rest day. For India it proved doubly symbolic.

Gooch and Boycott began again at 3 for o. Gooch provided Kirmani with his ninety-ninth Test dismissal and Boycott with his hundredth, but in the meantime Larkins went lbw first ball to Ghavri. Gower survived the hat-trick by hitting Ghavri for four and then played carefully until falling lbw to Kapil Dev. Brearley suffered the same fate and England were 58 for 5. Botham and Taylor then set about the second instalment of their double-act in a stand of common sense and professional application.

With the score at 85 Taylor was given out caught behind off

Kapil Dev. Taylor was clearly amazed and after Viswanath had intervened the decision was reversed. Boycott was also to earn a reprieve in the second innings. Whilst one applauds the sportsmanship of the Indians, one feels that umpires have a difficult enough job without players dictating their decisions for them and in each case it would perhaps have been better had the batsman unhesitatingly accepted the umpire's verdict. Nevertheless it made the Jubilee Test a completely happy occasion.

Taylor gave Botham admirable support and once more the Somerset all-rounder demonstrated his resolution and power. His timing was exact and he swept and pulled with precision. His driving was regal in its splendour, arrogant in its might. He hit 17 fours. The stand was worth 171, a sixth-wicket record for England against India, when Botham was lbw to Ghavri for 114. He had become the first man in the history of Test cricket to take five wickets in an innings and score a century in the same Test match three times. It was his sixth Test hundred and his second in succession. From a position of peril he had led England to within reach of India's score.

Taylor and Emburey resumed on the third day's play at 232 for 6. Taylor stayed for another hour, but was denied his fifty and it was left to John Lever and Graham Stevenson, who hit 27 in just over half an hour, to consolidate England's lead.

Going in again 54 runs behind, India made the worst possible start when Botham had Binny lbw without scoring. Their innings went from woe to woe as Botham and Lever swung the ball menacingly and extracted disconcerting bounce. At tea India were 72 for 6. Kapil Dev batted with aggression and determination and India lost only two more wickets in the final session, but on the fourth morning only one more run was scored as the last two wickets fell.

Botham's 7 for 48 brought his total to 13 wickets in the match and made him the first player in Test history to score a century and take ten wickets in a Test match. One was reminded of John Lever's comment on his Test colleague at the beginning of the 1978 season: simply, 'This bloke will rewrite all the record books'.

When Bob Taylor caught Shivlal Yadav off Botham on the fourth morning it was his tenth catch of the match so giving the Derbyshire 'keeper a world Test record. Rarely can two players have so dominated a match at this level.

Whatever hopes India had of victory were quickly dispelled by Gooch and Boycott who made no fuss in getting the 96 needed. So India was not to celebrate a Jubilee triumph, but the defeat could not detract from the assertion that they had a very fine side.

Eighty years ago Captain Philip Trevor could write disparagingly, and unchallenged, that in India 'there is cricket "of sorts".' He would be surprised if he was able to see the 'sort' of cricket produced today by Gavaskar, Kapil Dev, Viswanath, Kirmani and the rest, and I feel he would be gracious enough to join with all lovers of the game and say 'many happy returns'.

Sunday Telegraph, 20 February 1980

Fair and unfair play

The Laws of Cricket have been rewritten embodying in the 42 statutes a condemnation of and hopeful cure for the increasing moods of petulance and gamesmanship which have discoloured the spirit of the game, especially at international level.

Cricket lovers have had to endure this lowering of behaviour without being able to demonstrate their objections. They understood too that cricket's poor behaviour mirrors the 1970s in which many sporting virtues have been emasculated. Judging from my own correspondence a passive majority is now stirring and it will find a leader this year in S. C. Griffith, CBE, DFC, Cambridge University, Sussex, England, secretary of MCC, and now, in 1980, MCC's president.

His war-cry for the presidential year is good sportsmanship and fair play, and this month he sees the essence of his beliefs perpetuated in the rewritten Laws of Cricket. Billy Griffith was asked to reshape the laws in the early 1970s. He set about it in 1974 and the new code (1980) is now effective.

Only five times in over two hundred years have the Laws

been rewritten. This version replaces that of 1947 and, more copiously than any before, legislates for the spirit of the game. The fact that the Laws, approved by all International Cricket Councils, member countries, carry so much moral instruction is proof that all is not well with the modern game.

Billy Griffith, I feel, would have been even more drastic and punitive if those last words could have been used. His advisers along the line included F. G. Mann, who chaired a MCC Laws Sub-Committee, and the MCC Secretariat; T. E. Smith, the pillar of the Association of Umpires who assisted him throughout; and the ICC itself.

Even as it is the new Law 42, called Unfair Play, is now the longest. The repertoire of evil doings includes lifting the seam, changing the condition of the ball, incommoding the striker, obstruction of a batsman in running, the bowling of fast high full tosses, time-wasting, and players damaging the pitch.

In matters of dissent there is a strengthening of the Umpires' procedure of warning and ultimately reporting a player. For the barrage of bouncers which has so distorted the contest between bat and ball a fresh solution is adopted. A bouncer is now unfair if the umpire deems it an attempt to intimidate the striker.

The umpire must simply gauge the length, direction and the 'relative skill of the striker' and, if the very first bouncer a bowler sends down is thought to be intimidating, then the cautionary action starts. First a private warning, then the more public final warning and, for a third offence, the bowler must be taken off for the remainder of the innings.

This applies to all cricket although in first-class and Test cricket this year, the agreement of a maximum of one bouncer per over continues on an experimental basis.

The new law says that intimidation is no part of cricket. Many would disagree with that and claim that it always was; that it is fair for a fast bowler to test the courage of a batsman.

Unfortunately, players have always found ways around the laws whenever they have wanted. Now, in this case, all the batsman has to do is to make a show of being intimidated as he ducks a bouncer. There will be some great pretenders tricking umpires into issuing the warnings. What better way to draw the bowlers' sting? Stand-by for the theatricals.

Another law directed at the gamesmen in cricket is a brand new addition called 'Timed Out'. An incoming batsman has to set foot on the field within two minutes of the previous wicket falling. This is to prevent time-wasting. If he is late he is out, subject to an appeal by the opposition and after an investigation by the umpires. The umpires, who may visit the pavilion if necessary to check on illness or accident, must decide if the delay is wilful. Time taken for investigation is to be added on the day's play.

Previously, a two-minute law was hardly ever invoked because the batsman's failure to appear was taken as the whole team's refusal to play and so the fielding side could be awarded the match.

The story has always amused me of David Steele, who was said to have lost his way in the pavilion when going out to bat in his first Test for England at Lord's in 1975. Apparently, he went down one flight of stairs too many and ended up in the basement toilets. He would be wholly exonerated under the new 'Timed Out' law, but I wonder how many excuses can be dreamed up! How about a plea of a broken pad-strap, or split trousers or another call to the toilet, and so on?

Tucked in among this restrictive legislation is the one perfect cure for cheats and gamesmen: 'The captains are responsible at all times for ensuring that play is conducted within the spirit of the game as well as within the laws.'

So where have all the captains gone? It can be argued that, if cricket has the right captains, Law 42 on 'Unfair Play' could disappear in the perfect world. As it is, the players themselves have made it necessary to write it all down and to spell out what sporting behaviour the game expects.

Billy Griffth has cut a splendidly clear path through a jungle and it is appropriate that his fine efforts coincide with his year of MCC presidency. In the Laws and in his office, his message is clearly the same.

Sunday Telegraph, 13 April 1980

'Just talk to them'

In the days when I was playing first-class cricket, I was aware that an élite band of ball-by-ball commentators was at large but, like most practising players, I rarely had the chance to hear them work. Occasionally, at matches, the transistor radios in the crowd sent their commentaries booming across the field. Spectators were plugged in by one ear to those most popular personalities of the commentary box, and by one ear and two eyes to us. I remember having to retrieve a ball from the boundary three times in the same over. On the last time a red-faced man surrounded by icebox, binoculars, score-book, *Wisden*, umbrella, and radio to which he was attached by an ear-piece, shouted at me: 'Hey, Tony, mate. D'y know what Alan Gibson just called your captaincy? He called it eso . . . something . . . What was it, Fred?'

Fred, his colleague, was similarly connected to the ball-by-ballers, and because his volume level was well turned up he shouted his reply so loudly that everyone stopped and listened. 'He called 'im eso-bloody-teric, mate. That's what he called 'im: eso-bloody-teric.'

The first man turned back to me. 'Yes, Tony, mate: esoteric you are. Mind you, you don't look esoteric to me; y'look knackered.'

I record that with affection for Alan Gibson, a kindly commentator, who brought a delicious gift of language and style to the game of cricket. I got to know him better in the rugby season when we sidled up to each other in freezing Press boxes to write up match reports, or shared a railway carriage to one of his favourite far western fields, Redruth, Truro or perhaps Penzance. It was when I learned that he was part of the team which commentated ball-by-ball on cricket that I decided, for the first time, to squeeze in a little listening to Test matches in the summer.

So, oddly enough I arrived at Arlott through Gibson. I had known John probably longer than Alan but he was always perched distantly on his scaffold throne for television, or on the roof-top of Cardiff Athletic club, savouring delicious prawn sandwiches with a glass of wine, and broadcasting, of course.

I spent many hours with John Arlott roaming antique shops around the cricket circuit, picking up pieces of Sunderland lustre or glassware, or Stevengraphs or furniture. John supervised my first antique purchase, an oak chair from the Bown family of Pontypridd. There was time, too, to taste a little Vouvray at Turnbulls of Brighton, or a rich Rioja with Vintage Wines of Nottingham.

As soon as I heard John Arlott the commentator I knew that I would stay with the masses of listeners to the ball-by-ball men. His cricket knowledge, and his poet's art of condensing the actions and impulses of cricketers into a few rich words of description, trapped me. Indeed, I have never escaped the web of exquisite language which Gibson and Arlott spun around me. With respect to others, they got me listening to Test Match Special.

When I finished playing cricket in 1974 I continued my freelance work in writing, radio and television. There was plenty to do, most varied work too – presenting a Saturday morning sports programme on radio, Sport on Four; presenting and interviewing a light entertainment show from Birmingham, Saturday Night at the Mill; presenting HTV's Sports Arena programme from Cardiff; and writing as rugby and cricket correspondent for the Sunday Telegraph. I mention all these to make the point that, when Peter Baxter asked me in 1979 if I would like to try some commentary on cricket, I was not simply a raw recruit straight out of cricket. Even so, the idea of commentary brought on an almost nightmare fear of failure. Most of my broadcasting had been done from scripts. I had never been left alone with my mind, which I recognised as an extremely slow-moving, get-there-in-the-end sort of mind. In fact I had made two stumbling attempts at commentary before, which had put me off.

Once I had been flown in a helicopter up above the bustle and excitement of the British Open Golf Championships at Turnberry. In five minutes, all I spluttered into a microphone was: 'Ahead of me is the famous lighthouse and there is the sea and the green grass . . . and now I'm going over the green grass

over the sea and the famous white lighthouse is underneath me
. . . and now I'm coming back in from over the sea the green
grass and behind is the famous white lighthouse.' Back on the
ground my producer was shaking his head.

Another optimistic producer asked me to commentate on
part of the Arts Festival which accompanied the Commonwealth Games in Edmonton in 1978. In one of the city's squares
an African dancer was to climb a sixty-foot wooden pole and
dance at the top. How? Well, I was poised with my microphone
ready to tell everyone that. Yet, by the time I had come out with
'writhing muscles, his black silk skin, marble thighs entwined
around the pole, and now he is performing all sorts of gyrations
with his buttocks at the top', this producer shook his head too,
suggesting that radio in the seventies was not yet ready for my
particular brand of eroticism.

However, on a sunny day in June 1979 I took my place
behind the microphone at Edgbaston; West Indies were bowling to India in the Prudential World Cup, and I proceeded to
speak twice as quickly as Andy Roberts was bowling. Every so
often there was a message from Peter Baxter, master controlling from London: 'Would A. R. Lewis mind telling us the score
occasionally?'

On this debut day, fate, or clever selection, had placed me
alongside John Arlott. I hardly noticed him. I had put on
blinkers and I clung to the game's technicalities which I
understood best. Was it sunny, or cold, or cloudy? Was it
Sunday, or Monday, or Tuesday? Oh! and what was the score?
Of all of these facts the nation went uninformed. They were
tuned into a ranting Welshman, or was it an Indian, and all the
time the persevering Baxter was calling out, 'Would Lewis
have the kindness to let us know the score?'

Later in the day I ventured the question to John Arlott: 'How
did it go?' He dropped the corners of his mouth in the familiar
scowl, the thick eyebrows were raised in thought and the eyes
twinkled out the answer: 'You weren't good. In the first twenty
minutes you used two words which you would never have used
to me in conversation. You never call the bat the willow, and
the verb you used was so long I can't even remember it. Look,

[107]

don't broadcast to them; talk to them. Talk to the blind man at home, who, once upon a time, could see.'

Suitably chastened I moved on and in August came the proper debut, a Test match at Leeds. What a narrow commentary box! How wide Fred Trueman was! How splendidly Brian Johnston kept the pot boiling and stopped everyone taking themselves too seriously! How natural it all was!

As umpire, Dickie Bird was undergoing his usual trauma of whether play should start in blistering sunshine or not. I meant to say on the air, 'What the spectators need now is a quick, clear decision'. What I actually said was, 'What the spectators need now is a queer . . .' In leapt Brian Johnston with, 'Oh, no, A.R.L.! It's not going to be "welcome to another gay day at Headingley, is it?"'

By the Tuesday Peter Baxter was screaming uncontrollably down the line from London. 'Do tell that so-and-so Lewis to give us the so-and-so score.'

Relaxed as commentary should be there is a lot of learning to be done. Alan McGilvray issued me the stern complaint that I used the word 'we' when describing England, and that bias was not part of a commentator's art. I accepted the criticism but am still only at the half-way stage, referring instead to W'England.

If those were lessons, there was also experience to gather. Doing ball-by-ball commentaries from Bombay during the Jubilee Test match in 1980 had been a rare experience. Henry Blofeld and I sat in a large glass box, beautifully air-conditioned. The glass was so thick that it was impossible to hear a single crowd reaction through it. Henry began his commentary and I suddenly realised that I could not hear him. He was in some discomfort too and it turned out that he could not hear himself either. The earphones were just like ear muffs. 'We can't hear a thing,' pleaded Henry to our two women engineers. 'Ah! But you have no need to hear,' one gleamed so charmingly. 'Sound is coming out OK.'

'Yes,' insisted Henry, 'but I must hear what I am saying.'

'You wanna hear what you are saying? Oh dear! Indian commentators never want to hear what they are saying.'

Her eyes gleamed with misunderstanding but next day she

fixed the head sets and we were aware at last that there was a cricket match going on.

A lot of my friends say to me, 'What's it like in the commentary box?' I guess the short answer is that, architecturally, the boxes all differ slightly and have their special characteristics. What you find inside the box then depends on the listeners' habit of sending in presents. But, if you are looking for the spirit of the box, then I believe it is the same everywhere, no matter which commentators are involved. The Penates, the household gods, are itinerant . . .

I have been amazed by the reaction of people from all over the world to Test match commentaries. I was once telephoned at the Lord's commentary box from Saudi Arabia: 'This is Chris Syer, remember we first met when you came with the MCC to play Singapore. Well look, Tony, we have all been waiting all day for our commentary spell, and we only get ten minutes. Now it has the devil to rain. We have four minutes left of our allocation. Can't you do something to get them out there, or just say hello to us: we are sitting out in roasting sunshine around the radio'. I passed the message on to Brian Johnston who was talking on the air at the time, and he sent good wishes out east, speculating as he did on the nature of playing conditions in the desert areas of the world. To the next Test came a parcel containing a photograph of the golf course where Chris Syer and his friends play. It was rough dried-up earth with odd flags stuck in it. His last line was: 'Brian Johnston asked what the cricket conditions are like. Well . . . just take up the flags and then you'll know.' Not a blade of grass to be seen.

Lastly, to the spirit of the box. I can see that everyone who sits behind a microphone high above a Test match feels the privilege of being the eyes for so many who cannot be there. Every commentator loves the game. I am sure that comes over. Everyone admires the players, and the two summarisers, Fred Trueman and Trevor Bailey, respect the highest standards of the game, and will know very quickly if we are being treated to the authentic Test match piece or a bad imitation, and they will say so.

I have played the role of all-rounder on the team. I have done close-of-play summaries, those short Radio 2 reports, ball-by-ball commentary proper, and have also stood in for Fred or Trevor when they have been unable to be there: a sort of have-voice-will-travel role. Indeed it was at Manchester that Chris Martin-Jenkins rang through to say that he would be late arriving at the ground. He had unluckily been involved in a road accident. John Helm was producer that day and he whisked me straight out of the Press tent to fill in for Jenko for twenty minutes. As I prepared to sit in, Trevor Bailey informed the listeners of a late substitution and asked that they should be patient for a few seconds while he made a note of my number and inspected the studs of my boots.

The newcomer's arrival coincided with the Master's retirement. 1980 was John Arlott's last summer of commentary. We had dinner at Leeds when he was moved to advise me, 'Don't want too much and don't try too hard in this commentary game, just talk to them'.

He stepped out of the commentary box for the last time at Lord's in the Gillette Cup final. Why had he decided to make his departure so final? Surely he could come back; there must be more Arlott for us. Surely, there was too much romance left in cricket, I said to him, just to leave it like that?

He made the pause, set the scowl beneath the kindly eyes, sipped his claret, swilled a little around his palate and replied, 'What's more romantic than the clean break?'

How do we follow that?

Test Match Special, 1981

'Giff'

I have the strange feeling of having been to war alongside Norman Gifford. It is because we soldiered, on MCC's behalf, for five months through India, Sri Lanka and Pakistan. You need to know something of the heat, the crowds, the dust and the concrete grounds (not to mention the concrete beds) before you understand.

You need to imagine how spirits can be smashed by a bad umpiring decision on a blinding hot day in front of 85,000 home supporters, or what a sweat it was, in our case, to be shepherded everywhere by armed militia because we were receiving threats. Or how claustrophobic it was, surrounded by so many thousands of Indians whose great moment it was to shake your hand or at least to touch you.

Day after day we flopped on to the grubby seats in the team's bus outside the ground, and 'Giff' would start up his old war song, 'Keep right on to the end of the road'. Slowly everyone joined in, and by the time we had reached the hotel, the fun of a mock war was the balm that soothed the pain and raised the spirits for the evenings. Norman Gifford, more than anyone, knew when the moaning had to stop and the singing had to start.

I was captain and Giff was the senior pro. There was a lot of opposition to my idea that the senior pro was necessary in the modern context. As Alec Bedser used to argue against me, 'You are all professionals now, mate. The vice-captain is the senior pro . . .' Maybe the name is wrong, but the role is vital, as far as I am concerned. Vice-captains can be understandably over-ambitious. They want the top job. I prefer someone set in the old sergeant-major role, who is not going to take over if the war is lost. If the barracks is going to catch fire I like to know *before* the flames are licking the rooftops, and so, in the context of that touring team, Norman would come to me and say, 'Have a word with so-and-so, captain. I think he has got a complaint that you should look into, or whatever'.

The greatest compliment I can pay him as a bowler pure and simple is that, on merit, he displaced Derek Underwood from the Test team on that tour. Derek's low trajectory made him a medium-fast bowler without any spin at all. Norman, whose craft had been well learned by hours, days, seasons, decades of spin-bowling at Worcester, offered more variety.

I remember at Hyderabad, in Pakistan, Norman slaving in excessive heat, his lips and nose covered by protective white cream which itself frothed and bubbled under the scorching sun. In Pakistan's innings of 569 for 9 declared, he bowled 52 overs, 16 maidens, 3 wickets for 111. 'I turned two,' he said. 'That makes it only half a dozen balls that have turned in my whole Test career. What pitches! I've played on fourteen flat 'uns.'

It was the same in the next Test in Karachi. Gifford – 46 overs, 11 maidens, 2 for 99. But then on the fifth day at last a flicker of a turn . . . Gifford – 29 overs, 9 maidens, 5 for 55 and England almost forced a win before a riot ended the match.

All history now, but unforgettable for those who soldiered through it. And there was a postscript. When I broke down with knee trouble in the following English season, yet was asked if I would take the MCC to the West Indies, I replied thanking the Selectors for their confidence in me, but recommended instead the leadership qualities, the bowling talents and the balanced view of cricket of Norman Gifford. He was not chosen, but I have never had any reason since to think I was wrong.

'Giff', Worcestershire and England Testimonial Year, 1981

'Time to tighten up the nuts and bolts'

If the England visit to Barbados represents a half-way mark, and an assessment time for the tour of West Indies, then the conclusion must be that Ian Botham's party are heading for disintegration and ultimate oblivion. There is talk of a split in the camp and of uncommunicative captaincy. Some future careers at international level are threatened by the unequal struggle against superb opposition and, as with every ship that goes down, the instinct is to save oneself regardless of others.

As far as Ian Botham is concerned he will be learning that retreat requires a deeper understanding of the men and the game than attack. For instance, off the field he must be seen to be understanding the disappointments of those players who have had little opportunity to play on this disrupted tour.

On the field, there must be discipline in defeat. This was not in evidence on the fourth day of the Bridgetown Test when Clive Lloyd and Vivian Richards attacked the England bowling in order to set up the declaration leaving England 523 to win.

England were half-hearted, though there were exceptions, and the knowledge of bowling to a set line linked to carefully patterned field-placings was completely missing. Botham himself bowled splendidly through this session, so, in his heart, he knew what was expected, but others struggled.

Most surprising of all, was the decision not to bowl John Emburey. I would have nominated Emburey to bowl neatly, to have forced the batsmen to hit to predictable corners of the ground and to have given away only about three runs an over.

Captains of losing teams are always easy game for those who sit in the wings to criticise, but as my own cricket mentor, Wilfred Wooller, used to advise me, mainly with a loud voice in public, 'Unless you tighten up the nuts and bolts the damned wheels will come off'. It is worth passing on to all captains, and I think most of all to Ian Botham, the need to inspect the nuts and bolts of performance and team spirit diligently and daily. To retreat with merit requires from the leader a twenty-four-hour-a-day selfless slog.

The Barbados visit also presented problems which no captain could overcome. Because the Guyana Test was not played, the team was woefully short of match practice. This was most noticeable in the case of Graham Dilley, the man England rely upon to be their fast spearhead – Dilley's injured foot had kept him out of full practice and it was just too much for him to be presented with the new ball on a lively, helpful wicket on the first morning of the Test. Dilley scarcely made the batsmen play; his line was adrift, not by much, but by enough to waste Botham's advantage of having won the toss and putting West Indies in to bat.

After half-an-hour's bowling Rohan Kanhai, the former West Indian captain, said in the Press box, 'This young lad is losing you this match'. Unfortunate for Dilley, who had to be patient in his fight against injury during the week. Even so, Botham would have got the five wickets he needed on that first morning if David Bairstow had held a straightforward catch standing back.

A deeper problem still was that this England team, one week ago, thought that it was on the way home [because of Robin Jackman's link with South Africa], and then was bustled into a Test match in the next. It was almost like starting again. There is a custom also that the players' wives and families do not join the side during the first five weeks of a tour. Unfortunately this time they arrived in Barbados in the middle of what was, from a team point of view, a second start.

I appreciate that wives were once upon a time taken to war, but somehow I feel that wives being taken to work by cricketers who are fighting the toughest of campaigns is a distraction and an extra domestic responsibility which some carry off less well than others.

One last observation is that England were asked, for the first time in their touring history, to pay a fee to net bowlers. Whoever suggested it deprived a lot of young Bajan bowlers the delight of having had a tilt at Geoff Boycott and others in the nets, because the England management refused to be drawn into such private enterprise.

The conclusion must be that, for next time, an England tour

of the West Indies should begin in Barbados where practice facilities are plentiful and where there will certainly be fast bowling in every opposition. Also that the period reserved for wives and families should be a fairly innocuous fortnight of the tour, if necessary built in for the purpose of more relaxed cricket.

News arrived in the Caribbean last week that Peter May will replace Alec Bedser as chairman of the England selectors. The change is long overdue, not because Alec Bedser did it poorly – he was tireless – but because a fresh approach is urgently needed. Indeed, as a critic of the system rather than the people involved, I hope that the new chairman will institute a reform of the process which selects the selectors.

Choosing four from the only five or six men available in the country has never made sense in a professional game. That is not to say that amateur leadership at May's level is not what is wanted. Indeed, it is preferable that the chairman and vice-chairman are men of such wide and independent vision, and that his advisers are men who are deeply involved in the professional game. England cricket needs leadership.

Finally to the tragedy of the week, the sudden death of Ken Barrington. Players openly wept when the tributes were paid and there was a lot more weeping done in private. Cricket is a generous game and Ken Barrington set the finest example of the expert player with time and interest to help others. He knew the touring scene well and was masterly in the way he smoothed the path for the team through practices and matches and in their everyday life.

When I flew into Barbados, Kenny was at the airport to meet his wife, Ann. While he was waiting for her, he came over to me, volunteering to get me up-to-date. He looked fitter than ever in his England tracksuit and he talked about all the batting and bowling he had been doing in the nets. It was a lucky turn for me that he was there, so that I could learn so much about the tour so soon. He would have done the same for anyone and that was his way.

It would be wrong to fill his assistant manager's position now, because no-one could strike the rich harmony with the players which he had built up over the years. Perhaps for the remaining three weeks it is as well that Geoff Miller is given more duties and the responsibilities as vice-captain and that Alan Smith, yet another demon net bowler, extends his interests to the cricket side.

It has been a torrid tour and the England party have an ocean of sympathy going with them to Antigua for the next Test match. It is a desperate feeling to start a match with nothing but a hammering to anticipate.

Let it be written, however, that the West Indians in Barbados have been generous in victory. There has been no bullying of the shell-shocked English victims. One British home-owner on the island jokingly chided his butler, Moore, for returning from the Test match each day with a wide, silent grin on his face. 'Ah,' exclaimed Moore, re-setting the dutiful straight face. 'A Scout smiles and whistles in all difficulties.'

Difficulties! The only difficulty Moore's West Indian cricketers appear to have at the moment is how they can stop themselves from winning four-nil.

Sunday Telegraph, 22 March 1981

Professional guru

Mike Brearley returns. Immediately England, the habitual losers, become the winners. What is more, they win matches they should certainly lose. What does this man have? A mystique has settled over him. He no longer wears whites and carries a bat; he plays in a cloak and waves a wand.

However, there are intangibles. One is his effect on the team. There was bound to be loyalty because these are mainly the players who came together under his captaincy. They enjoyed success, they made more money than anyone had ever dreamed of making from cricket and, above all, they found that they could rely on his inquiring mind to unknot the problems, apply reason to a profession which was fogged by tradition and, when on the field, he was clear-sighted and positive.

Following Ian Botham's rather groping reign – and that is understandable too because Botham is 25 and Brearley 39 – the England players badly needed someone to follow. When the captaincy is uncertain, the group fragments into camps of mini-leaders.

When Brearley came back at Headingley, England played badly, but they were at least all striving in the same direction.

Also intangible is the effect he has had on two of the cricketers who have exploded back to their best, Bob Willis and Ian Botham. Willis now runs in as if he has a rocket tied to his tail and Botham's vast energy has snorted out in the Australians' faces, whereas before, when he was in charge, the true Botham was painfully contained and repressed in the mould of the selfless man he thought he ought to be.

Brearley's return has briefly solved the captaincy dilemma, but the selectors must learn one lesson. If they are to give it to a young man again, then it will take him time. David Gower, like Ian Botham, might find, given the responsibility, that his playing standards too would dip. . . .

Every captaincy is different because it reflects the mind and the personality of the leader. On the field it is easier to dissect. This is where Brearley puts down his wand and proves his understanding of the game and of the players on his own side and those against him.

Defending those small totals in the last innings at Leeds and Birmingham were meticulous demonstrations of who to bowl, when, at whom and to what field-setting. Balancing the ring of close fielders for Emburey with those protecting the boundary was delicately done. Most of all, he had to create a false situation in the minds of the Australians, and the hustle around the crease transfixed them, even though the ball only turned a little.

It was clever captaincy, but Mike Brearley would admit that he is not in possession of super-knowledge. The image of the grey-haired guru, or the academic head awash with Cambridge degrees is false. Mike Brearley is a thorough professional, and proud of it.

In many ways he has led the profession of cricketer into the

1980s. He plays the game hard and for money. He has made a particular point of not allowing the various media to make their livings off his back without getting his recompense. He has rationalised the profession. No longer do agency photographers snap the England side and sell their prints for profit – not without first paying the players.

Maybe it is the combination of his roles – managing director off the field and captain on it – which has sealed his support and has given his players the confidence in themselves to attack Australia and hound them mercilessly into two astonishing defeats.

His example should silence forever those who argue that captaincy is not all that important and that, in Australian style, eleven men should be chosen and the best captain from their number.

As for Australia and England, they have proved themselves to be like a couple of lightweight boxers, both with glass jaws. Daily in this current series one of them hits the canvas with such a bump you would think they would never get up again.

Unfortunately for Australia, luckily for England, Hughes and his men have frozen when about to deliver the knock-out punch. They have allowed Brearley's boys to stagger to their feet and play desperately with fast bowling, over-aggressive fields and the mock torture of Emburey's off-spin. The events of Headingley and Edgbaston have made not one tiny grain of cricket sense, but England's advantage over Australia is in the mind and that is why they are 2–1 up and not 3–0 down.

Sunday Telegraph, 9 August 1981

Botham at Old Trafford

Ian Botham enriched the already glamorous history of Old Trafford with a truly unforgettable visit to the crease. He turned a funereal England innings on its end and ridiculed every effort that had gone before him by taking a dazzling century off Australia in 102 balls. His 118 was in the heroic vein, but then everything Botham does is in the charging manner. Even his first ball dismissal in the first innings had the awesome impact of Goliath ducking into the fatal stone.

This time the aggression, the strength, the timing and the natural instinct to apply the right stroke to the right ball, slew Australia. England ended the day with 345 for seven on the board giving them an overall lead of 446 with two days to go.

Could Australia have bowled better at him? After all they had received the Botham treatment before at Leeds and may have worked out the antidote. It is possible that they could have tried Bright a little earlier to confine Botham to strokes on the leg side. However, it is all a question of perhaps and maybe. It will be more comforting for the tourists to face the truth that they went into this match with the weakest attack of the series, both Lawson and Hogg injured. They will frankly see that there is a limit these days to Dennis Lillee's fire and at this late stage in the tour to Alderman's endurance.

There is the more bitter fact that the Ashes are finally scattering through their fingertips when they might have sat securely in the palm of the hand.

England's early batting was a grim bore. Twenty-nine runs were gathered before lunch; four wickets were lost. When the score was 104 for five, Botham joined Tavaré. Tavaré was then 41. When Botham reached his hundred Tavaré had moved on to 68. When Botham was out the score was 253 for six.

To change the course of a match as he has more than once by a single performance requires a deep resource of natural talent, and the ego, even arrogance, of the performer who reaches out to his widest potential when on stage. By contrast Tavaré, his partner, who was almost everyone's partner, struggled for his rightful expression. Tavaré's seven-hour innings had the value of binding the team effort as many around him failed, but without Botham there would be no smiles in the England dressing-room and talk of declaration.

Brearley may work out that on this blameless pitch it is possible for a Test side to score 450 or thereabouts to win – shades of Don Bradman's victory at Leeds in 1948. Those were different days and different men, but so are England and so this captain may take the appropriate caution.

For the first two days this Test was a party, enjoyed from the edge of the seat by delirious viewers and listeners all over the world, everyone following the riveting spectacle of the communal batting collapse. Neither Australia nor England disappointed. The heroes were the bowlers and the catchers, especially the combination of Willis and Botham. Willis extracted unexpected life from a tired pitch and the ball, edged by the pathetic prodding bats of Dyson, Yallop and Marsh flew into the nutcracker hands of Botham.

Willis is proof that, in fast bowling terms, there is life after death. Injuries and lack of success for his county had appeared to have killed off his international career. Maybe because there have been no obvious replacements he has sustained it, but, this summer has seen him run in to bowl with the fixed eye of a very determined man.

His action is all effort. From the stuttering, foot-faulting start to the high knee-raising approach you can almost hear the clank of machinery, the knees are the pistons and the pumping arm the crank pushing him faster and faster to the wicket. In the middle of his run he veers away like a steeple-chaser about to run out at the last fence, but then he swings back to complete the contorted action which breaks all the classic guidelines. His chest is open, his arms whirl to slant the ball inwards. However, he gets bounce, movement off the seam and, at his best, he gets the wickets of the best players.

Apart from Botham and Willis the other player who gave England a lead of 101 on the first innings was Allott, the debutant. He played straight and had all the luck a no. 10 deserves. The 56 runs he put on with Willis for the last wicket represented a huge advantage.

At the start of the third day the capacity crowd had long been in their seats, considering how quickly England could build on their lead of 101. Australia had only one option, to bowl tightly, to set the field carefully, and to contain the attacking aspirations of the England batsmen.

The shock by lunchtime was that England had scored only

29 runs and had lost the wickets of Boycott and Gower. Lillee and Alderman trundled away heroically on the slow pitch but there was no logic to the passive approach to the batting.

Tavaré scored nine runs before lunch; Boycott was lbw nudging across the line; Gower fell to a brilliant catch at mid-wicket; Gatting was trapped by a ball which kept low. To repair his run of modest performances in this series Gower might digest the fact that he has been 'out caught' in all ten Test innings so far.

Gatting has been lbw six times. The gloom of mediocrity was raised, first by a brilliant catch by Marsh, diving down leg side to dismiss Brearley, and then, in mid-afternoon, by Botham.

When he first came to the crease Botham looked as if he had been programmed like the others to a long grasping stay, hoping that runs would accrue slowly. More likely he had been implored by his captain to take a good look at the pitch and the bowling before throwing bat at ball.

When he broke loose, he made everyone's journey worth-while. Hughes gambled by taking the new ball: Botham hooked it, cut it, lofted it over extra-cover and drove it to all parts. He reached his fifty in sixty balls.

As Botham took the limelight, so Tavaré settled neatly and unobtrusively into a rich, secondary role. He began to follow through with his drives, and tucked away crisp fours off the legs. Yet, for his own safety's sake, he could have done with a tin hat at the non-striking end.

Australia trailed off at tea 327 runs behind and all hope of revival gone. They knew they had just suffered a nightmare, a very real one. Not only had the fortunes of this particular Test turned against them, but the hope of winning the Ashes had also disappeared.

Eight overs of the second new ball cost 76 runs. Lillee fancied the bouncer trap, with two fielders on the long-leg boundary for the catch. Botham simply hooked harder and higher for three sixes. He treated Alderman to a taste of the lofted off-drive. It was superhuman batting of a wholly different tempo from everything in this series, save for Botham's century at Leeds. He reached this one with a six, swept over Lillee's upstretched hand at long-leg. It had taken him 86 balls, one less than that at Headingley. He fell to Whitney and normal cricket was resumed.

Tavaré's seven-hour vigil was ended by Alderman – a surprise bouncer which lobbed off glove or shoulder of bat to Kent at first slip. His 78 runs had taken him far too long. His contribution made sense alongside Botham's outrageously fast century, but otherwise his style was cramped by the instinct for survival. Plodding foot-forward defensive could have been turned into positive attack by a free follow-through. It may yet come for, to his credit, he is one of the few to have made any sense of the England no. 3 spot.

Knott, however, found his old confidence, even impertinence, when driving Lillee through the covers, and cutting and sweeping Bright. Emburey joined the assault as Australia, tired and disappointed no doubt, were by now clock-watching and the close could not for them come quickly enough. By then England were 345 for seven, 446 runs ahead. Knott was 56 not out.

Sunday Telegraph, 16 August 1981

Cashing in on the last ball

It was a lovely day for the first NatWest final and all the more so for the presence of Derbyshire and Northamptonshire, two clubs whose rare visits to the big time brought the romantic lustre of anti-heroes.

The flags were limp on the pavilion poles. In front of the Tavern the partisans congregated, Northants, rather chic and French in the maroon and white flat caps, the Tudor Rose pinned on; Derbyshire much more the British day-trippers in porkpie sunhats, chocolate, amber and pale blue with the rose and crown imprinted. So this, too, was a battle of the roses.

The ground was dry, and the pitch firm. Wood won the toss for Derbyshire and chose to field first. The louder the followers chanted 'Darbyshur, Darbyshur', the farther Larkins and Cook hit the ball. Indeed every time the ball was stroked for four the rallying songs burst out with blinder loyalty . . .

Larkins and Cook provided a flow of delightful runs, though they were restricted by the combination of Wood and wicket-keeper Taylor, standing up to the stumps. Larkins lofted Wood for six over square-leg and whipped Newman off his toes to the same area. Cook was slower but correct and steady. It took him longer to risk the shuffle down the pitch to drive Steele over his head and, next ball, through the covers for four.

The batsmen played in blue helmets which were obviously heavy, hot and blatantly of the wrong colour. Larkins called for his maroon cap, I was happier with that. He was not. Two balls later he holed out at square-leg. Lightheaded, maybe? 99 for 1 in the 29th over.

Derbyshire fielded well in spite of the lightning fast outfield. Newman, the young fast bowler, looked quick enough, but, for a while, laboured a little on his extra-long run. However, he came back strongly and found greater profit once his line had moved from the leg stump to off.

Cook completed a splendid century off 142 balls with a crisp boundary through mid-wicket off Hendrick. But his side lost their way once he had gone. Run-outs, mostly initiated by Wood's agile fielding, ripped open the batting order and turned a powerful innings of huge potential into a modest self-sacrifice. Lamb and Willey especially were far too valuable a pair of wickets to throw away.

Wood's fielders retreated to the boundary lines with three overs to go. They found themselves in surprising control: 204 for 4 had become 235 for 9 at the end of the 60 overs and Derbyshire had given themselves a real chance of winning a limited-over contest for the very first time.

If there was a surge of confidence in the Derbyshire dressing-room between innings, they may not have imagined how the opening bowlers, Sarfraz and Griffiths, would swing the new ball. Wright and Hill were pushy and tentative. Control of the tempo was intriguingly back with Northamptonshire.

Hill collected 14 runs in 14 overs before mistiming a pull

shot. Wright towered correctly over the pitch of every ball but he and his normally prolific partner Kirsten could not match the earlier fluency of Larkins and Cook.

Wright and Kirsten then became the spoilsports of the whole season. Used as we all were to a collapse around every corner, here two foreigners, New Zealander and South African, combined, saw a good pitch, played straight and collected a couple of half-centuries. It was stark efficiency for a long time, then eventually Wright revealed the virtuoso touches, down the wicket to Sarfraz, or back on the stumps thumping the ball through extra-cover or mid-wicket. Kirsten matched him; Northants were now under pressure.

Relief arrived in the form of Mallender, bowling from the Nursery End. Twice in an over he struck the pad and got the verdict from the umpire, Constant. Wright and Kirsten were gone. Could this be the way back into the contest for Northants? 60 runs were needed off ten overs, Northants had exhausted their ideas of slow bowling after Willey's immaculate contribution and a poor imitation by Williams. Back to Sarfraz.

Wood paraded with a chestful of confidence but Sarfraz had the answer to him with a ball that was slanted into his off stump, moving off the seam. So it was seven overs in which to score 47 and Barnett playing with the full flourish every ball. Steele was castled but still the Derbyshire chorus had retained enough voice at the Tavern to yell through a few military marches adapted to simple lyrics such as 'Darbyshur, Darbyshur'.

Out flowed the heroics – the brilliant fielding of Sarfraz off his own bowling, tight running between the wickets by Barnett and Miller. The light chilled. The Dickie Bird light metre would have had them off the field.

34 off four overs – the field, bar two, goes back to the fence, the fielders themselves have trouble in sighting the ball off the bat. They did not need to see Miller's six to square-leg off Sarfraz. Twenty off three, five wickets in hand. Barnett was run out. Well, that's how it happens at this stage.

Northants were winning – no they weren't. Tunnicliffe

whacked fours square and straight. Twelve came off Sarfraz's last over.

Seven required off the last over. Two off the first ball by Miller; then a single. Then three runs needed off two. It was dark. Darbyshur, Darbyshur, where were Northants?

Two runs now off the last ball – ah! but one run would do, a tie would make Derbyshire the winners, because they had lost fewer wickets.

The final ball was bowled to Tunnicliffe. Miller, backing up, appeared to overtake it in flight. It hit Tunnicliffe's pad. Miller arrived like the cow in the china-shop and no Northants player could turn to throw to the bowler's end. It was over. Derbyshire had won and now it was worth singing for.

Sunday Telegraph, 6 September 1981

For the benefit of Govind

When I read that England's cricketers were planning to end their already exhausting tour by nipping back from Sri Lanka to Southern India to play a benefit match for the senior baggage bearer, I thought, 'Well done, lads'. Every England cricketer who has ever toured out there will want to be identified with the effort. The story of Govind Bawji ought to be told.

Govind has looked after visiting teams and their kit since the Commonwealth tour of India in 1950–51. He is especially devoted to England or, as he insists on calling it, MCC. His father had worked a lifetime for the British High Commission in the Raj days. Govind remembers clearly and wishes those times were back. 'When British rule, Sahib, everyone know where he is.'

Almost with tenderness he has eased the passages of six England tours and fussed loyally about their captains, Howard, Dexter, Smith, Lewis, Greig and now Fletcher.

Govind is a chubby, giggling forty or maybe fifty, or perhaps thirty or even sixty. He is rotund and looks well; his black hair is always smartly greased and parted.

Greeting is one of his specialities. At the start of the present tour I got the amiable bear hug followed by the prolonged double-handed hand-shake. 'Captain, Sahib! How is Memsahib? I tell my sons Memsahib Lewis kind lady. I have two sons. Sahib will meet them in MCC dressing-room, they are with me now for very first time. I will present them.'

So it is a family affair now. Govind has long been the senior of three bearers who are appointed by the Indian Board of Control to serve every whim of the England party and to transport the kit, 'Doctor' Thomas's medicine chests, the cases of booze and any odd suitcase that does not find a place on the flight.

His khaki trousers and tunic smell of constant laundering and the silver badge of the Indian Board of Control shines on his chest. That badge is precious. It gives him identity among the masses. He is official. He knows where he is.

As Keith Fletcher's boys were flying from Madras to Indore this week, Govind's tiny army was asleep with the England bags on the floor of the luggage van of some dusty, dirty, overloaded train which hissed and crawled its way northwards through night and day. It arrived at Indore twenty-six hours later.

Govind has his favourite England players. He will put his arm around one of them and whisper, 'Sahib up late last night? Sahib naughty boy? Drink too much? Sahib definitely not look well. Have cup of tea . . . or Sahib prefer salt drink for long day fielding?'

I recall a rough hotel, the Lantern Hotel at Indore. I had a room only wide enough to accommodate the large fan grinding away on the ceiling. There was no window, just a grilled outlet. It was too dark to read a book there at mid-day. Perhaps it was a horsebox.

One evening the team went out for dinner. I had pulled a calf muscle and had to stay behind. No hopes of a decent meal. Suddenly Govind arrived. 'Special dinner is ready for Captain Sahib. In manager's room.'

Donald Carr did have a slightly grander room, and between two false pillars was a table laid out with a white crisp, table

cloth and a vase of flowers. For the next couple of hours I dined
with the mock eminence of a make-believe Viceroy as Govind
manned the double doors and announced each course. A
wizened old waiter in crumpled white with brass buttons, red
epaulettes and plumed headgear limped in and out.

'Fresh eggs, just collected for Captain Sahib . . . fresh
chickens I have just killed for Sahib . . . pudding of rice and
fruit I recommend for Sahib . . . fresh fruit deliciously picked
for Sahib one hour ago only.' (What next, petits fours from
Fortnum's?)

Govind's very special dinner ended with a surprise touch of
pathos, as he played out his British Raj charade. 'You see,
Sahib, without the cricket visits I lack money. Then I do not
know where I am. With money I could buy a good job.
Everyone has price in India.' Govind can coax out a rupee as
well as anyone else but I hope England can fit in his benefit
match. I hope too his price is met because I guess for Govind
Bawji, when tours end, the in-between times are not so good.

Sunday Telegraph, 24 January 1982

Cue Sri Lanka, transmission on

England have played out their match at Kandy and have gone
down to Colombo, but I have moved even deeper, and certainly
higher, into the mountain heart of Sri Lanka. My surroundings
invite imaginings of the old days.

After a gentle round of golf with friends at the Nuwara-Eliya
Club, I am now poised over my typewriter in the old Hill Club,
once the exclusive resort of gentlemen whose business was
mainly coffee, chinchona and tea. The cheetah crest still stands
firm and upright on the large teapots. The golf clubhouse light
bulbs are so dim they might well be the originals. But hard as
time is trying to drag me backwards, in the shadow of the
island's highest peak, Mount Pedro, there is the symbol of the
1980s poised on the mountain top.

It is the country's main television transmitter. It was placed on its vantage point by choppers, spectacular stuff for the casual, friendly folk, many of whom have heard that national television arrived here two years ago, but have yet to understand the presence of the very rare domestic TV roof-aerial popping up above the coconut trees. This is Sri Lanka's beauty. Whisky soda is 'in', new fangled television is 'out'.

It is television this week, ball-by-ball from the first Test-cricket match ever played by their own team, which will spread the historic news. From next Wednesday, Sri Lanka will become humanly and statistically, and highly emotionally, a Test-match country. The hour is at hand.

Sri Lanka has always been the country where Test sides called on the way to somewhere else. Stories abound of friendships in the game, and of personal experiences. Maybe this week gives everyone licence to recall his own point of contact with Sri Lankan cricket.

The deep voice from the dark corners of the golf clubhouse told of terror as he faced up to the demon West Indian, Prior Jones, in 1950, and of how Clyde Walcott caught him and then let the ball slip out on purpose, smiling and saying: 'You gave us some party last night. Have a decent knock, enjoy yourself'.

Members of the John Keells Company are renowned for the warmth of their welcome to MCC touring sides. By coincidence, I flew out here with a former director, who had not been back for twenty-five years. 'Remember a cracking night with the England lads in the early 1930s.' It was Harry Elliot, of Derbyshire, who tumbled into his room one night and because he had not seen a mosquito net before went to sleep underneath the bed. 'I stirred him in the morning with a prairie oyster – always worked, y'know. Ole Harry swallowed it without opening his eyes and stayed asleep there on the floor for hours.'

It is exactly a hundred years since Sri Lanka first played against an English side. The Hon. Ivo Bligh's team was on the way to Australia. Reports are conflicting, but I will go for the one which says England beat Eighteen of Ceylon in a two-day match and then set sail on the *Peshawar*. Unfortunately, the *Peshawar* was not far out of harbour before she collided with the *Glenroy*. So back to Colombo went the England party and they were persuaded to play a one-day match against the Dublin Fusiliers. Not a testing experience, I would imagine. In fact the match was not completed. The ship repairs were finished sooner than expected and so the teams shook hands and went their separate ways in the mid-afternoon.

In many ways, this was always Ceylon's trouble: how to be taken seriously. They were so obviously excellent cricketers, but they were always facing up to Test teams who were building up to a major Test series or cooling down from one. Colombo is on the direct line sea route between England and Australia.

In many ways Ceylon cricket was done an injustice. Their fight for Test-match recognition has been long and painful, full of toil and tears. They invited investigation, always stood up to the inquisition on the field, but never satisfied the ICC off it.

So, back to the great day on Wednesday, and that television aerial. The ICC were always concerned that Sri Lanka could not sustain a Test-match programme. Where else could they stage a match other than at Colombo? They have provided startling truth. Once ICC agreed to their inclusion, money has spilled into the reshaping of the ground at Kandy called the Asgiriya Stadium. They literally moved a mountain.

Around the ground there, and at Colombo, are advertising hoardings, every bit as numerous as at Lord's or Melbourne. The key to the incoming funds? Television. The Old Boy brigade have learned quickly, and if admitting Sri Lanka makes more sense now than it did ten years ago, it is because television has arrived.

Through TV screens also, the administrators of the game – who have a cricket foundation which is starting to tend to the youngsters – want to disseminate the game's fun and skills. They want television coverage of matches to spread the gospel and encourage the formation of a district competition. Sponsors will be easy to find. The chief evangelist will be Brian Taber, the former Australian wicket-keeper, who is shortly to take up the national cricket coaching post.

Much was made of Sri Lanka's vote on the ICC when they were allowed in. Would they not tilt the balance four-three black against white? What about South Africa's chances then? I have met only one response to my question: 'We trade with South Africa, don't we!'

So all looks well. Sri Lanka's hour has indeed come. On Wednesday morning, Mariamma, the long-serving grounds-woman, will tug her roller by rope as ever, and set up the stumps for a new history.

Tolerance and understanding will be required. The Sri Lankans are desperately keen to prove themselves worthy. I think they will be glad when the fanfares are over, the birds have been released and the balloons floated away. Once the first dot has gone into the score book they are official for the first time.

Sunday Telegraph, 14 February 1982

The richest, loneliest men in cricket?

Sad week. Silly week. Cricketer talking nursery politics: politicians spouting Boy's Own cricket; traders with South Africa, heads down, collars up, business as usual. It was a shock, but there has been plenty of dressing-room discussion about tripping off to South Africa. South Africans have let it be known that there is money available.

To be honest, when England were thrown out of Guyana last year because Robin Jackman had strong associations with South Africa, all of us, players and Press, felt humiliated. Some were angry. Why should we have moral guilt poured on us by an angry little country like Guyana? What right has it got to influence the choice of our side? Is a South African connection any worse than a Russian one? Most of us cooled down agreeing never to visit Guyana again.

Some players were struck less by a hot reaction than by a cold realisation that the cricket world might split into two circuits, black and white, and that the real money would be made in the white half. Some were not even prepared to wait and see Oxychem Ltd was their company, set up and registered on 5

October, and a tour to South Africa was a serious proposition.

It was a total secret during the recent Indian and Sri Lankan tour, as far as I was concerned. Ian Botham's solicitor did make a rushed and rather feverish visit to Bangalore without appearing to notice that there was a Test match on. I had a cup of tea with him and Reg Hayter, head of a Fleet Street sports news agency, who was on the same mission. I wondered why they were so happy to talk about broadcasting.

However, if you want to talk treachery, let us start, not with the England players, but with the International Cricket Conference.

A couple of summers ago I spent time in the company of two of the finest Springbok cricketers, Jack McGlew, skipper in the 1950s and 1960s, and the virtuoso strokemaker Roy McLean. They were in London on business. They talked about how the greatest promise of the lot had been broken. Following the D'Oliveira Affair in 1968, the South Africans were told that they could not expect another England side to tour there until their cricket was multi-racial at all levels. They told me of the astonishing courage the cricketers have shown in the face of an unresponsive government and how, in cricket, they have managed to run through many of the racial laws of the land, how their cricket is now completely multi-racial.

The multi-racial South African Cricket Union (SACU) replaced the all-white Association. The late president, Rachid Varachia, was an Indian of much tact and strength, holding all races together. By 1979 the International Cricket Conference was ready to send out a fact-finding group, and it returned with recommendations that multi-racial sides should be sent on tours of South Africa; that now the basic effort had been made, England should encourage the game out there by contact and communication.

What has happened? Nothing. What has ICC done? Nothing. What has our home Board of Control done? Nothing. The South Africans have despaired. Last summer, after putting their case again, one of their representatives, Geoff Dakin, told me that this was the end of patience and tolerance for them. What more could they do? They had been promised re-entry to international cricket if their game was multi-racial. It was. These were broken promises. Better not to have promised at all. I can see Jack McGlew pleading, 'We are like kids who have had to crawl through ten years of barbed wire to reach Father Christmas. And Christ, Tony, when we get there, he's got nothing to give us. That's cruel, man.'

Probably the England cricketers were moved to go out on this tour more by money than ideology; but you can be sure that by now they feel the surge of an honest campaign in their hearts. It was like that with Kerry Packer's recruits in Australia. Mercenaries thrown together without a cause suddenly have to find the ideal for which to die. Otherwise the Boycott-Gooch army will not be weighed down by the morality of the situation. They may suffer a twinge of concern for the county professionals at home who may feel the financial effects if this summer's tours against India and Pakistan are cancelled, but, as Graham Gooch stated, 'I am a cricketer by profession and I am free to earn my living where I can'. Ten thousand pounds a week for a month in South Africa is nice work if you can get it. Test players tend to throw their briefcases into dressing-rooms before their kitbags these days, and settling the family mortgage in half-a-dozen innings is attractive. You have to admit it.

The secrecy did not surprise me. That is how Tony Greig collected his Packer forces. Also, if you remember that cricketers these days think of themselves as businessmen more than games players, then you must expect business tactics to apply. Tycoons do not give advance warnings of dawn raids in the City.

At this point the understanding, tolerant vein of my thinking ends. The Boycott venture is greedy, selfish and myopic. Was this not the same Boycott who wrote of his hatred of apartheid in a recent book, the book which Mrs Indira Gandhi, the Prime Minister of India, considered decent proof of his and England's attitude to South Africa before she allowed the last Indian tour to go on? Boycott, at the same time, was raising troops for a South African tour. Hates apartheid, loves krugerrands! Tell that to the Indians. Is it the same Chris Old who bleated away that he was not prepared to play in the same side as Geoffrey

Boycott in Yorkshire? I suppose they are room-mates in Port Elizabeth.

The repercussions are these. The game of cricket in England might lose an estimated income of £1,700,000 if the summer tours are cancelled. Counties might go to the wall. Professionals of average talent will be sacked if the money does not go round. The game, which was a team game played for team ends, is now obviously a black pool of private graft and individual subterfuge. There may be mistrust in the England dressing-room where there once was harmony and a delight in the honour of wearing the England sweater.

South Africa, suitably encouraged, will now launch annual tournaments. The 'Dirty Dozen' may never see an England sweater again, but they could be committed for years ahead to play tournaments in South Africa. They could be the richest, loneliest men in cricket. That would not change life greatly for Mr Boycott, but for Mr Gooch it would be a tragedy.

What will happen to Gooch? Will England choose him? No. Will Essex sack him? I doubt it. Ever since Kerry Packer taught English cricket administrators a brutal lesson in restraint of trade some five years ago the Board of Control has been neutered. The Board has led without power. The ICC, even more pathetically, lies flabby on top of world cricket like a blind, toothless, clawless lion. While we are obsessed for the moment by riposte and reaction, it is as well to realise that international cricket needs a board of directors. It is a mighty entertainment business run on archaic unbusinesslike lines. Perhaps that is why the game has not kept pace with the hard-nosed element which has turned itself into a mercenary army, to everyone's embarrassment. Perhaps that is why there is a pirate team in South Africa.

And then, when everyone has counted the cost of this tour, the one figure which should remain in all minds is the 387 racial laws in South Africa, where your black skin is equated with statutory crime. That is one for *Wisden* . . . or maybe it is not cricket.

Sunday Telegraph, 8 March 1982

1983–1985

The Prudential World Cup

At 1am on Sunday 26 June 1983 a public holiday was declared in India. The Indian cricket team had just won the Prudential World Cup at Lord's. Only an hour earlier the handsome skipper, Kapil Dev, had stepped proudly forward on the balcony of the pavilion and received the Cup from the President of MCC, Sir Anthony Tuke.

Television had taken live pictures of the whole day's play to India for the first time. Soon the stories were returning of how streets were jammed as thousands stood outside banks and stores where sets were put on display. Oxcarts stopped in their tracks. Apparently firemen motoring to put out a fire found a vantage point for seeing the cricket: they stood on top of their fire engine, stopped ringing their bell, removed their protective clothing and settled down for the day, no doubt, while Bombay burned. In Haryana Kapil Dev's name was god. This was the young man, only twenty-three years old, who grew up among them, who had never seen a Test match until he was actually chosen to play in one, now leading his country by instinct and example. Where was the Indian team which could not master one-day cricket? Whither the small men, helpless against the fast men of West Indies? Gone.

This was wonderful for the health of cricket, for its propagation as a world game of honour, skill and of equal opportunity. India were supposed to have no chance of beating the West Indies in this World Cup Final, but they did.

[134]

Forget the romance for a moment. India were underrated. As I write, of the last six one-day internationals they have played against West Indies, who were rated the best in the world, they have won three. In the group stage of this World Cup they beat them at the start. Also, and much more significantly, they had won a match in Berbice in Guyana on their recent tour.

On the eve of this Lord's final I attended a cocktail party given by the Indian team. The invitations were rushed out, because before the semi-final against England two days before, they must have imagined themselves soon back home. England with all their ground advantage and their run of success in the competitions were favourites. It was a typical Indian drinks party. I got there three-quarters of an hour late with Abid Ali, the former Indian cricketer, and we were the first there! I heard how Dilip Sardesai, another former Test player, had heard of the great semi-final win against England and announced to his wife, 'We win semis. I go to London'. A simple enough message. And so Indians flew into Britain from all directions. Four from Belgium paid £70 each for tickets on the black market. On the morning of the match the same £10 tickets were going for £20.

India's success had repercussions outside India. It gave identity to so many expatriates living in Britain. In a strange and surprising way it brought out a patriotism for India among the sons of exiles who had never set foot in the land of their fathers. A Sikh raced up to me as I left Lord's on Saturday evening and said in broad London accent, 'We wunnit, mate'.

Cricket in this Prudential Cup competition was a unifying factor; there were many more supporters from overseas than there have ever been before. This was because of the arrangement of the elimination matches into groups with league tables. It used to be a straight knock-out contest, now each of the eight teams played at least six matches in their group before going out. The great performance of the series was appropriately by Kapil Dev. India were on their way out of the whole competition when, in their last but one group match, they were reduced to 17 for 5 against Zimbabwe. Kapil Dev came in and scored 175 not out. He was the last recognised batsman. It is a

World Cup record; astonishing, even allowing that his mammoth hitting was on the delightful but small Tunbridge Wells ground.

What went wrong with England? That was obviously a disappointment to millions. Bob Willis led a successful campaign until a first group match was lost v. New Zealand at Birmingham. Then, the shifting of Botham up the batting order did not help, neither Botham nor his team. There were careless moments, untidy wicket-keeping and a needless sacrificing of the innings before the sixty overs were up. Tremors of the undisciplined Australian winter tour of 1982–83 shook the nuts and bolts loose again. Sure enough by the time the semi-final came around when the pressure was on, when it required high skills performed in tight matches, England flopped. There is no doubt that the two finalists were the best sides in the competition.

It was surprising how much teams depended on the success of one player. New Zealand for example, who had beaten England in all five out of five previous one-day internationals, found that their medium-fast bowlers did not get the bounce on English pitches which they had got in New Zealand and Australia. They needed some fine innings by Glenn Turner. He failed and so did they.

England were waiting for Botham to fire. His bowling is now expensive, he was pulled out of the front line of attack; the big, bludgeoning innings never came. Pakistan were a major disappointment but showed how much they depend on the bowling spearhead of Imran Khan to give the whole team a cutting edge. His inability to bowl because of his stress fracture to his left ankle was the neutering of Pakistan.

In their way, despite the army of fast bowlers, West Indies knew that if Viv Richards got a long innings they would win the match. His form got better and better through the competition, but on Final day, he threw his wicket away and the cluster of youngsters, Gomes, Bacchus and Dujon were left in gentle confusion in the middle order.

Zimbabwe's important player, the former league professional Duncan Fletcher, did have a wonderful series of individual performances, but he lacked all-round support. Zimbabwe played good cricket, they beat Australia but never fired on all cylinders.

Sri Lanka proved that they could bat. Mendis, the skipper, was the man with the flashing blade, Wettimuny the solid anchor, but only de Mel was a threat as a bowler. Lack of depth in the bowling department made them unlikely winners. Australia had looked to several individuals to help them repeat their one-day triumphs of the winter. Two famous ones failed, Lillee and Thomson. Dennis admitted that he should not have toured Sri Lanka with Australia just before the World Cup. He should have stayed at home to build up his injured knee. As it was, he was never fully fit and never happy. Thommo looked as if he needed a month's practice to get line and length into his system. He bowled an Australian length, short, looking for high bounce. English pitches do not help that approach.

So we come to the reason for India's great triumph. Sunil Gavaskar their finest batsman, failed. Immediately, the depth of Indian batting was to be seen. Everyone made contributions. Apart from Kapil Dev's blinding world record innings, it was a team effort – Amarnath, Srikkanth, Patil, Vengsarkar, Yashpal Sharma – they all came off.

Benson & Hedges Cricket Year, Second Edition, 1984

Time to ban helmets in the field

Ban helmets for fielders! They are not used to protect the innocent from a dreadful blow, but to push forward troops behind their skills into territory where they can trample the batsman's nerve and win the psychological war.

Because of helmets, cricket is suffering in three ways. It is on the brink of seeing someone killed as the result of being hit; it has fed the instinct for cheating close to the bat, fielders claiming catches they know to be not out, batsmen acting cool and indignant when they know they have hit the ball; also, indirectly, the cage of close fielders a couple of feet from the bat is killing off a large part of the spin bowler's repertoire.

As for the danger, I do not need persuading that a helmet can save a life. Indeed, I was on the field, standing at gully, when Glamorgan's Roger Davis was hit on the head and, minutes later, was declared dead by the doctor. The kiss of life saved him and, thankfully, the only post-mortem was about the sanity of fielding at short square-leg. Next day Tony Cordle turned up prepared to stand in the bat-pad position if he could wear a boxer's sparring head protector. He was brave enough. I said yes.

I now think I was wrong.

There is more wisdom in the conversation with Mike Smith who was in the Warwickshire side that day. He himself was one of the finest short-leg fielders. He was sure that Roger had been fielding far too close. He had been drawn in by a slow pitch with very little bounce and a batsman, Neil Abberley, who tended to prod at his forward strokes.

However, I had failed to put into the reckoning the fact that Malcolm Nash was a medium-fast bowler who would swing the ball into Neil's pads; one flip at a full-length half-volley and short leg would have no chance. And so it proved. Roger had advanced beyond the point where he had a realistic hope of taking evasive action.

Roger Davis had the skills to field close: some do not, but are bolstered by helmets. A lot more play Russian Roulette. Football shin guards are worn, foam chest protection, gum shields, helmets and visors. Imagine where it might lead. A batsman might soon look down on this clutch of shiny helmets as Rome's enemies once looked down from the castle ramparts on the testudo – the tortoise, a tight formation of soldiers who, interlocking their shields above their heads, created the impression of the polished scales of the tortoise.

A batsman cannot pour molten tar or boiling oil down on the modern testudo, but soon he is sure to opt for playing much more aggressively. Who wants to go meekly to a catch off bat and pad?

It is safer to field close on the off side than on the leg because the warning signals are clear, especially a batsman's high backlift. Even then, if the reactions of the fielders are slower than those of a Gower, a Botham or a Radley, then someone may soon be seriously hurt.

The game, historically, has always had a pendulum swinging the advantage between bat and ball, and the bat is about to fight back. De-helmeting to persuade fielders to stand a safe distance is therefore advocated.

As for the cheating, who will deny it? Some call it fair to leave all adjudication to the umpire, to wash their hands and their conscience of responsibility when they appeal for a catch which came off the pad.

Fine, but do not act out the lie. Do not leap around congratulating a catcher – that is cheating. Equally the batsman who knows he has been caught by some prostrate helmeted hero at short square-leg and who acts out his surprise, even annoyance, is a cheat. Stand and wait? But how can you if you are being out-acted by the fielding side?

The game close to the bat has lost a deal of honesty. The umpires have an impossible job. Soon the only way of discovering the truth will be to march cricketers off to a small windowless room at the back of Lord's, interrogate them under a swinging light bulb, with them tied up to the lie detector, and wait for the pen to scratch out the truth on the graph paper. Take the helmets away, and make fielders calculate seriously how near they should stand to the batsman and a little will be done to defuse the situation.

The third flush of concern for the game close to the wickets came about when I watched Nick Cook bowl in the second innings of the last Test match [at Lord's against New Zealand]. In the first innings he had given the ball a little air. He had taken five wickets for 35 in his first Test. Second time out, however, he sent the ball whizzing down without loop or noticeable flight and we saw in action the modern fixation – not his but everyone's – with getting wickets from bat-and-pad tickles.

So often this approach works well, especially when a batsman is new at the crease or is one who pushes willy-nilly on to the front foot into the spin and bounce. These are the circum-stances which persuade a left-arm spinner to fire the ball in at middle-stump, to wait for the batsman to get in a tangle and squeeze out a catch. We have seen some brilliant catches as a result.

Yet there is an alternative game . . . and it is disappearing. In fact, it used to be the main-line game, born of the desire to see batsmen play positive strokes at the spin.

A spinner enjoyed seeing the bat follow through. It meant that the gap between bat and pad would open, that the edges would carry to slip and gully, that a backward short-leg – one of the finest 'trap' positions in the game – could be in play, and that a fielder could be set for the miscued drive.

Richie Benaud, who knew a thing or two about spinning people out, never liked to bowl into a circle of close fielders. 'A bowler smells danger, that one of his team may be seriously hit. So he plays it safe and fires the ball in low and straight.'

Benaud preferred to run through his repertoire to a slip and a leg-slip with, maybe, a man on the drive at short mid-off; or wherever he felt mistakes may come according to the batsmen. He never forsook flight, spin, bounce: the true arts. That is not to say that he ignored the chance to pressurise a batsman. He did it to Colin Cowdrey, who was blocking to draw the Lord's Test in 1956. Cowdrey, attacked by very close fielders, played back for once and was lbw.

The fixation with bat-pad dismissals is eroding the art of spin. Helmets first gave players the courage to get in too close and, helmeted or not, it is now a habit. At Headingley, Edmonds bowled over thirty overs to Edgar and Wright to such fields without taking a wicket. Cook in that second innings at Lord's was almost medium-paced on a turning pitch.

The loss of spinning skills is not unconnected with the cage field-placing mentality.

Sunday Telegraph, 21 August 1983

[140]

Where the joy, where the humility?

A week of living in the aftermath of Harrogate makes it impossible to be optimistic for Yorkshire cricket, and, although it is a cliché thought, it is a fact that England will be the weaker for Yorkshire's continued mediocrity.

In that Special Meeting, the reformers, the advocates of the clean sweep, had their way: the resignation of the whole committee and the reinstatement of Geoffrey Boycott as a Yorkshire player.

A clean sweep would have been the abandonment of Boycott, too, because he had been the focus of the club's most bitter private arguments for many years. Now his presence will be even more divisive because his opponents have been wounded in public.

Harrogate was not a vote. It was civil war. The established administration of the county was overthrown by a paramilitary campaign. Leaders of the victorious Members' Group '84 left the battle brandishing 'V' for victory signs. In the vast media spaces lovingly allotted to iconoclasts, they romped on the graves of the vanquished. But the stench of civil war does not blow away on the first breeze. This war will run.

Meanwhile the detached non-combatant, Geoffrey Boycott, received news of his reprieve with joy and 'humility'.

Whatever the make-up of the future committee, it cannot flout the Harrogate vote. It does not make sense for a members' ballot box to make professional cricket decisions, but it is understandable that the majority should want their hero back. He is the centre of attraction in a losing team. His statistical record is staggering. It is understandable that he gets a vote of confidence in his cricket. The only dispute about Boycott as a player will come when pundits try to decide whether he has been great or nearly great.

As the recent battle heat grew, Boycott, the superlative batsman, became the martyr wronged by a vindictive committee. Eventually the argument was so distorted that the committee could not win. Whenever they criticised Boycott they lost respect and when they remained honourably silent they were said to be guilty of failing to explain the extraordinary sequence of thinking which gave Boycott a testimonial for 1984, but no contract.

Cricket war historians will review the carnage one day and see the truth in the one massive unexplained fact, that the body of Yorkshire cricketers – past and present – fought on the committee side against Boycott.

Why no explanation? Honour, pride, loyalty cricketer to cricketer, no dirty washing. Cricket is not a game for school sneaks.

However, it is extraordinary that Boycott, the difficult pupil, now holds new sway, whereas the long-serving, much respected captains of the school, Norman Yardley, Michael Crawford, Robin Feather, loyal to the end, have been driven to self-expulsion. Geoffrey Boycott will stand for election to the committee as a representative for Wakefield. He might well unseat the devoted Dr Turner, he might score 2,000 runs next summer, but who then will insist that he leaves? Again the war might erupt. Again Boycott might even become captain; he might play until he is fifty; he might become director-general.

The special meeting cost £28,000, give or take a law suit or two. It would need only two or three more such meetings to dispute future Boycott contracts to impoverish the club.

What is good for Yorkshire? Best is surely peaceful solutions of the club's problems, all solved in the interests of the club's future. Lessons can be drawn from the trouble. Committee decisions regarding any player's future must be made early and firmly. Every cricketer deserves to know where he is and where he is likely to go.

The development of young talents is a delicate business; it can only be done with the bolster of experienced players alongside them. Yorkshire's senior players, therefore, like any others, have a responsibility to recognise the aspirations of the learners.

But can there be optimism? Mr Michael Crawford, the resigned club chairman, pleaded along the road to Harrogate that a Special Meeting and the taking of sides would split the club for a long time. He was right. There can be no peace now.

It is even more obvious that one person stands between York-shire and harmony, and yet that same person is their one link with greatness, too: Geoffrey Boycott. Only his removal, at the latest after his testimonial year, can unite the county.

Harrogate was an unpleasant experience for the Yorkshire cricket club and its members. And as for joy and humility – the whole campaign was devoid of both.

Sunday Telegraph, 29 January 1984

The ills of whistle-stop cricket

Pakistan won [the 1983–84 home] series against England for the first time in history but very few people turned up to watch. The local view is that tickets are too pricey, one-day matches are more exciting and, in any case, it is much more comfortable to stay at home and watch on television.

It begs a question. If this whistle-stop cluster of international matches is not being put on for the Pakistan cricket lovers, who is benefiting? Who wins? The cricketers? Cricket itself?

For the last three weeks I have witnessed Test-match over-kill. It is not a pretty sight: empty terraces, dusty, scalding, lifeless, unresponsive to the play. I watched England struggling to acclimatise to Pakistan during actual Test-match play, not in a programme of matches leading up to the internationals.

Before they came, only Willis, Botham and Gower were known by the cricket fans. In order to attract more gate-money the Tests needed more heroes. If England had played two or three zonal matches first then others would have caught the eye, built up their fan mail. With no Willis or Botham by the end, England came and went anonymously under white sun-hats.

The one rescue act came from Faisalabad. A small ground, but it was full up with their 12,000 a day. The scarcity value. Lahore and Karachi look played out.

So who wins on short tours? As far as I can see, only the players do and that only in a bank-balance way. There has

[143]

spread from Australia the notion that international cricket is marketable all the year round. The players themselves yearned to make their jobs full-time. The Boards of Control, in order to find the high fees, simply had to stage more cricket, especially in the poorer countries: West Indies, India and Pakistan.

The Pakistan players in this series received £750 a match. England's players averaged £10,000 a man for the winter tour, and in a whole year, a regular England team member would raise his income to £25,000 from match fees.

The Test and County Cricket Board is sharply aware that too much international cricket is debasing the product, but they are always being pressed to send a side abroad to help pay the wages elsewhere. There is an additional consideration. If the Board does not provide winter cricket for our top players, then more of them might be attracted to contract in South Africa and be banned like the rest. On this tour, which has been exclusively international cricket since the second Test in Christchurch on 3 January, it must be argued that the cricketers have lost as well, not just the two series, but in other ways.

Players left out of the Test side, like Tavaré, never have the opportunity to play their way back in. Dilley was reduced to a net bowler, and not a very conscientious one either, freely overstepping the crease in a rather casual way. When he was called on to replace Willis at Faisalabad, he brought to the middle an action which looked like a clockwork toy with its wires crossed.

If it is hard to break into a side, it is conversely difficult to get dropped because you are the man in Test-match practice. Lamb was in this position. He has gone adrift technically: far more open-chested on front and back foot than he was, and, besides technical considerations, I doubt if he had the clear mind to sort it all out. In ways, I feel sorry for the players. As Ian Botham rightly pointed out, life on tour these days is about hotel room service, a drink in the team-room each evening, a video and more travel. Touring life has changed.

Too much cricket breeds stale performance. Too much international cricket puts too great a physical burden on the busiest players. The three finest all-rounders, Ian Botham, Kapil Dev and Imran Khan, might well be finished and we are too busy writing down our scorecards from Kandy, Port of Spain and Lahore to notice. So we are left with the last question. Is cricket itself winning? The answer is emphatically 'No'. Test cricket has become a commercial cocoon which has separated itself from the body of the game. The England caravan – a comfortable, five-star, private club – moves swiftly from Test to Test. It no longer throws down roots. There were no small boys in Sialkot glorying in the sight of a David Gower cover-drive, none of the faithful in Peshawar or, 'Pindi went home talking about the might of Ian Botham. England never went there.

Cricket tours faithfully reflect the ever-quickening society. Yes, I accept that. But are those who present them to the public carrying on the traditional MCC creed: that every decision be made in the interests of cricket and cricketers? Whistle-stop Test cricket will eventually self-destruct.

Sunday Telegraph, 25 March 1984

Why Richards dabbles in the supernatural

As the first Test approaches, on Thursday at Edgbaston, David Gower, the England captain, may do what others have done before him: study the run-scoring chart of the opposition's most dangerous batsman. He could see where Vivian Richards got his 189 not out at Old Trafford and his 84 not out at Lord's, and set a field accordingly.

He might toy with fielders in odd positions on the leg side where the ball has been flying in the air – a close, straight mid-wicket perhaps, or maybe a man lurking between square-leg and deep square-leg. But then it all depends where the bowlers bowl . . . or does it?

On the evidence of the Texaco games, Gower needs three men at least standing in the crowd behind the mid-wicket boundary and one over long-off. I have only once seen a finer stroke than the lofted drive which struck a ball from Willis for six over mid-off at Old Trafford and that was when Richards himself advanced down the pitch to Dennis Lillee at Melbourne in 1979 and sent the ball skimming for four over Jeff Thomson's upstretched hand – also at mid-off – a savage flat-batted drive.

The whole country is in shock after Richards' recent batting. He has brought consternation to one father who stopped me in the village this week and asked me what he should do about his son. 'It's James,' he said with the mortification of a father who has just discovered that his son has sneaked mother's favourite putter back to school for the summer term. 'What do I do? Every ball on or outside off stump, he tries to flip over mid-wicket for six.'

D'y'see how bad this Richards has been for us? Has he never heard of Harry Crabtree and the massed forward defensive stroke? Does he not know that balls on the off must be played to the off?

I suggested to the agitated dad that natural justice would prevail. Once his James had heard the constant rattle of timbers behind him he would conclude that Viv's game is strictly the preserve of Viv. Not even Sir Don or Sir Gary played like that.

Then, again, I pictured Viv Richards playing across the line of flight and middling the ball so sweetly, and I worked out that it may not be quite so risky as it looks. He gets his front foot across and forward with speed. Even if he misses the ball it hits the pad which is usually too far up the pitch to give out and often outside the line of off-stump. . . .

In the new biography of Viv Richards by Trevor McDonald, you can read about Viv's first entanglement with traditional coaching. He was twenty-one. He came to England to attend the Alf Gover Cricket School in South London. Andy Roberts, fellow Antiguan, was with him, freezing cold by night in Putney digs and going to Wandsworth to be tutored by Alf Gover by day.

Richards recalls: 'I was playing a lot of cricket and making a lot of runs, but I had never been coached as such. I found it difficult to adapt myself to the business of being coached. I had played my cricket naturally. No-one really told me what to do.

'I came to Alf Gover with a wide-open stance. That suited me well, because I was playing on hard wickets in Antigua and I could hit through the line of the ball. Alf tried first to make me change my grip. He wanted to try to teach me to play with the left elbow well cocked. But he had problems getting me to do that. I felt it was too defensive a stance and it didn't seem to give me enough time to hit out if I wanted to.

'I did try to listen to what Alf said, though, about playing with bat and pad close together. I think he made me realise – although I didn't let on at the time – the importance of being technically correct, whether you're playing a defensive shot or trying to cover-drive. That's the most important thing I learned.'

When you consider the incredible 189 not out he scored at Old Trafford last week you have to concede that he rarely looked technically vulnerable on an extremely slow pitch which turned square. As the innings went on, I kept reminding myself that I was watching something historic. It is so difficult to appreciate that an innings, when it is actually happening, is about to take its place among the finest ever played.

There was an important turning-point. Richards had played some uppish shots through wide mid-on. One dropped over a fielder's head and rolled to the outfield. It was an easy three. Richards and partner ran one.

He hated the imperfection of the shot.

He was annoyed with himself, because, maybe as a legacy of Alf Gover or other helpers along the way, he does set himself high technical standards. It is just that this idea of perfection is not based on any conception of orthodoxy. His range of possibilities is still rooted in the determination of the young Antiguan who wanted to belt the ball gloriously to all parts, who was fiercely proud of his birth and his Rastafarian belief in Africa as the spiritual home.

Taunt him on any of these subjects, say you have found a way to get him out or, as Tony Greig famously boasted, of making his team grovel, and you have the batting wrath of Vivian Richards with which to cope, based on enough technique to make the magic work.

Young James had better not be deceived. Without an understanding of technique, Richards would be vulnerable and erratic.

Another father I met this week told me that he walked into the bedroom of his ten-year-old son, Tom, and caught him doing violent press-ups. The father was Roger Davis, my former Glamorgan colleague. Roger advised the young man to take it easy.

'Viv does seventy a day,' came the reply from floor level.

'Oh!' said Roger, and closed the door behind him on the way out. For David Gower's problem, too, there may be no answer.

Sunday Telegraph, 10 June 1984

Are the West Indies legal?

This past year proved again that there are two types of cricket, the one played by the West Indies, the other by everyone else. The West Indies won series against India, Australia and England, never losing a match. They did it mainly by fast bowling which was often pitched short and directed well above the stumps to the batsman's head. By including so many fast bowlers who, relentlessly through a day's play, base their attack on intimidation as much as skill, they have distorted the very nature of the game. No longer is the object to bowl at wickets in order to knock them over, it is to shock batsmen into a rushed defensive jumble of gloves, helmets and bat-handles.

Andy Roberts, Colin Croft, Michael Holding, Malcolm Marshall, Wayne Daniel, Winston Davis, Joel Garner, have unwittingly, by their high speed and by an eye for the maximum effect, turned batting into an attritious war of self-defence. Illegal? The cricket Law 42 is clear. It comes under the heading Unfair Play, Paragraph no. 8:

[148]

The bowling of fast, short pitched balls is unfair if, in the opinion of the umpire at the bowler's end, it constitutes an attempt to intimidate the striker. . . . Umpires shall consider intimidation to be the deliberate bowling of fast short pitched balls which by their length, height and direction are intended or likely to inflict physical injury on the striker. The relative skill of the striker shall also be taken into consideration.

There follows the system of progressive warnings which leads to the umpire removing an offending bowler from the attack.

Defenders of the West Indies will argue that their world superiority comes from team-work, and they will be right: Clive Lloyd's is a splendid side. They will put forward Viv Richards's genius, point out that Lloyd himself headed the batting averages in India, that Desmond Haynes averaged 93.60 against Australia, Richie Richardson 81.75, and Gordon Greenidge 78.60. We can follow that up with glorious descriptions of the two double-centuries scored by Gordon Greenidge in the series against England, and of the quiet dedication of Larry Gomes. Nor must one forget the all-round skills of Jeffrey Dujon or the considerable promise of the off-spinner Roger Harper. Yet we come back to the brutal, irresistible force which denies hope to any opponent – the high ingredient of physical intimidation in their bowling.

Now, wait a minute, I hear you say. How often have we heard short-pitched fast bowling praised? Alongside me in the BBC Radio Commentary box I hear Trevor Bailey congratulate Malcolm Marshall on sending down a 'beautiful bouncer' – and Trevor would have his own memories of Lindwall and Miller bouncers hitting him or flying past his temple.

In my playing days I have ducked under bouncers from Fred Trueman, Frank Tyson, Wesley Hall, Charlie Griffith, Brian Statham, John Snow and a host of others. Batsmanship has always been to do with personal courage as well as skill. The bouncer was the legitimate surprise weapon in the fast bowler's armoury. Ah! Surprise. That is the difference.

As far as England were concerned it began with Dennis Lillee and Jeff Thomson in 1974–75 on the tour to Australia under Mike Denness. With Max Walker a third, lively fast-medium bowler, there was a day-long rotation of fast short-pitched bowling. Experienced and talented batsmen like John Edrich, Dennis Amiss, David Lloyd, Denness himself, Keith Fletcher, were never quite the same again. They were shell-shocked.

Lillee boasted that he aimed for the ribcage and he did. That was intimidation in speech and in action.

The Australians, however, would tell you that Ray Illingworth started the planned attacks on the body by instructing John Snow greatly to increase the number of short-pitched balls in Australia in 1970–71. We could go back to Jardine with Larwood and Voce in the 1930s. The truth is that top-class fast bowling is usually decisive and the more of it you have in your side, the more decisive your victories.

Back to Law 42, no. 8. Why do the umpires not uphold it? There were official warnings of West Indians during the summer in England, but the truth is probably that the strictest application of the law would be sensational, a volte-face, and the umpires rightly fear that their stand would not be supported by the Boards of Control.

The West Indies barrage of bowling aimed at the man not the stumps has become habit. The West Indies themselves would be the last to appreciate how they have eroded the pleasurable side of cricket. It is time for the International Cricket Conference, which meets annually in London each summer, to argue the issue and pledge universal support for umpires by instructing them to eliminate intimidation from cricket.

The game has always been richest when bowlers are trying to hit wickets not batsmen, and as soon as they begin to do so again, the old skills will return of swing, flight, spin and seam, and batsmen will stop shuffling in defensive parries under suits of armour. They will all have the confidence to move to the ball again.

Benson & Hedges Cricket Year, 1984 (Third edition)

General Gower

A most interesting study on England's victorious tour of India was the batting of the captain, David Gower. He went as an established international batsman and yet got to the last match with a Test average of 11.00.

If you had to bet on anyone to take a tour captaincy in his stride you would have gone for Gower because of his calm, even flippant attitude to big occasions, his long experience as an England player and the high class of his batting. However his form dipped; his talent almost disappeared.

It is easily done – ask Kim Hughes – but not for the reasons which many would believe, of the so-called burden of the job or of sleepless nights spent drawing diagrams of field placings on the back of supper napkins.

The truth is, it is easy as a batting captain to relegate one's own individual performance. You put a mass of thought and nervous energy into a day's play and when you flop into the seat on the bus back to the hotel, you feel as if you have given as much as the bowler who has taken five wickets or the batsman who has got a century.

Gower is what is known in the trade as a touch player: his batting is instinctive and elegant. It all clicks smoothly according to some divine hand-out of natural ability. However, when a touch player loses form he often finds it more difficult to recover than others whose game weighs heavily on technique, like Geoff Boycott.

The extra talent can be a cheat, because even in the middle of his low scores, Gower was always able to improvise, to manufacture the odd stroke even in short stays at the crease, but apart from elegant wafts at the ball he appeared to set off aimlessly on each innings.

He got more and more withdrawn and tentative, he pushed and paddled the ball instead of playing through it. I am sure he was concerned about his lack of runs. He tried hard in the nets. He was certainly the victim of two bad umpiring decisions in the Tests. He denies that he worried and I am sure that Norman Gifford encouraged him with his usual rallying call that 'talent hides in some funny places, but it never disappears altogether'.

A prolonged run of poor form in a good-class player is usually to do with the attitude of mind. I recall Bernard Hedges, a humorous and wise Glamorgan player, advising a young batsman out of form that there must be positive objectives in the mind. Glamorgan had lost a match against Derbyshire in two days and we were going through the humiliating business of practising on the third day on the youth pitch.

The young player was still getting out dismally every other over. 'You think you are trying,' said Bernard. 'But you are not. You have not a single positive thought in your head. Try to hit 12 runs off the next over. And in the over after that win the game for us, we need another eight.'

So the batsman did, with perfect strokes to many parts. David Gower at last got his motivation in the final Test at Kanpur. All the tour's scheming and hard-earned success was going to be tossed away if the middle-order collapse continued and if Gavaskar made England follow-on. A definite objective led to positive thought and positive play – the captain got 78 and 32 not out.

This battle with his talent will help Gower mature as a captain. Already he will know much more about himself and his batting.

He led a brilliant campaign and this coming summer will have the chance to prove that he can skipper, bat, field close, take Ian Botham back on board, and beat Australia in six Tests. I think he will do it.

Sunday Telegraph, 10 February 1985

Crude oil on cricket palms

I enjoyed my cricket in Sharjah. It looked like cricket anywhere else, but every time a ball was bowled or a stroke played, I kept thinking of the Great Arabian Desert underneath and all around us, concluding that the neat concrete stadium with its green, grassy centre, was either a miracle or a mirage.

Just to sharpen the reality of the achievement, the 18-hole golf course up the road, the Sharjah Wanderers Club, does not boast a single blade of grass. It is 7,000-odd yards of soft sand; the biggest single bunker in the world.

The Four-Nations cricket tournament was played hard. The players were obviously spurred by pride and prize money. England came last and left with $US 1,000 apiece. The winners and still world champions, India, were worth three times as much, plus Man of the Match awards.

Yet the very success prompts questions. Where does Sharjah fit into the run of cricket fixtures? Should England have sent a full team? Are top players overloading themselves for the sake of money? It is also worth asking if there is too much money available. If a tournament here offers, as it does, more prize money than the Prudential World Cup, is it elevated in the players' eyes to pole position in the calendar? It would be in the interest of the Boards of Control if the prize money was regulated, and Sharjah cricket given a respectable, but financially less spectacular place.

Sharjah offers perfect off-shore cricket for India and Pakistan; a handsome donor to the benefit funds of former Pakistan and Indian Test cricketers it might be possible in future to link with the Cricketers' Association in England so that, whenever an England team plays here, a donation can be made to the association or even to the beneficiaries of the year. It is more likely, though, that benefit monies will be directed back into the game in general.

England are unlikely to visit Sharjah on an annual basis; for example, next year at this time, they should be in West Indies. No doubt Asif Iqbal, the Cricket Organiser, can invent enough competitions to retain the interest of all the Boards of Control who have supported and attended, like Donald Carr and Peter Lush representing the Test and County Cricket Board.

I would guess that night cricket is a natural for the Gulf. A day-night series involving Dubai Television would have a strong following from the 700,000 expatriate Asians. The working week is strictly six days, but government offices open early and close at one o'clock, so it would suit the public.

[153]

I imagine the stadium could be developed to include boxes for sponsors. There is talk of a three-match tournament in late autumn between India and the Rest of the World. For Sharjah, from now on, I predict only success.

Incidentally, the pitch is a spinners' joy which made interesting cricket but a lot of attention will have to be given to the soil mixtures and grass quality from now on.

England disappointed many by not sending a full team. The Board did not include Sharjah in the players' winter contracts, believing that some might want to spend time with family or resting before the home season begins. This is surely right, and it opens the way for popular cricketers who are out of the Test scene at the moment, like Derek Randall or Kim Hughes of Australia, and for one-day specialists like Dean Jones or India's Srikkanth.

Young players like Bailey of Northants, French of Notts, Wells of Sussex, can join in too. However, if the Board agrees to support these competitions it would create more goodwill and keep faith with the efforts to make an authentic international atmosphere if the current England captain or vice-captain leads the side. This is not criticism of Norman Gifford who did, and who bowled better than anyone.

Unofficially, India played Pakistan yesterday at the Isa Town Stadium in Bahrain. Gavaskar, Kapil Dev, Shastri and Azharuddin were joined by seven Indian club cricketers to play against seven Pakistani club players with Mohsin Khan, Zaheer, Javed Miandad and Imran. There was a lot of money at stake on a rough wicket; the whole event being run by what a Bahrain journalist described to me as the 'spiv' element in Gulf sport.

It makes more sense for Gavaskar to be taking the hat around at the end of a long, successful career than it does for the young talent of Azharuddin to be exposed to fairground entertainment. Without the guidance of his Board of Control he might develop more into a tournament jouster than a master of the art of batsmanship.

Sunday Telegraph, 31 March 1985

[154]

The Sri Lankans at Lord's

This was Sri Lanka's first Test Match in England and, of course, to play it at Lord's meant a milestone of fruition and maturity for the country which was only eleven Tests old. That they played so magnificently to get the better of a draw is now history. If I relished anything in the commentary box it was the underestimation of the Sri Lankans by Fred Trueman and Trevor Bailey.

Fred said that he thought Paul Allott was not being bowled by Gower because his place on the winter tour to India was safe and that Gower was probably giving others a chance. (Sri Lanka were about to score 491 for 7 in their first innings over two days and 90 minutes!) Trevor suggested before the match that we were about to watch the worst collection of 22 cricketers ever assembled for a Test match. He later conceded that Sri Lanka could bat. I was amused because I had led two MCC tours to Ceylon in 1970 and 1973, in the days when they were building up steadily to Test-match status. I had seen how strongly they batted. I had sweated with my bowlers at the Colombo Oval trying to prise the ever-so-correct and durable Sri Lankans out. I could not expect Trevor and Fred to know as much, but I was delighted to see their views change during the five days. Their expert eyes did not miss the quality of technique nor the range of strokeplay among the batsmen.

In the Test Match Special box with us was a Sri Lankan who now lives in exile in Sydney, Australia, Gamini Goonesena, once a fine leg-spin and googly bowler for Cambridge University, Notts and Ceylon. Gammy had a tricky time at Lord's, balancing his social performance with the requirements of the summarisers' rota in the box. His return to this country after long absence brought his long-denied disciples out of hiding, demanding a sight, a touch and a few words from the great man. Fred Trueman, tired of looking around the box for Gammy, next on air, kept groaning, 'Where's the phantom tea-planter gone now?' When provocatively asked if he remembered playing against Gammy at Fenners or Trent Bridge,

Fred said that he only recalled a little black head on its knees behind the bat-handle, praying! How a head kneels you will have to work out for yourself.

Brian Johnston immediately confused everyone with several pronunciations of the same Sri Lankan name. He rejoiced when it was announced that of the twelve Sri Lankans on the scorecard, Samaranayake would be left out and John included. Easy. That was until we requested a Sri Lankan reserve player to help with the identification and Brian had to turn to 'our good friend here, who has come up to the box from the dressing-room to help us with the recognising of his colleagues, now, after three days, we've got their names'. And turning to the helper said, 'Now your name is Anusha Samar . . . Oh! no!'

The start of the match was surprising. David Gower won the toss and put Sri Lanka in to bat on a pitch which had no serious growth of grass on a roaring, sunny day. He said after Sri Lanka's mammoth first innings that he thought the ball would have swung. For optimism unsupported by facts this rivalled Bob Willis's putting Australia in at Adelaide in 1982–83. I have never heard of sunshine and heat alone recommending an 'insertion'. Oppressiveness, heavy atmosphere, seaside conditions and others, perhaps, but in too many cases, the decision to put in to bat purely for swing-bowling proves wrong.

On this occasion the ball did not swing for long and Sidath Wettimuny played the innings of a lifetime, 190, and a model for young boys to copy. Trevor and Fred firmly pointed out the merits of his technique and we all observed that he had rolled back the years a couple of decades. He played a long innings, for two days, but it never lost its aesthetic appeal. He played the game sideways; he moved right back when he was back and right forward when he was forward. Simple ancient truths, not followed by the bulk of England players these days.

To find the quality and the spirit of Sri Lankan cricket you must look to the colleges, the most famous of which are Royal and St Thomas's. Gammy Goonesena described for the listeners the crowds of 10,000 who attend the annual dust-up called the Royal-Thomian, Battle of the Blues. It is over a hundred years old. So you might guess that Sri Lankan cricket is based on college disciplines too. Players are always perfectly turned out, shoes whitened, flannels pressed. Their sportsmanship is fairly rooted in the best of the Old Boy morality. It is not surprising in this Test match to hear that they had addressed the umpires David Evans and Dickie Bird as 'Sir'. Sadly, it was also no surprise to learn that the umpires had to talk to Gower, the England captain, in order to check the flow of bad language coming from some of the England side.

Wettimuny's performance must have been received with great joy in Sri Lanka as we talked them through it ball-by-ball. Then came Ranatunga, now an old man of twenty! He was strong and much more controlled in his choice of strokes than when I last saw him in Sri Lanka's inaugural Test in Colombo in 1982. He got 84, putting on 148 with Wettimuny.

The major virtuoso performance was still to come. The captain, Duleep Mendis, a short man of ample girth and powerful forearms played an innings which is unforgettable for its wide range of strokes and improvisation. If I had to recall one particular shot, it was the hook that found the ball had bounced a little higher than Mendis had gauged. Then with a regal flip of the wrists he adjusted to bring the meat of the bat smack against the centre of the ball, firing it like a bullet into the Mound Stand.

Wettimuny and Mendis put on 150, Mendis's share 111. Maybe just to prove that his skill is no fluke he repeated the treatment of England's bowlers in the second innings. Before this match he had already scored a century in each innings of a Test against India. He came alarmingly close this time, too, scoring 94 the second time around.

The England compensations were few but Allan Lamb's fourth century of the summer underlines the need to persevere with a player who has the talent even when he has a bad patch. His winter form was awful. However, the three centuries against the West Indies fast bowling must rank as one of the finest series ever by an England batsman. If this last one against less formidable bowling on a perfect pitch was less difficult to achieve, it still remained England's only piece of authority in the five days' play.

Towards the end of the match Neil Chanmugan, the Sri Lankan tour manager, came up into the commentary box to join our ball-by-ball descriptions. Neil was a fine cricketer, hard and competitive and, with others I played against in the early 1970s like Michael Tissera and Anura Tennakoon, prepared the way for Test acceptance by their own high standards. Nor is he a stranger to the microphone because in Sri Lanka he broadcast on the inaugural Test for his island's station.

His thoughts at Lord's were these. 'I hope that our example has stimulated Sri Lankan businessmen. We need sponsorship both for players and for matches. I imagine that the way ahead for us now that we are accepted as decent cricketers is to set up a semi-professional life for our best players . . . retained by businesses perhaps but free to play cricket at the top level.

'Also we need advertising support to bring monies into the game. Our country does have rich natural resources and plenty of trading activity, and our cricket is now on TV.'

Most of the competitive cricket in Sri Lanka is played by clubs in Colombo. There is a new four-day match competition to prepare youngsters for the skills and tempo of Test cricket. Yet the miracle of their first Test at Lord's is that they more than held the best that Britain can offer and it is likely that their strong emphasis on college cricket will soon see them beating England for the first time.

Test Match Special 3, 1985

Make way for Mister Dickie Bird

The scene is a busy Colombo street. Right in the middle of the traffic comes the sound of a loud Yorkshire voice. The traffic jostles and hoots: there are no courtesies of the road. It is a free-for-all. The whole jumble stops. The Yorkshireman gets out of his car on the wrong side. Everyone shouts, 'Mister Dickie Bird. Mister Dickie Bird.' The pale Yorkshireman, now surrounded by hooting vehicles, signals four byes and the crowd applauds: then a 'sixer' and then, with a scowl and an upward sweep of the right forefinger, he gives the driver of an auto-rickshaw out, 'That's owt, son: obstructing t'field. Mister Dickie Bird says so. Mister Dickie Bird.'

Dickie Bird and David (weren't you the preacher?) Shepherd have been the neutral umpires through Sri Lanka and Sharjah. David Shepherd was, of course, the rotund striker of the ball who played for Gloucestershire. They arrived to find relationships between Pakistan and Sri Lanka explosive but they defused them in the very first game of the Asia Cup and everyone delighted in a good old-fashioned demonstration of British justice. When a Pakistan player complained about the shape of the ball and threw it petulantly to Shepherd, he inspected it and tossed it straight back. Nothing special but the whole stadium erupted. Indecisive umpiring has so often led to shambles.

Bird and Shepherd are the only umpires I have ever heard having their decisions clapped. However, when Mister Bird gave out Asantha de Mel caught behind, the batsman left rubbing his arm. Next day a local newspaper carried the shock news: 'English umpires Dickie Bird and David Shepherd flew back home last night following complaints about the controversial dismissal of de Mel in yesterday's match. The English umpires were brought down to the Asia Cup to avert such shocking decisions. The local umpires' union boss Upali Mahanama said: "My lips are sealed".'

My telephone rang time and again in the hotel. Why was Mister Bird upset? Could not the Reverend David have persuaded him to stay?

At last a call from a friend advised me to take note of the date, April 1. Mister Dickie Bird, in fact, was taking a full breakfast of fresh pineapple, mango and York ham ('York, y'see. Must be the best in t'world, mustn't it?') in Room 324 of the Oberoi.

Television witnessed his great deeds. Thereafter doors were never closed to him. He even waltzed through the most stiff, poker-faced immigration officialdom at the airport on his departure, simply saying: 'Mister Dickie Bird, Mister Dickie Bird', the passwords: repeat them and the whole of Sri Lanka parts and genuflects before you.

Sunday Telegraph, 13 April 1986

Jim Laker

Jim Laker would not want any word-monger to gush about his passing. He was devoted to proper professional cricket and, on the field, he let actions say everything.

He loved the television commentary of cricket – the professional sort – he deplored wafflers. Cricket and television cricket he saw as team games. He acknowledged that broadcasters, like bowlers, have to be concerned about their own performances, but only inasmuch as they were contributing their best to the team.

Cricket for Jim was a high art form. He scorned the way that cricket in his day was often run by, as he wrote, 'well-meaning gentlemen with but the scantiest knowledge of the game, as happens with so many county committees'. He therefore accepted his BBC commentaries as a serious responsibility. Not a word too many, not a word too few.

Our playing careers overlapped marginally. I remember playing just inside the line of three off-spinners in a row and beating them with the defensive middle of the bat. For the fourth I lurked in a similar position and was astonished when I missed it. The ball shaved the bat and I heard the bowler's snort, followed by the glare which said that a priceless quartet of deliveries had been wasted on the likes of me.

I mentioned it a few seasons ago and he remembered. How could he? He must have passed a million novice, outside-edges in his time. He brought clarity of recall to his commentaries, too. He knew what true cricket quality was; he had seen it and remembered it. You could not sell Jim Laker a poser.

Our broadcasting careers have gone side by side for a long time. We first worked together on 28 July 1971. He was at my first effort, a match that turned out to be famous: Lancs. v. Glos. in the Gillette semi-final which finished in the dusk after nine o'clock.

Suddenly our outside broadcast was joined by all sorts of programmes requiring updated reports including a live performance by Jim on the Nine o'clock News. He was, as always, succinct and balanced, even as David Hughes was hitting John Mortimore's off-spin for 24 runs in an over.

It was pandemonium outside and inside our box. When it was all over, I asked: 'How do you keep so cool?' With his lovely wry humour, he replied: 'Well, could be worse. I could be out there bowling.'

Sunday Telegraph, 30 April 1986

Crowe flies high

New Zealand batted with a pleasant combination of good sense and style and moved remorselessly on to England's total of 307. At tea they were just 35 runs behind with six wickets standing.

England were handicapped by the injury to Willey which, on paper, deprived them of an off-spinner. Not that Willey can be described as a bowling force. He has taken only three first-class wickets this season at the cost of 83 runs each.

The truth was that England's attack rarely threatened. Dilley was lively, using his height to get much more lift than Radford. Foster strayed too often and too expensively wide of off stump, but he had a problem with line. Radford urgently needed a device on length. He pitched too short.

Instead, the inspired batting of Martin Crowe dominated on a peaceful pitch. His stroke-play had a distinct punch about it; he likes to stand up to play his strokes, not using a high back-lift, but favouring the on-drive more than any international player other than Viv Richards. His partner, Edgar, was gritty and sensibly cautious as long as his partner was in such good form. These two put on 210 for the third wicket which beat the New Zealand third-wicket record against England, which was 190 by Hastings and Congdon at Lord's in 1973.

England's most effective moments were when Gooch was helping out the best bowler on the side, Edmonds. Edmonds floated and flighted many variations from the Nursery End: Gooch got as much movement as any of the seamers from the Pavilion. Within a scope of three runs, when the score was 215 and then 218, both Edgar and Crowe were gone. England had the chance of a breakthrough.

The overnight scorecard had had a symmetrical look about it – two ducks, two not out 52's and two wickets to Dilley. New Zealand were on 127 for two and a depleted England side faced a hard day on a good pitch.

At this point we must talk of the wounded because it was the gossip of the day in the big crowd. Willey could not field because he had a swollen knee. Prichard of Essex substituted. Foster, rumoured to have what was described as a 'stiff' back, surprised those who claimed contrary dressing-room knowledge by racing in to bowl the first over of the day from the Nursery End.

The injury on Friday to French, the wicket-keeper, and his replacement by the retired England 'keeper, Bob Taylor of

Derbyshire, belonged to the world of fond fables told to grand-children in the flickering half-light of the Christmas hearth. You will have heard how Taylor, who now attends Test matches to represent Cornhill Insurance and attend on their clients, was called from his lunch to pad up and substitute for poor French, who was hit on the back of the helmet by a ball from Hadlee. The event gave rise to a long list of questions, and not all of the answers are available.

Why was medical attention so long in reaching French, who had staggered, sagged and eventually lay motionless in the crease? Why was there no ordinary, flat stretcher available? French departed in what looked like an invalid cradle chair which had to be carried, wheels held manfully off the ground, and with a hand placed under his head for support.

Why was French, whose head wound needed two stitches, not taken then to hospital for further examination? Apparently he had admitted to losing the power of his arms and legs and could not speak. If he had been taken, it might have been established earlier that he would fail to take the field yesterday.

Why did Coney, the New Zealand captain, allow someone as expert as Taylor to take French's place? In the case of a sub-stitute wicket-keeper, the opposing captain has the right to object. Why did he not insist that Gatting continued with Athey, the first stand-in? Coney is clearly a most sporting fellow.

But even if you allow the indulgence of letting the forty-five-year-old Taylor go to work again after a two-year lay-off, it did appear generous 'beyond the call' to allow the England selec-tors to ring up Test hopefuls in the morning to see who had a day off.

Bobby Parks of Hampshire was just about to give his wife her only Saturday out in the season when the telephone rang. By 12.50 he was crouching behind the stumps at Lord's waiting for Radford to bowl to Martin Crowe from the Pavilion End. Why did the selectors not call Parks on Friday night?

Why do the playing conditions not either rule out altogether the right to object to a replacement 'keeper or alternatively ban a specialist substitute in that position? I favour the latter. Surely a fascinating aspect of Test matches is the need for captains and teams to improvise when a key player is injured or absent.

Perhaps Coney was right in the end, his generosity was appreciated and he probably knew that it mattered not who stood behind the stumps as long as Martin Crowe and Edgar stood in front of them. These two were not separated by lunch when the score was 193 for 2.

Crowe completed his superb century straight after lunch but when he and Edgar had gone, England took the second new ball. It did not produce the collapse hoped for. Coney and Jeff Crowe dug in and when the evening session began, Gatting had once again turned to Edmonds. Later New Zealand had taken their score to 310 for 7 wickets.

Sunday Telegraph, 27 July 1986

Exit without a tear

The great sadness of Geoffrey Boycott's exit from first-class cricket is that there is not one moist eye within the game. A fine player should not go like that, especially in a team game. Yet it had to be this way; it has long been obvious.

Unfortunately, he reached his personal pinnacle the lonely way, by denial not expansiveness. He was even more frugal with his strokes and former colleagues say with his money, with his consideration of others in the team. They complain that his generous moments turned out to be exercises in public relations or schemes to go onwards and upwards financially. Yet he was a marvellous player.

That single-mindedness which made him one of the prolific run-getters of all time adapted easily to his skirmishes off the field. You have seen it in all his battles with Yorkshire committees. He has played all their bouncers stoically off the front foot with his faithful solicitor batting patiently at the other end – about the only one he did not run out – and even now their partnership may ride again.

There are thousands who are hypnotised by Boycott, the cult

figure, and they will be heard again, no doubt marching on Headingley chanting out the message – 48,426 runs; 8,114 runs in 108 Tests, second only to Gavaskar: 151 first-class centuries and even this year top of the Yorkshire averages. Boycott has been a magnificent batsman; not the talent of Sobers or Richards, but with superb technique built with devoted care and attention.

No player leaves county cricket happy, there is usually disappointment and often disaffection. Even W. G. Grace in his fifties gave the Gloucestershire Committee a blast when he felt the icy dagger coming his way, and he left. There is a difference, though. W.G. was an obese non-bender, and was not getting many runs. Boycott is still fit and could play on even though his runs come more slowly these days. He will, therefore, be hurt that after all these years, since 1962, his emotional umbilical with Yorkshire cricket has been severed. Harder still, it has been done by people with whom he played: Brian Close, the Yorkshire Cricket Chairman, Phil Sharpe and Brian Stott. Also the former Yorkshire and England player, Bob Appleyard.

Boycott is seen by many as their victim, yet Close's committee is saying, as were many committees before them, that it is Yorkshire cricket which has been the victim of Boycott.

It astonishes outsiders to hear Yorkshire members go against their committees so often. Why, although committeemen give up a lot of spare time to help administer the playing side of the club, the moment they lay a hand on Boycott, half of the membership erupts in Boycott's favour? The truth is the same now as it always has been and it is not encased in Test or Yorkshire averages. It is closeted within the dressing-room walls. Now through Close, Sharpe, Stott and Appleyard, the dressing-room speaks.

It is no idle tribute to Boycott's play to say that he would still be the most dependable opener to play against Australia this winter; the five-day game could still cope with his slow tempo. Yet three-day county games are too short for him. He has never been a great winner of county matches. So if he is not going to win matches for Yorkshire, the only point in continuing the Boycott career is for him to get more and more runs.

[165]

The end of his playing days is sad and, because of the mountain of his achievement, even tragic.

Sunday Telegraph, 28 September 1986

Gower policy shift

David Gower was co-opted on to the England selection-committee this week, joining manager Peter Lush, assistant Micky Stewart, captain Mike Gatting and John Emburey, the vice-captain. It is the first grain of responsibility Gower has been offered since he was so publicly stripped of the leadership and reduced to the ranks. The selectors at home certainly did not include him in the decision-making group.

Their treatment of Gower has been the most shameful pulping of a player's confidence I have ever seen. They are entirely responsible for the man who has been wandering around with the current England touring team, wounded and uninterested.

Gower must wonder – as Ian Botham might too – how for a series or two, while they were England's captains, their cricket intelligence was rated so highly then, suddenly, they were not given the responsibility of looking after the dressing-room key when the team was practising.

Players who once looked up to them soon lose respect and, in Gower's case, he has strolled around the nets aimlessly; always unlikely to take any game seriously outside a Test match. Therefore it is no accident of form that he went into the Brisbane Test runless; nor, of course, was it a surprise that he responded to the big occasion. That is why he is such an outstanding cricketer.

It is important to remember that we are discussing a captain who led England to an Ashes win and to a Test victory against India away from home, the very side which, this year, has just beaten England in England.

His blemishes are well known – annihilation by the West Indies twice and a personality which infuriates some because of an excessively casual look. I once before suggested he looked like Christopher Robin dragging Pooh Bear up the wooden hill at the very moment the nation expected a blowing on the bugle and the sound of a battle charge. However, Gower is his own man and what eventually lost him the leadership, when he was given that demeaning last chance in the first Test of the 1986 season, was his refusal to jump through the particular hoop set out by the selectors who were trying to change the team image.

How much less sanguine it would have been to have appointed a new captain at the start of that series. Stripping Gower of all responsibility in that way, followed by the loss of Leicestershire's captaincy, has virtually cut loose one of the most consistent Test batsmen of his generation. To be averaging 45 in Tests makes him a precious commodity for England and his former tour manager, Tony Brown, always thought him to have a first-class cricket brain. Happily, it has been recognised again on this trip, or maybe someone realised suddenly that a tour committee had been appointed by those at home in which only Emburey had played a Test match in Australia!

There is Gower, there is Botham, both debadged Test and county captains. But there will be a difference when history compares their situations: Botham's England captaincy was followed by the return and success of Mike Brearley; Gower's by an encumbent – Gatting – who went on to lose to India at home and New Zealand, and still has it all to do.

There persists the reek of the scapegoat about Gower. His morale needs repairing. This week's move on tour to include him in the policy chats is wise indeed and may sustain his interest and keep his talent going.

Sunday Telegraph, 16 November 1986

Sensational Botham at Brisbane

Before the first Test Australia were lauded for their drawn series in India and manager Bobby Simpson was telling everyone how a renaissance was magically in process and how their team had grown a certain 'togetherness' on tour, staying in each other's company and talking cricket.

Those of us who know a bit about cricketing in India, and love the place, recognised this as propaganda. What else do you do of an evening in Jamshedpur, for example, but retreat from the heat and dust to the team room, open a can of beer and talk about cricket as if you had invented it? So there was nothing special so far.

However, I must start at the beginning, because nothing would have been possible without Bill Athey who, in his correct, sideways style, reversed the tide of the tour so far. He defended with such determination on the first day that he played himself into a strokeless state.

Luckily, Gatting and Lamb kept the scoreboard clicking, then Athey found his nudge to leg, next his pull and hook and then, at last, a straight-drive. His was the foundation on which all others built attractively and Ian Botham built sumptuously.

There were shocks at the start of the second day. Athey, who had batted through the first day, and Lamb were both out without a run being added, and England went from 198–2 to 198–4.

Then Gower gave Australia prolonged slip-catching practice but they never held him and he began to play well, with Botham talking him into a competitive mind. Indeed, Gower was unlucky to find his thunderous pull shot arrive in the hands of a shocked mid-wicket, but he had had his luck and could not complain.

Botham's innings was unforgettable, however. He played seriously and straight and the Australians were bowling much more accurately on this second day. However, the extreme delight of Botham lies in his ability not only to ignore convention but to rupture it. So fifteen minutes before lunch, when everyone was saying 'My word, if Gower and Botham could only stay till the afternoon', he slashed a bat at the fast and lively Hughes and cut the ball square on the off side for a six, which I promise you scarcely got above head-high all the way to the greyhound track in front of the stands.

Well, we thought, that is his pre-lunch madness over. The next ball he hit on the up, over mid-on for four. Gower had a word with him. Whack! Over the covers for another four. Botham's 50 came up in 72 balls and included a six and six fours.

Other batsmen came and went, DeFreitas more delightfully than others, but it was Botham who gave everyone a day to remember . . . unhelmeted, hair tinted blond, slipping and sliding along the green edges of the mown pitch in rubber-soled shoes – as ever doing so much wrong but a lot more right.

He beat an England record for this particular ground of 126 by Maurice Leyland. Gabba folk did not care. They wanted more and he did not disappoint them.

Hughes, the fiery, heavily moustached fast man, the one renowned for a short fuse and even shorter vocabulary, ran in to bowl an over to Botham, who had reached 97. Botham hit a two and Border called in the fielders to save the single. In snorted Hughes again and was just getting through his action when the ball whistled back over his right shoulder to crash into the sight screen for the boundary which gave Botham his century. He hit 22 runs off that particular over, and for most of the time made the orthodox ring of fielders who usually try to save the single as relevant as foot soldiers in a missile attack. He was sensational.

Brisbane, 1986, will be remembered as one of the days when the mood took him to play with the utmost loyalty and dedication to the cause, and yet to transcend the values of others. He will be happy to couple with his great innings the name of Bill Athey, who prepared the way.

Sunday Telegraph, 16 November 1986

Micky Stewart

Micky Stewart's full-time employment as England's cricket manager begins this month. I was one who doubted if there was such a role to play.

What happens when the captain is strong and wants to run

all of the cricket himself? When Mike Brearley was captain there was no room in the nets for Ken Barrington. Did Ray Illingworth not prove at Yorkshire that a former player trying to run a side is in danger of ending up back on the field again, thus proving that good captaincy is all that is required?

Bob Willis, who was the assistant manager in charge of cricket on the last England tour of the West Indies, found his job was mainly to put up nets and play ball-boy. However, here in Sharjah, where England are engaged in a four-nation tournament, Micky Stewart has tried to persuade me that his is a most important job. 'Organising, coaching, advising and leading individuals to a correct outlook . . . it's a tough job,' he says.

'I have to be flexible to fit in with a tour manager and with various captains, but the quality of England's cricket and who plays it is surely the priority. When I was working for Slazenger it was the same there, different approaches for different people. You wouldn't sell a tennis racquet in Sunderland with the same approach as you'd sell one in Southampton.'

Although he did not mention it at first, clearly team selection is where he will have most to contribute. England's selectors, often busy men, never see enough cricket – especially abroad. Players will be encouraged to think that there is a professional selector and Stewart's looks like being the most authoritative voice on the selection committee.

In this connection, he has positive ideas too for the enlarging of the England pool of players. 'I do not want to be a Bobby Robson and do it all myself. Then it depends only on results. But we do need continuity because something important has changed since the days when I was playing for Surrey and you were in the Glamorgan side . . . not the game itself, but the people playing it.

'Now they expect to work daily at their cricket . . . they see it as a twelve-month-a-year occupation; they want to be led to a high fitness level and they want their profession well run.' Indeed, on this rest day he was last seen going off to the nets just to help one player, Robert Bailey.

Certainly, international cricket is proliferating to allow those professional aspirations to take shape. This tournament in

Sharjah is an example of serious competition and soon there will be another international event in Dubai.

'I have been astonished by the excellence of the cricket in Sharjah,' said Stewart. 'People back home have no idea what a truly international atmosphere we've got out here. I believe that England should play everywhere and get involved all the time, all over the world if the cricket is there.

'But I do not believe in sticking to the same team. Some reach the time when they would benefit from a rest. I think it was absolutely right for Graham Gooch to take last winter off and for Ian Botham to give up touring, and quite frankly I can only congratulate David Gower for getting through the Australian tour so well and so successfully when he was clearly struggling to get into the right frame of mind.'

The handsome Sharjah stadium with its 17,000 fanatics screaming India or Pakistan to victory is superb preparation for Neil Fairbrother, James Whittaker, David Capel and Robert Bailey. Stewart agrees: 'It's a tough Test atmosphere. I believe if we can have more players used to cricket at this level we can come here and win for a change. It is wrong to think that only the Gattings, Gowers and Lambs can bat for England: there are several county players who could be introduced tomorrow who would do well.'

So, the excess of cricket often complained of these days would be turned to England's advantage if more players were involved at the top. Therefore, allowing that such a new breed of professional does exist and with the ease of international travel likely to proliferate England's commitments in the future, Stewart anticipates an important job. As a player himself he was never one who toyed with the game or his fitness and he appears to be a natural to take England along the road he knows well. Whether it is the right road will be fascinating to see.

Sunday Telegraph, 5 April 1987

Noughts anonymous

Scores of 0, 0, 27, 27, 2 not out, 0, 0 – and I thought all we would now find of Goochy was a pile of clothes on Clacton sands.

Then came the brief shower in his arid desert – 53 not out and renewed hope that the England selectors would remember his bowling and take him into the Texaco Trophy squad as an all-rounder. But come Friday, another duck, fourth ball.

A club cricketer can sneak into a new season with a run of ducks, but when an outstanding Test batsman starts to lay the blade at fresh air every time he goes to the crease he becomes a public curiosity. His fate-of-the-day becomes a sportsnews headline, and all Goochy has been able to do is pretend to relax nonchalantly on the pavilion balconies, phoning imaginary numbers on that portable telephone of his while others are doing the batting.

Noughts Anonymous – is that who he is talking to? Why haven't I thought of that before? Cricketers are vulnerable souls. Golfers survive disasters on the first hole, snooker players can miss the red triangle completely on the break but still be around to win on the black, tennis players can be two sets down and ahead by the end of the fifth.

It is not like that for a batsman – and I write with the authority of one who collected a pair of ducks in a day at Hove sometime in the 1960s. Batting is sudden death.

Did you know that there was a professional batsman who sent a piece of paper up the chimney to Santa every Christmas with one request written on it: '1,000 runs please'? Just look at a county player when he pulls a wishbone. He does not long for wealth or a Georgian mansion, he just mumbles helplessly: 'Please, God, let me get off the mark on Friday'.

What shall I tell Goochy if he has to ring Noughts Anonymous? I had better tell him seriously how easy it is when you are captain to relegate your own concentration with the bat, even to the point of letting someone else have prime time and the best of the pitch in the practice nets.

I had better say that he will have flaws in technique but also that they multiply once the brain fogs up with self-doubt. When

Gooch is playing badly his front foot never gets far enough out to the pitch of the ball, and in backward defence his body gets turned around, chest facing down the pitch. When he is playing well, however, his front foot never gets far enough to the pitch of the ball and in backward defence his body gets turned around . . . that is not a lot of help to him.

Consolation is probably the best bet of the counsellor. Remember Denis Compton, I shall say. The Compton bubble burst on the tour of Australia in 1950–51, most apparently in Tests. His scores were 3, 0, 0, 23, 5, 0, 11 and 11 not out. Aggregate 53, average 7.57. He was even given one-off-the-mark by his pal Bill Johnston in the Adelaide Test, but hit a deliberate long-hop straight into the hands of the substitute fielder, Sam Loxton, at mid-wicket. Compo went to the Don.

The following is taken from *Cricket and All That* by Compton and Bill Edrich: 'Whereupon the great man [Don Bradman] produced a bat from beneath a bed in his hotel room at Melbourne and proceeded to give me a ten-minute display of magic strokes and footwork with an imaginary ball. He reckoned I was playing across the line, was not using my feet properly and had lost confidence.'

So much for the diagnosis. Compo listened and took the action which returned his game to the peak of genius forever – he never again had a single gin and tonic, only doubles, and swopped early nights for late. Batting was never a trouble to him after that.

So maybe we will see a tired and emotional Gooch weaving his way into The Oval on Thursday for the first one-day international. Or perhaps I should recommend first what Majid Khan did when he was out of runs.

He brought out of the attic an old favourite of a bat. Then, when he failed again – I recall it was at Derby – he went and obtained a saw from the groundsman and sawed it in half. At least after that he knew it was not the fault of the bat. Eliminate the problems . . . good advice?

P.S. If you do need to contact Noughts Anonymous, do ring . . . Alf Gover.

Sunday Telegraph, 17 May 1987

Trouble in the pavilion

Phillip DeFreitas is missing from the England party at Head-ingley; his career has skidded into a U-turn.

The dressing-room politics at Leicester are well beyond me, but anyone who has played first-class cricket recognises the symptoms of a peculiar disease which often afflicts those whizzed to stardom in the crown-and-three-lions, but who return to their county sides on a wet Wednesday and perform like a lame fox, wilting roses, blunted sabres or whatever imagery you choose.

When I read that DeFreitas's kit had been tipped out of the dressing-room window I remembered what happened to me in the early 1960s on the morning I rejoined Glamorgan after playing in the University match at Lord's.

It was at the old Cardiff Arms Park ground. My kit went missing. I found it eventually, scattered on the corrugated roof of the low members' stand in front of the dressing-room window: Cambridge blue blazer, sweaters, boots and box, the lot. I suspect it was just Brian Evans' way of telling me that he would prefer I left that sort of kit at home.

If DeFreitas thought for a moment that Leicester was just a resting place before the next Test match, if his Dominican exuberance for the England life was spilling over, he could not have crashed into two more sanguine hatchet men of the spirit than Ken Higgs, the county's coach, and Peter Willey, the captain.

Both of these are superb professional craftsmen. They are only interested in performance – fine speeches are for weddings, hard-luck stories for the dead and departed, dressing-room pranks for the kindergarten. They will know that self-confidence is vital to a top-class cricketer, but that confidence only comes from technical mastery of one's skills and a boat-load of guts. Higgs has invested a lot of hours getting DeFreitas to bowl close to the stumps and the profit was there for all to see in Australia. Willey, too, was in touch with him: which says a lot for the input of Leicestershire enthusiasm for the Ashes effort.

However, there is plenty of evidence that Test cricketers find it impossible to play as hard for their counties as for their country. Certainly DeFreitas has not been very successful this summer.

Somerset will testify to the merits of having eleven players on the field totally devoted to their cause rather than have Ian Botham and Viv Richards, who may have failed to find an ordinary day in the county championship important enough for absolute concentration.

What did not help DeFreitas were the recent doubts about his fitness. He was unlikely to get any charity then. Whatever agony he was in, if he decided not to play for Leicestershire then the old pros would come out with, 'Fit for England, but not fit for us, ay?'

So the brief set-back in his career is nothing to do with practical joking. I cannot believe that, apart from Agnew, whose salad DeFreitas over-salted, anyone raised an eyebrow at the dressing-room jape, even though it was unsubtle.

The best dressing-room jokes always make a point. Richie Benaud recalls how Colin McDonald at Johannesburg in 1957 was indulging in his latest penchant for Limburger and Gorgonzola cheeses, as ripe as possible. Unfortunately, after a couple of days' exposure, the cheese was not only stinking out the Australian dressing-room, but undermining the usual sang-froid of one who was locked into the dressing-room every minute of the day because he had a broken finger and was not playing. One Neil Harvey.

It was towards the end of the second day that Harv snapped. He was seen hurling McDonald's cheeses through the back window of the dressing-room into the rubbish area outside.

No dressing-room jape ever ends there. McDonald, when he discovered the loss of his cheese and how it had happened, and knowing that Harvey's and Benaud's playing lives depended on ample intake of a special elixir, Coca-Cola and milk drink, walked slowly to the cooler, removed every bottle of coke and jug of milk and emptied them down the sink. Harvey protested . . . but McDonald was bigger than Harvey.

No-one took their bat and ball home: no cricket writer considered it worthy of report. Honour was satisfied.

[175]

There is only one conclusion to be made. Captains of counties do have to be communicators and persuade their whole team, especially those returning from Tests, that what they are doing in a county sweater on any day of the week is the most important thing in their lives, because it is.

You can have a gilded image of yourself in Tests and the best players deserve the flattery. But it is the county game which tells you the truth: it is the image to be trusted.

As soon as DeFreitas sees this and sets out to prove the domestic jibers wrong, he will be back for England. Otherwise he may join the pathetic figures who think that by changing counties the problems of the very talented Test player may disappear.

Sunday Telegraph, 5 July 1987

Sunil's swansong

The MCC Bicentenary match has been a happy event, crammed with excellent cricket, and yesterday it provided cricket lovers in this country with a last, adoring sight of Sunil Gavaskar, the record breaker, in full flow. His long innings of 188 took the Rest of the World side to 392 for seven by tea. This was in answer to MCC's 455 for five declared and creates the possibility of an exciting match. . . .

Gavaskar's innings was a delightful exposition of his skills and concentration. He almost never carried his stroke-making into the risk area. He was nimble and compact, a joy to watch.

Imran Khan too was saying farewell. His bowling has pushed his batting into the shadows but he played strokes which were every bit a match for anything else on view.

There was time lost – half an hour in the morning – and after tea thunder and lightning edged closer to Lord's and umbrellas went up. However vicious the storm, nothing could spoil the magnificent party.

The sight of whales, water-hogs and the paraphernalia of drying equipment was a poor sight in the early morning, but

[176]

the depression of the big crowd vanished with the announcement of an 11.30 start. Would Sunil Gavaskar, who overnight
had announced his retirement from Test cricket, turn Lord's
from an unlucky ground into a stage for a glorious farewell? His
previous best here was 60.

In a television interview before play he revealed a recent fear
of the nineties; the last three times he got that far he got out.
Strange for the holder of a record 34 Test centuries who has
passed that way more often than anyone else.

Forgetting nerves, there was another obstacle, Malcolm
Marshall, easily the most dangerous bowler on both sides.
Umpires say that Marshall often walks back to his mark
nominating what he will do with the next ball: he is aiming for
records. He is a cold assassin. When he got Haynes out, his
Bajan mate, he ran past him without contact of word or eye:
another first-class victim in the bag. Marshall first dismissed
Dujon by a catch at third slip – and then proceeded either to
pass Imran's bat or snick the outside edge in a spell of 4-0-15-1.

Gavaskar *was* nervous: he nudged and pushed, scampered,
slipped and stopped. Nor were his jitters eased by the other
Bombay boy, Ravi Shastri, playing on the other side. Sunil is
his guru, coach and father confessor, but Shastri's bowling was
a model of slow, floating accuracy.

Then it came, the century and the standing ovation: the
brilliant exit from top-class cricket, yet with all his batting
virtues still intact – the head so still and right over the ball, the
precise footwork, allies to his natural eye.

The game this far had been tough going for the bowlers, none
of whom is used to being fodder at a batting feast. Gooch's
century had been full of thumping and it was hard to imagine a
more dominant innings than Gatting's 179. Yet somehow
Gavaskar's play was more even, containing fewer flaws.

It was just before lunch that hope appeared for bowlers. Both
Emburey and Shastri got occasional balls to turn sharply.
Imran Khan and Gavaskar applied their techniques seriously.
With Miandad nursing an injured back, a long partnership
between them was essential. In fact by lunch they had put on
91, the score 264 for four.

This is thoroughly modern cricket but if anything created the sensation of flicking through faded old photographs it was the fielding. These giants of the game, mature in their specialist skills, missed the camouflage of young athletes dashing about the field around them. There were no sliding stops, muddied trousers or crashes into perimeter advertisements. It was not exactly boot to ball, but one or two did appear to be running on the spot.

After his century Gavaskar recovered his fluency. Then, before anyone appeared to notice, Imran was also going well at the other end. A substantial partnership was building up.

Both Sunil and Imran strike me as batsmen who put in a lot of practice when young. Their sideways play is cultured and a model – Imran, the product of Aitchison's College, Lahore, and Sunil from the famous nursery of Bombay cricket, the Dadar Union. They put on 180 superb runs in which time Imran landed a huge six into the President's box.

It took another product of the Dadar Union to trick Gavaskar out. Shastri bowled beautifully to three fielders on the leg side who were rarely troubled. His rhythm was excellent and eventually he got the maestro driving too soon and took a caught and bowled.

Sunday Telegraph, 23 August 1987

Comeuppance time in the Reliance Cup

'Calcutta welcomes, cheers and sings.
Come and crown the cricketing kings.'

What the advertisers failed to mention to this tumultuous population was that India and Pakistan would not be playing in the great match – the final.

On our flight from Bombay to Calcutta there were 120 cancelled seats; there are hotel rooms available where only park benches were on offer. The unthinkable has happened. How can you have a World Cup final without the holders, India, and minus the bookies' favourite, Pakistan? Who has deprived the subcontinent of the final they wanted?

Whoever wins, or has already won, the Reliance Cup in Calcutta today, the protagonists, England and Australia, have done cricket a lot of good in these parts. Although the cricket-lovers here are still in shock – and will be for sometime – they needed to realise that the tag of world champions was too heavy for them and their team.

Whereas other teams would be happy to win a World Cup, to celebrate and move on to something else, Indians have elevated themselves with the national success, rather like Welshmen who get carried away when they have a great rugby side. Cricket since the 1983 World Cup has been a major slice of an Indian's identity: he has got the whole show out of proportion. Egos have become pumped up.

Winning a 50-overs tournament at cricket is tough, fun and delicious, but it is not life itself. It is still impossible to tell an Indian that. A spot of rain fell just after England had won in Bombay on Thursday and 45,000 spectators made a shocking silence. It was a national disaster.

When Australia won at Lahore on the day before, it was so quiet you could actually hear the Australian players out in the middle of the field back-slapping and making whoopee.

Only today, because India are not in the final, has the realisation struck – the 1983 World Cup is history, the glory road embarked on then has run out of ticker-tape. They are over the precipice into the swamp.

Even so, yesterday's newspapers in Calcutta published cricket supplements full of Indian and Pakistan photographs without a mention that England and Australia were playing in the final. The perfect party has been broken up, because India v. Pakistan would have erected the stage on which the last acts of two great careers were to be played out: of Imran and Gavaskar.

Last week we were besieged with stories of how Gavaskar had consulted his guru, Sai Baba, and received a gold ring with predictions of success. Vengsarkar went too but, despite encouraging mystical words, he missed the semi-final because he had flu!

Kapil Dev's mother has been much quoted, saying that prayer works better for her than watching her son play. I hope the dear lady was spared a vision of her handsome son's ugly stroke when India had England on the ropes.

Pakistan's fortunes are also talked about in heavenly terms with their manager, Haseeb Ahsan, saying 'Inshallah' – 'our success is in the hands of God'.

Thus, both Indians and Pakistanis appear to have elevated their cricketers above reality. They are not allowed human weaknesses. Handsome faces feature in glossy magazines, the movie-star treatment. You can pay up to £5,000 to hire a cricketer to do an advertisement for your business product.

The Shastris and Srikkanths move lithely into five-star hotels from cool cars behind the shades of sunglasses. There is an aura of arrogance with some – though not with those two – which cricket, cruel mistress that she is, has refused to tolerate any longer. Even Don Bradman saying farewell at The Oval in 1948 had to bow before her.

I must be careful not to equate Pakistan with India in too many ways, but both have their spokesmen who think that the headquarters of world cricket should be in Asia: Abdul Hafeez Kadar in Pakistan, and the politician Salve in India. They argue for the shift in the balance of playing power. I hope they are not claiming administration, too. Neither country is hot at answering letters, and telephone communication is still in a perpetual state of muddled infancy.

'Shall I end your call now, Sir?'

'No, not now.'

'You want Lucknow?'

Tomorrow at the ICC meeting, Mr Salve, who threatened to break up the ICC if it did not adopt a militant anti-apartheid stance, will receive the reprimand of a lifetime for breaking the confidence of the ICC in his recent, self-glorying book *The Story of the Reliance World Cup*.

Sensible Indians are relieved that their team and officials no longer parade as World Cup holders, and I believe that the players themselves, although having turned a pretty rupee on the back of it, will be pleased to feel the suffocating expectations of their countrymen recede. It was always going to be a test for both India and Pakistan to keep winning in front of their own crowds, who were insatiable for success.

These are still wonderful cricketing countries, fascinating to be in, friendly, enthusiastic and ever-helpful. Still, on the scorched maidan, boys bat and bowl, swarming like ants over a white handkerchief. There are smart games played in proper cricket clothes and peasant games between mud hovels; both dream one day of being Gavaskar or Imran Khan.

Like Bradman, these two great healers left international cricket by stumbling off stage over the trip-wire, yet their immense achievements will persist. I played Tests against Sunil fifteen years ago and believe he has always been the finest technician I have seen. Not only did he fashion a superb technique, he retained his strokeplay. He was no defensive item. Of course, he could play fast bowling well, but his complete sovereignty was over the spinners. With immaculate judgement of length, he knew when to go forward and when to go back.

As for Imran, Britain has seen more of him because of his contracts in county cricket. His game, like Gavaskar's, has been based on a complete understanding of technique, in his case both batting and bowling. Only the most serious dedication could have got him back from his crippling shin injury a few years ago and found him thundering in still at top speed in his middle thirties.

So, two genuine heroes go. Neither was patient with fans or officials who glorified in their country's cricket for the wrong reasons. Neither stooped to cheating nor offered excuses. Both will be missed because they set these high examples.

It is time for India and Pakistan to consider what they stood for and shrink a little before they grow.

And so we said farewell to the 1987 World Cup with fireworks climbing and exploding high above the giant stadium at Eden Gardens in Calcutta. None of the 90,000 Bengali crowd quit the ground early. It had been a glorious finale to a happy tournament. India and Pakistan had proved they could combine and succeed. Also, because the competition was played outside England for the first time, for a beautiful cup fashioned in Jaipur, it felt, for the first time, that the event belonged to the whole world.

Sunday Telegraph, 8/15 November 1987

TCCB has to stand up to moralisers

The ICC is to have its rules rewritten and probably its voting arrangements changed. Wise, but it will not truly matter.

After the Conference meets in January it is likely that every full member will be given an equal vote, with no right of veto retained by England or Australia. It will then vote to ban from international cricket every player who henceforth plays or coaches in South Africa. Those will be British professionals because only in Britain is there no cricket between September and March.

Then, before every England tour abroad, some sort of charade will be enacted: individual names may have to be presented for the approval of the host country. The Guyanans will say no to the Jackmans and there will be much huffing and puffing in the media. The British Test and County Cricket Board will have to go along with this game, but even now they know the outcome.

The cricketers of this country will insist on retaining their legal freedom. There is no way the Board can be outvoted and adhere to the International Conference majority decision. Either the Board withdraws from the ICC and sets up an alternative network or the cricketers will help start their own breakaway organisation of the Packer variety. There will be no shortage of money.

Already the TCCB has considered this alternative and done some sums. Of course it has a duty to help keep the cricket world intact, but there is dissatisfaction at the way it is going about it. By joining those who make moral judgements about South Africa it treads the dangerous high-and-mighty ground.

Furthermore, even by discussing the banning of an individual British cricketer because of his South African connections, they are toying with a citizen's civil liberties. Why does the Board not have the firmness to stand up and say that right now? Why the debate at all?

Criticism does not end there. Why does the Board pretend that South Africa does not exist? Sure, there are clandestine meetings and they listen to the pleas of the South African Board; but they stonewall.

It would be ideal to give every cricketing fraternity in the world a helping hand. Turning the back on South Africa is to deny the social advance which cricket is leading there; it is to be ignorant of facts like this – that the host of young black children who have recently been taught cricket in the South African Cricket Union schemes now want to play the game not only in season, but for twelve months of the year.

Turning the back on South Africa is to deny John Passmore's seventeen years of labour in the black township of Langa; it squashes the right of Monica Magadielo, the schoolmistress in Mamelodi, who umpires in the playground at 7am before school starts and coaches the off-drive at lunchtime and after lessons. It is as if Omar Henry, the first coloured cricketer to become a Springbok, had never played; it scorns the work of Freek Burger, the international referee who is now the full-time development officer for black cricket in the Western Province. And what will Lawrence Mvumvu, South Africa's first black cricket co-ordinator, tell his kids? You will never play at Lord's or Port of Spain.

Why has there been not even one word of encouragement for South African cricket? Why is there so much ignorance about it? There is a hope, however, that the centenary of South African Test cricket, to be celebrated next March, will see a large party of English administrators spending time at the party and seeing much more.

It is time the cricket authorities of the whole world stopped playing political theorists. It is definitely the moment for the

TCCB to come clean with our friends in the West Indies, India, Pakistan and Sri Lanka and advise them not to try trampling on the personal liberties of the British people.

It should make a simple statement that England will play anyone, anywhere. Join in if you want to. It is no use the seventeen counties presaging a collapsing financial structure and doing what is expedient, not what is right.

This leads to the fear of dividing the cricket world in two, black and white. So be it, but it must be understood that the burden for doing that must be placed firmly at the door of the West Indians and their backers who are trying to cage free British sportspeople behind political bars.

Sunday Telegraph, 10 July 1988

'Result' pitches

'Your Country Needs You' – that was the week's message from Raman Subba Row, chairman of the TCCB. He was asking the seventeen counties to extinguish the fires of self-interest which are blazing away at the roots of the English professional game.

County captains order groundsmen to prepare what they call 'result' pitches, often arguing, reasonably, that they are a precaution against boring drawn games.

But in practice it is more insidious than that: pitches are more often prepared, or under-prepared, to suit the home side. Conspicuously, Nottinghamshire made grassy, bouncy surfaces for Richard Hadlee and Clive Rice. Warwickshire's recent success coincides with poor pitches at Edgbaston and a bucket of wickets for their fast bowler Tony Merrick. Glamorgan have wanted turning surfaces at Swansea to suit Ontong and Shastri; in Essex, John Childs, the England spinner, is often left out of the side. The eyes blinked at Canterbury the other day to see the very ordinary medium-fast bowling of Graham Cowdrey darting all ways off the seam.

There are more examples. What captains are saying is: 'Give me a result, whoever wins'. If they win only half their games, at

[184]

least they are ahead of teams who play on flat, unresponsive pitches and who draw a lot of the time.

Club committees are happy – with playing success comes gate-money. Membership expands to give the club a much more solid financial base. Compare, for example, Hampshire's membership of 4,499, which brings in £113,395, with that of Northants – only 1,950 members subscribing £53,261.

Players want 'result' pitches at home because they are the victims of them away and it is hard for a captain to hold out against such demands in the dressing-room. They want to sign big, fast, overseas bowlers.

It is a fact that fast bowling works best on under-prepared wickets. Batsmen cannot deal with the difficulties so easily when they occur at 80mph. Derbyshire, for example, scarcely bother with the trivia of spin bowling and who can blame them? Most counties look overseas, especially to the West Indies, to hire their assassins. Only two can be registered at the moment and only one can be played at a time in the first team. But Northants are associated with four big names – Dennis Lillee, Winston Davis, Curtley Ambrose and, just in case spin is required, Roger Harper. The club has a good commercial argument – how can a county of sparse population compete unless it imports?

Yet there are losers and the first is the game of cricket itself. Some modern captains believe they cannot win a three-day match on a good pitch. Many do not know how to. Instead of the genuine bustle to score quickly on the first day, with the chance to bowl at the opposition for an hour before the close, they are content to graft on and on in the hope that the ball will 'do something', go through the top of the pitch, as it deteriorates.

Think of the bowling. If the pitch alone brings about the movement of the ball, the bowlers do not need the skills which were once taken for granted – control of length, line, seam, swing, flight and spin.

How few players understand that the famous trio of Indian spinners in the early 1970s – Bedi, Prasanna and Chandrasekhar – were better than ours in India because they spun the ball considerably on unresponsive surfaces. They had been brought up that way, forever trying to get batsmen out on sun-baked pitches. No bowler like Alec Bedser exists in England these days, a master of late in-swing with a brilliantly disguised leg-cutter. No-one practises as much as he did and no-one takes on his work-load in a summer.

If the pitch does not help, many bowlers, even at Test level, are lost. Also, the 'result' pitches have completely confused the selectors. Supporters of Jon Agnew of Leicestershire say he could get wickets even away from Grace Road where the seamer reigns. It is difficult to know for certain and he might be being unjustly assessed. As for the batsmen, the ones who succeed on these wickets are usually those with lots of experience – Gooch, Tavaré, Border, Barnett, Broad, Athey. The only young batsman to get through is Matthew Maynard at twenty-two.

Overseas cricketers cost about £15,000 a head, give or take the use of a house and a car. For the price of two of them a county could take on seven young players and deal flexibly in summer contracts for those at university or college.

The other loser is England's own cricket. The county game has schooled many of England's brilliant opponents like Andy Roberts and Malcolm Marshall.

'Result' pitches persuade cricketers to achieve success the short way. They wait for outside forces instead of building up the skills which could work for England.

There is no hiding place when they come up against the West Indies on the best pitch in the country, at The Oval. It is firm, has decent, even bounce for stroke-making and is not unhelpful to bowlers either if they bowl with control and know how to hit the seam of the ball or how to spin it.

The England team may contain eleven Surrey players in a few years' time. It just depends on the quality of the raw material they have.

The TCCB Pitches Sub-Committee, chaired by Donald Carr, claims it is cutting teeth and intends to use them. Obviously, the restoration of decent pitches will not make England suddenly a more successful Test team, but it will force cricketers to take the long-term view of their abilities and realise that the art of cricket is not going to fit into the world of fast food, fast travel, fast fortunes and quick solutions.

At the end of the last century, the county cricket clubs almost destroyed each other by their self-interest and in the end pleaded with the Marylebone Club to take over the administration of the game, which it did successfully, according to its creed 'in the interest of cricket and cricketers'. The game urgently needs the same sort of benevolent despotism and, as England are tested on the field and found wanting, so the Board of Control faces its own tests off it. The difference is this – the administrators cannot afford to fail!

Sunday Telegraph, 14 August 1988

SACU lashes apartheid

In a week when the Test and County Cricket Board combed every inch of its cricket world, it is alarming that a sensational Press release from the South African Cricket Union was kept secret. It was known about at Lord's but not communicated.

Unfortunately, treating South Africa as if it does not exist just continues to compound the ignorance which this country shares with every other within the ICC and fails to acknowledge the heroic campaign the South African cricket fraternity has launched against its government.

Yet South Africa has been central to all international cricket wrangling for twenty years. You would think, therefore, that it is a duty to possess and transmit every jot of information. You would expect England to do it above all because of its historical racial links. It is long overdue that someone talked to the Springbok bad boy who has been standing in the corner of the classroom for twenty years and begins to encourage his moves to repair his ways. Ignorance of South African cricket affairs is unpardonable.

The following is this week's statement from Dr Ali Bacher, managing director of the South African Cricket Union (SACU). It speaks for itself:

[187]

In view of the recent decisions of the municipal councils of Brakpan and Boksburg to discriminate against people of colour, the South African Cricket Union deems it necessary to reiterate its policy of non-racialism as it affects those who play cricket under its auspices at schools, private clubs and municipal and public grounds.

The SACU in the first instance believes in the freedom of association in that those who play cricket can do so against and with whom they choose. However, should this choice be made on the grounds of discriminating against people of colour then that choice is in direct opposition to the constitution of the SACU and will have serious consequences for those in transgression.

In the case of schools and clubs, they will be given no cricket subsidies, all coaching schemes will be withdrawn and no players will be eligible for selection for SACU provincial or national teams.

Should local or national laws prohibit people of colour as spectators or players at public, municipal or private grounds, then no cricket under the control of the SACU would be allowed there.

The decisions by the local authorities of Brakpan and Boksburg have done incalculable harm to South Africa both internally and abroad. These are decisions which must be deplored in the strongest possible way.

They have come at a time when it has become vital that all the people of South Africa should be getting together to work out a common future based on mutual co-operation and mutual respect. Anything less than this is retrogressive and the consequences will be terrible.

What is of constant concern is that there are apartheid laws on our statute books, such as the Group Areas Act and the Separate Amenities Act, which are the breeding ground for the racism that has come out of the Boksburg and Brakpan decisions.

The SACU cannot urge the government strongly enough to rid South Africa of all laws of this nature. Until that happens apartheid will not be dead in South Africa and South Africa itself will die if apartheid remains.

The SACU is committed to do everything in its power to bring about meaningful change on and off the fields of cricket.

And these are the people with whom we refuse to play cricket.

In January, England will be formally out-voted at the ICC and be forced to omit from Test selection players who work in South Africa. That probably means against Australia and New Zealand too, because those countries are submitting to third-world hegemony within the ICC quicker than we are – note the fuss that the New Zealand anti-apartheid organisation HART is kicking up about Gooch and company's forthcoming visit.

Of course, on the subject of South Africa, only the bad news sells.

Sunday Telegraph, 11 December 1988

Glamorgan – a personal view

The story of Glamorgan Cricket can make you laugh, make you weep; sometimes both at the same time, so sudden are at the moments of triumph, so deep and long the troughs of failure and frustration. The graph of progress from 1888 to the centenary year of 1988 is one of long, uphill scramble to playing respectability and financial solvency, a line jagged with pitfalls and occasional leaping achievement: even now, ninety-nine years later as I write, the team has managed seventeen seasons of mediocrity, save a losing appearance in a Gillette Cup final, and at the moment a beleaguered treasurer sometimes has to pretend he has lost the key to the Club purse. The history of Glamorgan C.C. makes *A Pilgrim's Progress* seem like a day in the life of Peter Rabbit.

Yet there is romance in all this, woven into tales which, if not exactly true, tell us what it was like at the time – tales of the 1930s spun by Dai Davies, staunch batsman between the World Wars and Test umpire afterwards, of Maurice Turnbull taking the team dancing after a full day's fielding in order to raise cash for their week's wage: 'Dance our feet off, we would,

[189]

and there would be the skipper at the door by midnight handing out the pay-packets'.

Was it really true that Frank Ryan, American born, long, left-arm spinner, lover of the alcoholic beverage, was found one early morning sleeping under the covers? Was it true that Mr John Clay could usually be seen in the Cowbridge High Street squeezing a firm rubber ball in his right hand to strengthen his fingers for spin? John Clay always referred to the 'rag-time days' when, as captain from 1924 to 1927, he was never sure he had eleven players until the bus left and even then not sure which eleven. Did it happen that they had only ten on the way to the Midlands one day in 1926, stopped at the crossroads in Tredegar, picked up a stranger named Jones who played the one match, got no runs and did not bowl, and was dropped off at the same corner on the way back without anyone knowing his Christian name? The statistical section at the end of *The History of Glamorgan County Cricket Club* suggests that our mystery man may be Edward Cyril Jones. But what was he doing at the crossroads in Tredegar? This tale may not be true, but the times were ripe for it to be so.

Glamorgan cricket has long lived in the shadow of Welsh rugby. Visit almost any of the club's grounds used for first-class cricket and you will see rugby posts at the other end of the ground. The Cardiff Arms Park ground which we used until 1967 was dwarfed by the giant north stand of the famous rugby ground next door. Rugby for many Welsh people is identity. Cricket excites a small, patriotic following, an emotional watering of the national daffodil every summer, but for most of the year we are a rugby nation. Glamorgan needs to be chasing the English County Championship before the masses turn out.

Glamorgan, in cricket terms, has come to mean the whole of Wales. It was always a strange feeling driving for five hours over the mountainous inland to play a Glamorgan home match in Colwyn Bay in Denbighshire on the North Wales coast. This was probably Wooller's Law. Wilfred Wooller, born in 1912 at Rhos-on-Sea, which is virtually part of Colwyn Bay, has been the colossus who has held North and South together, not only by his link with both but because his unwritten edict was that any young cricketer born or residing in Wales is 'ours'. He freely quoted the Act of Union of 1536 to include Monmouthshire and a lot of the Welsh Marches in that! There was no pussy-footing to Lord's with application forms to register any young player from Chester or Shrewsbury or Ludlow or Monmouth. They were Welsh until proved otherwise.

It is still an astonishment that Wilfred allowed Pat Pocock out of his Bangor birthplace in his nappies to go to London to become the Surrey and England off-spinner. David Green of Oxford University, Lancashire and Gloucestershire, born in Llanengan, Caernarvon, was another babe to side-step the Wooller minefield laid between Mold and Old Trafford. . . .

As long as I have known Glamorgan Cricket Club there has always been argument about identity, about Welshness. How much should Welsh talent be eased out of the team for signings from outside? On only the rare occasion has there been a team on the field composed entirely of Welshmen. There were the great Yorkshire saviours between the wars: Bates and Bell, then Arnold Dyson. In the 1948 Championship came the strong Middlesex influence of Len Muncer, Norman Hever and Jim Eaglestone. Ossie Wheatley in his day was the first non-Welsh captain, and in the 1969 Championship side there were two overseas cricketers, Majid Khan from Pakistan and Bryan Davis from Trinidad. The modern Glamorgan side frequently contains as few as three Welshmen.

Personally I do not believe the Welshness is the vital factor but I do believe that the side should contain a high percentage of locally reared talent. Otherwise what is the incentive for the young player? It is difficult enough to persuade teenagers to choose cricket at all now that much of school cricket has disintegrated. It is equally hard for our coaches to turn club players with poor techniques born of limited-over matches into cricketers capable of performing well in three-, four- or even five-day games. Yet this is the job facing us, and only evangelism at the grass roots level will send Glamorgan healthily into the next one hundred years. One day surely we must turn the patchwork history into something richer and more reliable.

from Foreword to *The History of Glamorgan County Cricket, 1989*

$$\boxed{1989\text{--}1990}$$

Theorist as England's saviour

Ted Dexter's behaviour is often Batmanesque although he is far too singular and private to put up with a Robin.

Take his departure from Lord's on a Test match evening. He strides in fine clothes away from the television chatter, out through the Grace Gates. Within two minutes a motorcycle of a million ccs, BMW with automatic breaking (the latest, of course), thunders down Grove End Road, leaving MCC ties flapping in its wake.

Who knows that the man beneath the leathers and shining jumbo helmet is no overpaid yuppie, high on Moscow Mules, but the aforesaid gentleman: Edward R. Dexter?

See him leave Lord's by car at the North Gate and it is the Lord Edward you expect, the dashing driver of machines of distinction. Alas, the trusty, red Aston Martin has gone: how we wept in the commentary box, and all the more so because our hero once again fell for a theory, this one purveyed by a salesman weaving a web of turbo-talk. To be short, it is a Porsche now.

Then again there is Dexter the owner of racing greyhounds, impossible to pick out in a crowd despite the noble profile. If the odds sound right and the dog is ready, he has been known to beat the landspeed record between Ealing and Skewen dog-track, which greyhound cognoscenti will know is near Neath in South Wales. There, lurking beneath ratting-cap, is the man who once stood as Conservative candidate for Cardiff against someone called Callaghan.

The latest I have from the stable yard is that he has pulled out of syndicated ownership of a slow racehorse, but he will know the form book daily. Oh and by the way, the aircraft which once he piloted even as far as Australia with his family on board is gone too.

He may need another. He is about to run England's representative cricket and so another cell has been grafted on to the already busy Ted Dexter and Associates, experts in sports sponsorship. Airborne he could see Maynard bat at Swansea before lunch, Agnew bowl in Leicester before tea, Moxon see off the new ball at Headingley up to 6.30 and be home for dinner at eight.

Personally, I am sad to lose Ted as one of my regular interviewees on television: his keenly prepared theories happily balanced my own random stroll through technicalities. How often has he arrived with the words 'I've got it', and the theories unfold on back-lift or bouncer. What is more, I think he is crazy to take on England.

It is not fair that his popularity will mirror England's success at cricket, but it will. At least in his contract there should be an arrangement for a quiet bed in Forest Mere for September. However, there is nothing I can write which will stop Dexter the quiet theorist from turning action-man again. Once convinced, he acts.

As a winner of the President's Putter and currently handicapped two strokes (back from four after surgeons got at his bad back), the new England chairman knows how much top golfers work at their games and how little, by comparison, do top cricketers. He is not the coach but the influence. Apparently he will communicate TCCB policy and run the England business.

But what of his patience? I cannot see him sitting for long watching all this cricket. And is there any point in trying to streamline England's affairs when junior cricket is in such chaos at most comprehensive schools? The answer is yes. Often a professional player involved with the England squad can

[193]

spread good thinking and methods downwards into the county system.

In truth, England cricket is fortunate that Ted Dexter has been attracted to the new role and, indeed, is a contributor to its creation. The theory is fine: a plan was needed. But it will take more than plans to win Tests. It will take talent, guts, practice and pride. I must just keep him out of the dug-out, forbid him to wear a track-suit or, more important still, stop him padding up again.

I rang him up to ask for his own thoughts. 'Out. At Sunningdale,' I was politely informed. And that is another tip for you. Work out the fastest route from Ealing to Sunningdale, and stay off it. The Batmobile has it down to fourteen minutes!

Sunday Telegraph, 5 February 1989

Waugh lords it

Steve Waugh's centuries in the first two Test matches [of 1989] were models of style and technique. They were composed and sustained with blinkered concentration, and his movements at the crease were simple and sideways.

Twenty years ago these virtues would not have been worth more than a quiet tick of approval, but now, compared with the humble unorthodoxies practised by every one of the England batsmen, they need to be underlined and starred.

In his stance, Waugh's feet are wider apart than is recommended in coaching manuals but he is perfectly balanced and, above all, still. This prepares for his greatest strength, the ability to strike the ball with equal punch off the front and back foot. His body stays sideways – note the back-foot strokes played with foot parallel to the popping crease – and he is always just inside the line of the ball so he has room for a straight bat to flow forwards.

It is embarrassing to list the England players who thump a front foot down into the line of the ball's flight, bring the right shoulder heavily into the stroke and play around the pad and therefore across the line, but you can start with Gooch, Broad, Gatting, Smith, and Barnett. Ian Botham is the best example of a sideways-on batsman in England's Test squad.

Steve Waugh has an easy stance, bat on ground. It is interesting to see how Australia and England, who have been battered by the West Indies for a decade or so, come out of the experience differently. England batsmen are twitching, shifting and often locked into the raised bat stance, while the Australians have clung to orthodoxy.

Waugh uses a bat which weighs 2lb 7oz, not the 3lb thumper. You must go back to Leonard Hutton for the 2lb 2oz bat and then, in the early 1960s, to Richie Benaud who first asked Gray Nicolls to make him a couple of 2lb 7oz bats which he believed was the right combination of weight and manoeuvrability.

Waugh plays right back or right forward. He is not as tall as Graham Gooch but he reaches twice as far. The tempo of his two superb Test centuries has been perfect – never holding back on his attacking strokes but playing every ball on merit.

Had you walked into a ground to watch a fine player, say like Bill Lawry, you would not have known whether he had scored 20 or 200. In Test matches the best players appear to have set their course by automatic pilot.

Lawry was a sideways player. Who else was? Compton, Peter May (even though he was a strong on-side player), Norman O'Neill, Ted Dexter and the modern model for all, Sunil Gavaskar.

It is unfair to hail Steve Waugh in these terms just yet because it has taken him 27 matches to get his first Test century, but he is on the way.

Then again it is right to inquire who succeeded in Tests without being a sideways player. Ken Barrington's is the name which comes first, and then a concession that Doug Walters had a style all his own. Even so, the Barrington supporters argue that he squared up his shoulders first of all to play the West Indian fast bowlers and that if he was not hooking or ducking he quickly got into sideways positions.

Of course, batsmen slip into habits unknown to them. It often takes a team-mate to point out some small unorthodoxy which has crept in. When Geoff Boycott returned from England's 1980–81 tour of the Caribbean, Ray Illingworth, then Yorkshire's cricket manager, spotted that Boycott had opened his stance to such an extent that he was never quite getting back to the sideways position in the stroke. The bat was being tugged slightly across the line, off the leg. He videoed Boycott from the bowler's end in the nets and within a minute of viewing it Boycott agreed the flaw.

England cricket-lovers who feel depressed about the game at present must be careful not to blame one-day cricket for all the ills because Steve Waugh emerged on the international stage as primarily a one-day player. If anything, it is his bowling which has not transferred well to Tests. This is surprising because Waugh is used to bowling Australia's final overs in one-day internationals, yet his control appears to have deserted him for the moment.

For the future health of England's cricket, I recommend a study of Waugh and the use of video cameras. Even the best coaches often advise players in vain: perhaps only discovery for oneself will bring the whole technical horror-story home.

Sunday Telegraph, 28 June 1989

'Theez Creekeet'

I am asked if the cricket taught to Africans in the black townships of South Africa is a white man's gimmick to persuade the sporting world that apartheid does not exist in sport. I reply immediately that the inquiry would offend the black community and infuriate everyone else.

What the black people call 'Theez creekeet' is now a passion and it is not taught them by a white organisation but by the South African Cricket Union which does not allow any racist element within their constitution. Two years ago, when SACU decided to take cricket to the townships, it did not realise that it was pressing a button which would start first a flow of interest and then a torrent. The first stage was mini-cricket and already

[196]

there are two black boys chosen on merit for the Transvaal Under-15 representative team. Walter and Billy live and practise in Alexandra but their team plays white state schools and also the fee-paying pupils of independent schools which are open to all colours.

I need hardly remind you that South African society is mysteriously and sometimes menacingly preserved according to laws of separate racial development. Cricket for the young is a point of communication. When apartheid is finally negotiated out of existence these may be the young men sitting opposite each other at the debate and they will both know how to speak to each other because they have done it before, if only in appeals for lbw and a 'thanks for the game'.

Over 60,000 black children have been learning cricket and there are millions more clamouring to join in. Coaches are being trained every week, many under the national scheme which has Hylton Ackerman, the former Northants cricketer, as tutor-in-chief. 70% of his coaches are lady teachers.

Let me tell you about a visit my wife and I made to the township of Atteridgeville near Pretoria. We arrived just before 2pm on the rough ground which serves as the playground for the Patogong High Primary School. Thirty-two youngsters, all turned out neatly in mini-cricket tee shirts and tracksuits, practised in two nets, one of which was supervised by the young Leicestershire professional Russell Cobb and the other by one of the senior masters, black and delightfully vociferous, Charles Kekana. Charles, in his fifties, was in grey tracksuit trousers, mini-cricket tee shirt and colourful peaked cap.

The nets were good, level artificial surface and the netting flawless. 'Come on, Nicodemus,' urged Charles, 'theez creekeet eez a sideways game.'

There was a lunch break. The boys either opened packets of food which they had brought from home or took delivery, from the van parked outside the fence, of a hot concoction on a cardboard plate which was school catering of the unofficial kind.

'Now, mini-creekeet,' announced Charles, and they rushed to the only open space and set themselves out in traditional fielding positions. As a couple of batsmen padded up Charles pointed at a boy:

'What eez theez?'

'Meed-on.'

'What eez theez?'

'Extra-cover.'

'What eez he?'

'Non-striking batsman.'

'And who eez theez?'

'Seelly point.'

When the batsmen had taken their guard, the mini-cricket game was soon in progress. But it was not the disorganised affair dominated by a couple of skilful lads which I recall playing on the Gnoll School Yard in Neath in the 1940s. First of all, every boy bowled two overs and the batsmen had to run every time they hit the ball. Secondly the bowler dare not take a stride until Charles had given the order, 'Bowl one, bowl two', etc.

In Atteridgeville, as in all other townships, there is a mini-cricket league, all very competitive. There are 26 schools, each one with two teams, under-10 and under-12 overs per innings. It was no surprise to learn that Charles had got boys to change schools in order to get the best under his charge.

He said he had loved the game from the moment he first saw it. 'Theez creekeet I saw at Wanderers. I saw the man with sloping walk, Slasher Mackay. I loved him. He only aimed the bat at the straight ones. Richie Benaud, a great spinner', and then, going soft and throaty to conjure up old magic, he almost whispered, 'That Neil Harvey. He was so little and he stroked the ball so far and all the time'.

I was so entranced by my afternoon on this small playground that I went there again later on during my visit. The scene was amazing. The nets were all in full use. There were four different matches of mini-cricket going on, shoulder to shoulder and – would you believe it, the latest development! – forty girls being taught the basics of the game by a lady teacher – catching, the bowling action, batting, and so on.

What happens next? There is a need for new cricket grounds

and many more leagues throughout South Africa. Outside Port Elizabeth, for example, they are developing 'buffer grounds', land between white areas and black where sporting facilities are being installed for the use of both races. In Western Province, the cricket ground in the coloured Langa is so developed that English touring teams play there and recently the Cape Town schools mini-cricket tournament was held there. White parents went into a coloured township, some for the first time in their lives. In Cape Town too Bob Woolmer does heroic work with the coloured cricketers, though his problem and sadness is SACOS, the South African Council of Sport, which is the body created not so much to administer sports as to be a political instrument against apartheid. Woolmer's boys have dropped out because SACOS' members have thrown petrol bombs at their homes or threatened their families. Their approval is reserved only for non-cooperation with white people.

Bob Woolmer is even more worried that the motives are becoming more and more religious. SACOS is a Muslim stronghold. Christians beware. . . .

The Rugby Club of London Brochure, Autumn 1989

Sabina Park, 1990

Prior to this first Test match there had been much talk about the pitch. You could see your face in it and, consequently, both sides had been keen to bat first because the recent history of the pitch suggests that wickets fall quickly later in the game when the bounce gets very low.

Although the bounce is good, even the best batsmen now talk with trepidation of the 'rat ball' which scuttles along the ground. Another version is the 'zandolee ball' – named after the Caribbean snake.

Gooch had wanted to bat first but lost the toss and took a side into the field which contained no spinner at all, Hemmings having been omitted from the twelve. This gave Test-match debuts to Alec Stewart and Nasser Hussain. By including the extra batsman, rather than a spin bowler, England's approach was defensive but this was sensible. A draw would be a most satisfying conclusion here in Jamaica because few of the England party are at the top of their form. Even if they were they would have to play, as Gooch put it, 'out of their skins'.

If England are to win the series it is likely to be by the odd Test and that would surely be the third one on the Port of Spain pitch in Trinidad which is slower and helps spin. Remember how a spinner of Border's ordinary talents bowled the West Indies to defeat? Gooch will need Medlycott, his left-arm spinner, confident and in form by that time, if there is to be any hope of emulating the Australians.

As it was, Gooch could be well satisfied with the bowling performance of Small. He kept a line strictly on or outside off stump and, on one occasion, surprised Greenidge with a bouncer which struck the batsman's left shoulder and passed the outside edge of his bat. He was tidy and gave Gooch control in a first spell of 7-2-25-0.

At the other end Malcolm, who had been billed as England's attempt to meet fire with fire, was hostile, gave both batsmen uncomfortable moments but also sent down some half-volleys and some short balls which fed Greenidge's endless appetite for the square-cut. Greenidge played some memorable strokes, flipping a high square-cut square – and driving Small, again, for one bounce for four through mid-on. England needed early wickets but they were not coming.

No opening partnership has performed as long as Greenidge and Haynes. They came together in 1978 and have opened for the West Indies in almost every match since. Greenidge is among the finest openers of all time, positive and often savage in his strokeplay, while Haynes is a tremendous hooker of the ball.

The outfield was fast. During the off-season youth soccer is played at Sabina Park and the cricketers have complained about a rough fielding surface. So an extra heavy roller has been used. Sometimes the batsmen only coaxed the ball, but it still raced for four.

Despite their almost telepathic understanding, however, Fraser managed to keep a good line and length but Malcolm, despite his bursts of genuine speed in front of his home town, was erratic. It must be said, however, that he would have been helped by an earlier placing of a mid-off. All bowlers would have suffered with England's abysmal ground fielding.

As it was, Fraser, who did a superb job, was bowling when the first wicket fell in astonishing fashion. Greenidge turned the ball to fine-leg. Malcolm, having moved awkwardly to it, fumbled. Off went Greenidge for the second run but Malcolm, now recovered, sent in a low, flat throw of breathtaking speed and accuracy and Greenidge was left stranded. 62 for 1.

Richardson was looking to paddle a short ball to leg when he was caught off his glove and Haynes, seeing a rare ball straight on the stumps, launched into a fatal drive to give a caught-and-bowled.

It was hard to believe one's eyes: West Indians fidgeting nervously, fencing at shadows, surviving throaty shouts for leg before. Was it really happening?

Sunday Telegraph, 25 February 1990

Country before county

The TCCB will decide in early March whether or not to introduce a programme of four-day County Championship matches in 1991. Many arguments can be made for and against but the priority is clear to see — country must come before county.

To begin with, it is wrong to think that three-day cricket is played in the way it was. The present generation of players has been nurtured on limited-over matches – sometimes as short as 20 overs-a-side in school – and, in approach, they have turned the three-day game into a one-day extension.

In three-day cricket, as bonus points come into view, negative bowling and field placing serves them well, as does slogging for the batting side, although this mini-charade is a mere sideshow compared with the circuses that are sometimes set up on the final day.

The ratio of three-day to one-day cricket hardly matters: the one has become equal to the other and, therefore, the time has come to introduce the more thoughtful four-day game to induce proper skills and buy time until a wider base of preparation can be set up.

A misconception is that the TCCB Cricket Committee which, with the Marketing Committee, has proposed a four-day Championship, refused to reduce the amount of limited-over cricket played, for example the Sunday League. The contrary is true. The four-day structure was devised because at the December meetings the counties themselves did not favour a reduction in one-days.

As for the players, the captains unanimously declared support for the four-day programme and I would argue too that professional players would benefit from less cricket; remember there would be eight days less championship play – that is until Durham come in.

County batsmen do not attach the right degree of importance to a visit to the crease. There are too many in a week. England needs a breed of hungrier batsmen, keener not to get out, who put a high value on their wicket. Four-day first-class cricket is the norm, except in New Zealand.

This rearrangement would leave more time for practice. Consider the shambles of technique displayed by England's Test players over the past few years. Is that the sort of England you want? If not, what do you suggest?

Bowlers nowadays are often wicket-takers by defensive means. They need to get out good batsmen on good pitches: four-day cricket would make that imperative. English bowling needs a return to flight, spin, swing and the hard-learned deceit which comes not from landing a ball with a big seam on a rough pitch or from a slogging opposition.

Four-day cricket would breed better pitches. It is in no-one's interest to make a poor surface for a match which would last only two days. Out of 51 four-day matches played in 1988 and 1989 only two finished inside two days.

This programme does not debar counties from setting up their traditional festivals and local derbies. Of course, it would mean a reduction in the number of grounds used but counties would have Test players more often. Indeed, the debate is very much about priorities, and I appreciate that counties place members at the top of their considerations. But it is essential that the members are presented with the wider marketing facts.

It is important not to think that professional cricket, the commercial product, is where it was. It is the responsibility of the Board, especially of those who market the game, to think ahead: in business, anticipation is everything.

In 1989 the aggregate income from international cricket in the UK was £9.5 million, approximately 50 per cent of overall income. England cricket is high-profile but it is also the least successful, barring Sri Lanka, where there is a civil war. Do you imagine that there will be a constant desire from television to programme a product with fading appeal? And if they retreat, what is there to attract the big sponsors?

It is not surprising that the world's best cricket team, West Indies, has the world's strongest marketing agent, IMG, handling its commercial affairs. Marketing income is sure to be threatened by any further decline in international and, indeed, domestic performance. If cricket becomes a low-profile sport, it is possible that county clubs would be forced to increase substantially their membership fees, anyway.

Counties should be brave enough to ride a possible £30,000 marketing downturn to ensure that the massive income which accrues to the TCCB from Tests is sustained and increased. Those recommending the status quo are putting at risk, on the field and off it, the very game they are trying to save.

Sunday Telegraph, 25 February 1990

Protect foot soldiers from heavy artillery

The International Cricket Council will have to legislate against four fast bowlers in a side. The sight of batsmen being hit, bones being cracked and heads being split no longer has the fascination of a joust between two men. It is more like putting a man against the wall and four others stoning him.

The West Indians did not try to knock English heads off [in the 1989–90 series], though it is easy to conclude that they did after seeing a televised sequence of bouncers edited together. Those pictures suggest a bombardment which did not happen until the final Test. The series was not about deliberate intimidation: it was all a matter of weaponry.

The West Indies had three fast bowlers standing over 6ft 6in. and they bowled their fastest. England had three fast-medium bowlers and Devon Malcolm.

Those West Indians did not have to pitch the ball particularly short to get it up to the batsmen's chest. The sheer height of Ambrose, Bishop and Walsh has destroyed the old geometry of cricket: a short ball from them is often a hand-cruncher.

Ezra Moseley, who is not very tall, got surprising lift at both Port of Spain and Bridgetown, and he broke Gooch's hand. It was not his fault, and nothing to do with intimidatory bowling. The Trinidad pitch was shocking: sometimes the ball leapt, sometimes it shot low. Malcolm Marshall in Barbados was not physically threatening at all.

There were most definitely balls in England's second innings in Antigua which should have been no-balled by the umpires under Law 42 – Unfair Play. Robin Smith was struck a blow on the jaw and the next ball from Walsh was a wicked bouncer. It is the frequency of the bouncer which equals intimidation and intimidation is illegal.

Walsh, too, slammed in bouncers at Jack Russell, who avoided them neatly enough, but that should have brought another warning. At the third warning, according to the Law, the bowler has to be taken off.

Ian Bishop had two successive balls flying past Smith's nose when the West Indies were pressing for victory. Illegal, yet no-one should say that the whole theme of West Indian play was intimidation. They just had four fast bowlers.

Continuous fast bowling has changed the character of the game. It is unattractive, monotonous and slow. The exciting dimensions of flight and spin are almost history. Only the West Indies bowled spinners: Richards and Hooper. Remember, too, that England's hourly over-rate matched the opposition's at about 11. West Indies fired guided missiles while England sniped away with pistols.

How do you play against the West Indies? They themselves would do it best because fast, short-pitched bowling is the favourite mode of attack from the time they start playing as children on the beach.

They dip a tennis ball in the sea and play wind cricket, which allows them to race in and throw the ball with a bent arm much faster than they could bowl it. They bounce it and it skids off towards the head. The batsmen can handle it, because the first stroke a West Indian must learn is the hook. Many club cricketers who visit the Caribbean for tours vow they will never return because fast, short-pitched bowling is the norm.

Umpires, who, by the way, were mostly good and positive in the last series, would not recognise a breach of Law 42 if they saw it. I doubt it has been invoked.

England tried their hardest before the tour to prepare for the short ball. They used softer balls in an effort to develop technique. Every morning of the tour Russell was to be seen batting on the outfield against a team-mate briefed to bowl from ten yards, under-arm, full-toss at his head. Russell either played a high defensive parry or dropped his gloves and watched the ball pass his helmet.

Geoff Boycott, an expert in this field, urged the England batsmen to use their upper body padding as a second line of defence. When young, one is often coached to play the ball with the bat, but to use the front pad as a second defensive barrier in case the ball turns inwards off the pitch and beats the bat. Now, so it seems, the need is to remove the bat from a ball that is about to smack into your ribs, and take the force on the chest-padding which was once considered to be either eccentric or cowardly.

What is wrong is the amount of fast bowling and the quality of the surface on which the bowlers perform. Forget theories of lengthening the pitch to change the angles of bounce. It means that Ambrose would have to bowl off 24 yards and Gladstone Small off 22. Forget also a line drawn across the pitch making it imperative for a bowler to land the ball on the batsman's side. The line would have to be in different colours for bowlers of different height: red for Walsh and Ambrose; blue for Marshall, Moseley and Fraser; and a green one perhaps for David Capel.

What a joke! Capel being warned for bowling two short deliveries. Many a batsman would long for him to try a couple of bouncers in Antigua where the best pitch of the series has been prepared.

England last year proposed that bouncers should be limited to one an over and were annoyed that the support for this among the Test-playing countries was distorted by the votes against the proposal by associate members, small national teams who have no experience of facing a day of fast bowling. In any case, however, one an over is far from a perfect solution. As soon as it has been bowled the batsman can get on to the front foot. But it is at least an effort to face the fact that Law 42 is not being enforced by umpires around the world.

Colin Cowdrey, when he took up his important post as Chairman of ICC for three years, announced his intention of discouraging bouncers. It will be hard to persuade the West Indians because they have an army of fast bowlers in reserve and there is no doubt that fast bowling wins matches.

Sunday Telegraph, 22 April 1990

Turner the turning-point

Chatting on television at the Test match, Richard Hadlee and I stumbled to a conclusion that Glenn Turner must have been the first of the modern New Zealand professionals who played both for their country and in English county cricket in their year's work.

Before Turner, New Zealand Test cricketers, once they had joined an English county, were not selected for their country again. Was there a prejudice against them, or a ban?

The following day Mr A. E. Johnson, of Ripon, North Yorkshire, wrote reminding me that New Zealanders have long been attracted to English cricket as a means of earning their living. 'I was an immigration officer stationed on the old complex of London Docks. One day I was engaged in checking passengers as they embarked on the *Rangitiki*, a New Zealand vessel, and a chap presented his passport with the name Ken James. Profession: cricketer.'

Certainly wicket-keeper Ken (K. C.) James, who played for Palmerston North and for New Zealand in eleven Tests, became a Northants player but, like the rest, never again appeared for New Zealand, according to television presenter Peter Williams, who was able to list names of New Zealanders in English cricket going back to Dan Reese who played for Essex in 1906 in New Zealand's pre-Test days.

C. S. Dempster, one of the greatest of all New Zealand batsmen, began in county cricket after his Test career of ten matches was over. He played mostly for Leicestershire (1935–39) where he was captain for three seasons.

Take the example of Tom Pritchard, a fine fast bowler, born in Kaupokonui, who played 170 first-class matches while with Warwickshire, taking 100 wickets in a season four times with a best of 172, average 18.75, in 1948. Why was he not selected for New Zealand's four-Test tour of England in 1949 when they were hard-pressed to find support for that durable seam bowler, Jack Cowie? Was this the ban working?

This mischievous ban theory happily was drowned in the Trent Bridge rains because Richard's father, Walter Hadlee, captain of that 1949 tour, was at hand to relate the simple fact. 'There was never a ban: it was just expected that when some of our best cricketers wanted to make a livelihood in cricket they travelled to the far side of the world to do it. It took months by boat so we never expected them back. In most cases they settled in England at least as long as they played.'

But then we found a New Zealander who did in fact play Tests while he turned out for Warwickshire, Martin Donnelly, the brilliant left-handed batsman and also a slow left-arm bowler. He played 20 matches for Warwickshire from 1948–50 and yet played all four Tests against England in 1949.

Walter Hadlee recalls: 'We asked Warwickshire for Martin Donnelly's release. We thought it was a bit much to ask for Pritchard's as well. We were very uncertain about ourselves in those formative days.' Donnelly, in fact, never played a Test in his native New Zealand.

So we concluded that air travel and the improvement in New Zealand cricket had led to the proliferation of Tests and to the commuting cricket profession which has been practised by many from Turner to Richard Hadlee.

There is one final observation to make: Glenn Turner, like John Parker who came to Worcestershire after him, both arrived in county cricket as youngsters trying to make the grade, not as Test players with proven talents.

Of such debates are rainy Test matches made.

Sunday Telegraph, 14 June 1990

Cowdrey's patient line

Colin Cowdrey is a patient man and needs to be. He is not a man to rush to decisions yet when he has listened to all views and makes up his mind, he is firm enough.

As chairman of the International Cricket Council he has been trying to get positive conclusions from the member countries. It has been like playing a big fish to the point of his own exhaustion because the ICC never tires of wriggling off the hook. How often have cricket writers tapped out top-class waffle after these mid-summer jamborees? Today, however, it is at least possible to see the stepping stones to a more decisive future.

Most important of all, the seven Test-playing countries have managed to form a break-away committee of their own. The need for this became obvious last year when England's proposal to restrict bouncers to one an over was voted out by a group of Associate members who seemed to think Marshall, Ambrose, Bishop and Walsh were a firm of solicitors, not a hit squad.

It has been voted out this year, too, but few were convinced that it was a proper solution to the intimidatory bowling which is changing the nature of the game. So in the autumn, action will be taken with regard to a code of conduct for players on the field, a panel of independent umpires and a match referee.

First of all, there was confirmation this week that all countries supported the 90-overs minimum per day of Test cricket. Cowdrey said: 'Both England and West Indies fell short of the 15 overs an hour required during the recent series, but when I talked to Clive Lloyd and Micky Stewart, both agreed that the target of 15 was right. Personally, I hope to raise it to 16 and upwards, peg by peg.'

In the matter of a code of conduct the Test countries might well move to a yellow-card and red-card system – a warning for any miscreant and next time, off. 'The system at the moment is flawed,' the chairman believes. 'For example the West Indies behaved badly in Australia when they were there last time but there was nothing the home authority could do about it. Boards find it difficult to act. We are looking for something swift in discipline. Rugby football has that in the "back 10 yards" rule when there is abusive language or dissent.'

It could work. A player shown a yellow card is going to look such a fool it may never happen. The two-card system could be most effective as a deterrent. It could also be a mess. When Javed Miandad threatened Mike Gatting with a bat in Pakistan, who would have been shown the card? When Greenidge threatened Gladstone Small, who was to blame?

It invites the professional foul, for example a side-of-the-mouth quotation from the Ian Chappell Book of Sledging could have a batsman receiving both yellow and red cards before he had cooled down. I am in favour of cards only for abuse of an umpire, incidents which usually occur when some petulant appeal has been turned down or a bat-pad catch has been given where no contact was made.

The move to a panel of independent umpires has become inevitable. The need became most apparent in matches in which Pakistan were concerned because they perfected theatrical appealing, but all countries are to blame. Pakistan had more opportunities to go wild because they have a high-class leg-spinner, Abdul Qadir, whose turn few can 'read' and who has one of the most fiery temperaments in the game.

When a ball from Qadir hits the pad and he spins on an umpire with one of his raging appeals, fielders leap around like animals. Independent umpires are essential to defuse such situations.

They are required also to reduce the incitement of crowds in some countries when they believe there has been a miscarriage of justice. When Kiran More, the Indian wicket-keeper, made that successful appeal against Viv Richards in the Jamaica Test a couple of years ago Richards pointed his bat at him. It was clear on television replays that Richards, given out caught behind the wicket, was not out. The Jamaican cricket-lovers, taking a tot or two of rum out on the uncovered stands needed no further invitation to riot. There followed sixteen minutes of bottle-throwing which required a peace patrol of the local boys, Walsh and Dujon, followed by Richards and Lloyd before play could continue.

Umpires seen to be neutral will help to quell that possible crowd disorder. The experiment in the Pakistan–India series recently was a success. Whenever the old enemies meet there are volcanic rumblings not far below the surface, if not among the players, in the crowds who pile into the one-day matches.

John Hampshire and John Holder, both from England, stood in those matches and though they made an odd mistake, as all umpires do, their decisions were instantly accepted by players and spectators.

The Test-playing countries will have to decide that all countries have umpires from the elected panel even though they are not obviously required in some. It will cost a lot of money but it is a conspicuous area of the game and should attract sponsorship.

There are 35 Tests to be played next year and Colin Cowdrey believes that the controlling body of Test-match play and behaviour should be the ICC itself. It makes sense because the decisions made in their meetings will be binding. In the past an agreement made by the ICC was sometimes flouted by an individual Board of Control.

'I would like to see this panel of umpires meet for a week and exchange views on interpretation of the laws,' says Cowdrey. 'Maybe we could get to a system of an ICC representative overseeing every Test. He could view it alongside the third umpire. Who knows, one day, there might be radio communication between the arbiter and the umpires in the middle helping to boost their confidence and authority?'

Presumably when Ian Bishop, for example, nearly takes the head off Robin Smith next time, the arbiter can whisper: 'Go for it, matey. Warn him. Next time stop him bowling.'

Cowdrey shares the concern expressed to him when he was in Trinidad by the former West Indies captain Gerry Gomez: 'Gerry has worked on the improvement of Caribbean umpires for twenty-five years and he feels his organisation will end now. English umpires have a lot of first-class experience in our county championship but the West Indian umpires have only 36 days of first-class play a year. They have so few opportunities to go out there and do it.'

A panel of independent umpires may blight the development of others: that is the cautionary message.

The efforts of Colin Cowdrey have been worthwhile. The ICC act is coming together, first by his appointment to the chair for a four-year term and by his endless flying around the world which has helped distil all opinions.

The importance of last week's meeting cannot be measured in current issues. What is exciting, even tense to watch, is that the angler appears to be reeling in the great big fish without as yet breaking his rod or his back.

Sunday Telegraph, 1 July 1990

Gooch – persevering but with a twinkle

Graham Gooch's innings of 333 at Lord's revealed some of the hardiest strains of the man's character. He perseveres when things go wrong, he is not prepared to be passive in the face of any opposition and there is a twinkle in the eye to signal that he sees the funny side.

The durability is well proven. There was the twenty-one-year-old who failed to score in both innings of his first Test match, against Australia at Edgbaston in 1975. Years later it is the same Gooch who was trapped game after game by Australia's Terry Alderman. His technique is not perfect but he works and works at his game. Whatever the playing disaster, he believes he can work it out.

His raised-bat stance and the tense swivelling of the head over the left shoulder towards the bowler are his trademarks. Personally, I would love to have seen a more orthodox Gooch stance with a lighter bat. He is a thumper, not a stroker. Yet he could easily have been a tough player. He has been successful not because of his upright stance and big bat. His talent would have got him his 333 runs in a Test match however he chose to stand at the crease.

The England captain is strong on principles. He is the man who chose South Africa instead of the established game, not only for the financial security of his family but because he truly believed that British cricketers should not be told how they can earn a living by foreign politicians.

Nor is he the sort to deal in double standards. Graham Gooch would not be happy to buy a diamond in Bombay which had been mined in Kimberley and then turn around to boycott South Africa. Also, having played with South African cricketers in Western Province and enjoyed their company, he would not ever turn his back on their cricket fraternity.

He persevered, too, at captaincy. He was voted captain of that rebel tour and later made captain of Essex. He did not bat well, he became introspective and was replaced by Keith Fletcher. Second time around, he has managed to combine the leadership with the responsibility of opening the innings as well as anyone in the history of the game. Indeed, he gives Essex massive direction but also the thrust of his batting. Unselfishly, and without regard for records, he can control tempo. Graham Gooch is unambivalent about the captaincy of England. He wanted the honour but the uniform alone is not enough for him: he wants to lead well from the front, and win.

His refusal to be passive was seen in the West Indies. Open a hotel curtain at any time of the early morning and you could see Gooch jogging on his first physical exercise of the day. He developed a compulsion for physical fitness. He led the way. This sharpened his reactions for the battle against the fast bowlers. He was fearless and demonstrated how to take on the fast stuff responsibly, simply by cutting out stray attacking shots and resolving to spend a long time in the middle.

He defused the explosive speeds with patience and looked like wearing them down until his hand was broken – the result of a freak ball, not a deliberate attempt to injure or intimidate. Ezra Moseley got uncomfortable lift from just short of a length; the ball struck the unguarded outside of Gooch's left hand.

If that had not happened, and had it not rained in Port of Spain, England would have taken a 2–0 lead in the 1989–90 series. Gooch's part in that volte-face of fortunes must never be understated.

Now thirty-seven, his maturity has become the most positive driving force in the new England. He is less wounded by criticism and more comfortable with the media. He has the regard of the whole side.

Tossing up at Lord's in the current Test, his old silver coin fell in favour of Azharuddin's call. There was a big smile from Gooch: 'No. I haven't lost it again, have I? What yer goin' to do with me this time, Azhar?' As history will record, Azhar said 'Field' and Goochy said: 'Oh! I'm not so worried now. I would have batted. I suppose this is the nearest I'll get to winning it.'

In his long innings, he demonstrated how his fitness training has given him both sharpness and stamina. His innings lasted six hours and 25 minutes and he was running fast singles even towards the end when Robin Smith was trying to squeeze out every run for his century.

Some batsmen have been good runners for their own runs but not quite so prepared to race around for someone else's. Gooch did tire, the bat suddenly looked too heavy and the legs got sluggish in the stroke. But there was nothing in his play that was at all calculated to get him to a record.

In fact, he took risks when England needed to be bowling, not batting. Down the pitch he went to Ravi Shastri and made powerful hits, but with the ball further from his body than he would have liked for safety. The team cause came first. It was a commendably unselfish charge at the ultimate individual batting record.

And why does the England captain sport such an unshaven visage? 'It's not unshaven: it's my beard. I just keep it short to keep all the grey out of it.' It would be a splendid contradiction if he did grow it full and white; the fittest grand old man of English cricket who might well approach Sir Garfield's record again. I hope he gets it.

Sunday Telegraph, 29 July 1990

Azharuddin takes fight to England

A brilliant century by Mohammad Azharuddin, full of natural strokes played without inhibition, sent India racing after England's 653 at Lord's yesterday. By the close, India's response was 376 for six, requiring another 78 to avoid the embarrassment of following-on and 277 more to draw level.

The day glowed with fine strokes and it was a nice coincidence that the captain and vice-captain of both sides scored centuries. Ravi Shastri's effort was crammed full of purpose and he will have been furious to have been removed by Hemmings's clever bowling just when he had England heads drooping in the field.

Often a side facing a mountain of runs plays a care-worn innings, ultra-defensively, so that they become enmeshed with close fielders and fail to move the scoreboard on. Not this India. When England bowled bad balls every batsman went for attacking strokes.

In Azharuddin's case he made good-length, straight balls into blitzing boundaries by meeting them with a flowing bat on the up. His ninth century, and fourth against England, was the fastest scored in this country for nine years. Indeed, it was only one ball slower than Ian Botham's century in 86 balls against the Australians at Old Trafford in 1981.

India began the day knowing that they had to bat for a long, long time. They had survived the second evening's assault and were 48–0 but there was still the small matter of being 585 runs behind. Even the base camp for the scaling of this peak, the avoidance of the follow-on, was a distance away at 454.

Indians, however, are more used to the contemplation of massive scores than the English, that is until this run-glut summer. And so it appeared as a five-finger exercise as Sidhu and Shastri went about their defensive business.

The pitch is sluggish, with a bounce which gets lower as the ball gets older. Defence was unlikely to be a problem but England did have one or two positive moves to make and, of course, they had so many runs in hand. Graham Gooch could keep his attacking fielders in position for the rest of the day.

The combination of Devon Malcolm's speed and Angus Fraser's accuracy was likely to be the biggest threat to India. Indeed, the first wicket came during that first long initial spell. Sidhu pushed forwards to a ball from Fraser and John Morris took a quick reflex catch at short square-leg.

Ravi Shastri and Manjrekar continued with studied defence. None of these cricketers can be intimidated by fast bowling. There were quaint recollections in the crowd of Indians cowering away from Fred Trueman in the 1950s. It is amazing how long it takes to kill that sort of reputation. Some of the great players of fast bowling have come from India – Pataudi, Gavaskar, Viswanath – and indeed of this side, there are those who scored centuries against the West Indies in the Caribbean only eighteen months ago: Sidhu, Shastri and Manjrekar.

Shastri is a correct batsman with limitations which he usually observes. His defence is upright and straight: he deflects the faster bowlers and repels the steep bounce with an angled bat. Runs came for him downwards behind square on both sides of the wicket, but he is a fine straight-driver too. Where he errs is in his lust for the lofted drive. It can be a damaging weapon and he can hit a bowler clean out of the attack. He also holes out far too often for a top-class player, and so he did yesterday.

First Manjrekar went to an inspired bowling change. Graham Gooch, obviously happy to continue centre-stage after his 333, took a four-over spell of bowling before lunch. Manjrekar tried to cut his third ball but instead snicked it to Russell who was standing up to the stumps.

Gooch got the ball to swing both ways. He was the first to manage that. Not that the dismissal was a matter of swing alone. It was probably the complete change of atmosphere as the fast men took sweaters and rested and the slower stuff was purveyed. Perhaps Manjrekar relaxed ever so slightly.

Gooch bowled only those four overs. Hemmings was brought on at the Pavilion End to bowl the 57th over. The ball turned much more than expected. It was difficult to gauge this in his first over because Ravi Shastri went from first gear to fourth, lofting the ball straight for four and then to mid-wicket for four and six: 14 off the over.

Hemmings smiled and thought. He set a fielder back at deep mid-wicket just beneath the Tavern Stand. There was still an ocean of space for Shastri over mid-on and mid-off.

In the third over of off-spin Shastri was down the wicket for another big drive. He did not quite get to the pitch of a ball which was allowed to turn a bit. It never got above head high and arrived in Gooch's safe hands at mid-on. That was 191–3, a wicket given away and Shastri was sore annoyed. He had compiled a century splendid in its own way, full of clever defence and concentration with crisp scoring shots, but in the context of India's plight it lacked the vital quality of longevity.

Who would provide the backbone next? Dilip Vengsarkar is a nervous starter. Something draws him to playing odd passes at balls outside off stump. He moves predictably forwards and this makes him a target for fast bowlers who can make the ball rise from a short length. Vengsarkar, however, is also a Lord's specialist. He has scored a century on every one of his past three

Tests here. This time he began better and looked likely to do the same again. It was batting of deep personal commitment.

The bravura touches came at the other end from Azharuddin, the captain. He was once hit on the helmet by Devon Malcolm but appeared to be prompted even further to go for his strokes. His whip shot through square mid-wicket is famous and he treated one or two disbelieving England bowlers to a sample.

More risky were his swats off the back foot through point. One floated the ball through the covers in the air for four, others were cut off by the excellent Chris Lewis who fielded well in spite of a pulled groin.

But the more Azhar played his strokes the louder was the crack of bat on ball. Memorable strokes off an over from Chris Lewis sent the ball scorching either side of extra-cover and then straight. Kapil kept him eccentric company to the end. India are on trial but, my word, they are 'wonderful' to watch.

Sunday Telegraph, 29 July 1990

A phoney season?

Should this 1990 season be struck from the record books?

Congratulations to the batsmen who filled their boots with runs, but the sight of an outstanding fast bowler unleashing a ball which bounced twice before the wicket-keeper was evidence that the competition has been phoney. The balance between bat and ball disappeared.

You will know that the seam of the ball was made less prominent and bowlers proved that only on exceptional days did it swing or move off the seam. Mostly it bounced conveniently to be struck by the middle of the bat, regardless of a batsman getting his foot to the pitch of the ball or no. I watched Glamorgan chasing 495 to beat Worcestershire on the last day at Abergavenny and getting as far as 493–6 when time ran out.

I also saw the South African, Alan Donald, last week at Edgbaston: a genuinely fast bowler rarely seeing his bowling rise above stump height. He bowled double-bouncers to the wicket-keeper on a lifeless pitch.

Pitch or ball? Which is to blame for the summer's distortion? The TCCB made a mistake. A more sensible experiment would have been to change either one or the other. Not both. Then it would have been a simple process of elimination.

Many cricketers believe that the best formula is to return to the ball with the higher seam (constructed of 15 strands of flax) but still play on pitches as they are, carefully prepared to be dry and not to incur a 25-point penalty in the Championship.

At the same time the lobby for uncovering pitches grows stronger, and you must seriously consider the argument that it may be wrong to keep the turf so dry. On these super-safe, chip-dry pitches ordinary batsmen looked very good, and the very good looked brilliant.

On the other hand, the TCCB would argue that 1990 was the season when the bowlers learned the lesson vital to England cricket that they were not half as good as they had appeared to be. No more landing the ball anywhere in the batsman's half to see it deviate off the seam every other ball. Bowlers this summer have suffered if they have not commanded a good and consistent length.

Angus Fraser survived: Philip DeFreitas did not. Those who just waited for things to come right again got their wickets expensively. Those who had the sense to school themselves with coaches, recovered and ended respectably.

The unhelpful surface and alien ball also meant that bowlers had to experiment to get some lateral movement. County captains screamed out for variations in attack and most counties played two spinners. The cry for the return of spinners was answered.

So there was greater concentration on the art of bowling and this must be the most salutary effect of the changes. Take a look at the national averages and see how those bowlers established as craftsmen still led the field.

The Board knows that good comes out of bad, and bad out of good. And so it has already anticipated the next trends. Firstly, fast bowling could become extinct. Just look at India. The reason why there are no fast bowlers in India is that it is the most unrewarding job when pitches provide no bounce. Could our young cricketers similarly soon prefer being clever, medium-fast bowlers and spinners to toiling with unproductive flat-out speed?

Secondly, the effect on batting may be equally damaging. This past season technique has gone out of the window when approximate footwork suffices to deal with balls which do not move at all over after over. A batting average of 35 once meant a useful county contribution, this year only 50-plus registers.

Of course, batting is much more than a bat and pad jammed together but generations have proved before that it is a sideways game when played most consistently. So the question is: How long will it be before batting becomes the simple exercise bowling became before the changes? Just a matter of getting on the field fit and going through the motions. Would it be wrong to make changes quickly and to what? In which direction should the game go?

The advocates for uncovered wickets believe rain-affected pitches will bring back the spinners. That is not entirely correct. Often the most effective bowlers after rain are faster bowlers.

They do believe that the more natural surface will breed better batsmen and better bowlers. They see the return of variety. I am with them as long as uncovered pitches mean a bounce which mirrors the effort a bowler has exerted.

Strong voices urge no change at all, arguing that the lessons of 1990 are yet to be learned. So within the game there are three voices: for the old ball but present pitches; for uncovered pitches; and for the status quo. . . .

Personally, I am not for tinkering with the ball as much as I favour serious change in the surfaces on which the game is played. That sight of Alan Donald's embarrassing double-bouncing has lingered with me the longer. Equally the sight of batsmen of limited talent looking like world-beaters – or, as Geoff Boycott puts it, 'Bad players gettin' 'undreds' – persuades me that uncovered pitches will be best for the game. Cricket is rich because of its variety. Since pitches have been dry, some of the zest has gone out of the game. The Board has been guilty of too much change in a short space of time. As a result, we have years of discussion ahead about pitch-covering, of seams on balls, and of three-day and four-day cricket. The balance between bat and ball is delicate and achieved by a gentler touch than tinkering with the lot at once.

Sunday Telegraph, 23 September 1990

England must re-learn the sideways skills

England may win a Test, even regain the Ashes, but if success against all the odds should come, Union Flags should not be waved over the game in Britain, which has most definitely lost its way.

Not only the England Test team but the whole of the professional game has become a hotch-potch of commercially produced mediocrity which stumbles from season to season, series to series.

Although England, in the famous MCC touring sweaters, still has the trappings of a great Test-playing country, the team is not a lot more than a collection of unorthodox cricketers born of the fashionable one-day game, spiced with the immigrant grandsons of old colonials who learnt their game as batsmen in the schools of South Africa or as bowlers on rough ground in the West Indies.

In a Test match of thirty hours' duration, if you have only one bowler, Angus Fraser, who can match the accepted method of bowling from close to the stumps, then you must have lots of runs. Runs, in this context, means not only a first-innings lead, which England have achieved in the first two Tests in Australia in the 1990–91 series, but in the second innings as well.

The techniques of all England batsmen, excepting Atherton, are too flawed for that. The weakness is in the mind and in the technique, and often the mental infirmity leads to the technical one. To be positive in defence is as much a state of mind as position of feet. Bruce Reid, England's destroyer, bowling left-arm over the wicket, did not swing the ball but slanted it across the right-handed batsmen. So what did they see?

Firstly they saw a ball wide enough to give them alluring space outside the off stump in which to swing the bat in its full arc – always inviting. Yet to hit the ball to the off side was to play across the line and this would only be a safe option if the front foot was across to the pitch of a full half-volley. Anything less would be to play the ball on the up with the face of the bat open. Easy prey.

Professional players are reluctant, however, to talk about technique when a mini-innings or a few quick wickets make them heroes in limited-over cricket.

The time has therefore come to abandon the Sunday 40-over competition, and, for the moment, to play more four-day cricket while the old skills are learnt again.

Some argue for the uncovering of pitches and for three-day matches. This is a reasonable proposal but badly timed. It may soon be worth an experiment but not while the TCCB is trying to sort out whether the ball with nine strands or the dry pitches or the exceptionally dry weather have tilted the advantage to the batsmen. One thing at a time.

It is time for England to abandon Micky Stewart's football squad mentality; time for Gooch and Co to burn their tracksuits and spend their time practising what they have to do in the game – bat or bowl or field.

Cricket is a sideways game both in batting and bowling. Durability is best developed by repeating those actions. Nothing gets a batsman fitter than a long innings. Nothing hones a bowler's sharpness more efficiently than bowling, often to an empty net.

Watching the England team running around hotel after hotel, ground after ground, is like seeing Stephen Hendry train for potting snooker balls in a swimming pool, and what is more absurd than having Allan Lamb pulling a muscle on a jog from ground to hotel? They have, admittedly, not been helped by the itinerary in Australia, with a quicksand month of one-day games.

Many sages blame county coaches for the lame products at the top. That is wrong. Much more dangerous is the National Cricket Association's idea for giving the equivalent of a degree for coaches after a three-year course.

Coaching cricket is simple. It is no academic pursuit. England does not need courses or young stars called to NW8 but, rather, local enthusiasts who take lads to the net with a basket of balls and throw them one at a time saying, as that wise man the late Cyril Coote used to say to undergraduates at Cambridge in the 1950s: 'Wait for it, sir. Stand still till it's in the air. Hit the ball coming on the off to the off, the straight one straight and the one on the leg . . . open the front pad and hit it to mid-on. But above all . . . stay sideways and wait, sir.'

Anyone who believes that cricket is a more complicated business, only to be performed in tracksuit, is an enemy to progress. Most of cricket is played in the head and you do not need a course for that. A teacher, yes. But then you need listeners too and that, many good coaches believe, is what is most lacking.

The resuscitation of England cricket is indeed a grass-roots job.

Sunday Telegraph, 31 December 1990

Afterword

When I was appointed cricket and rugby football correspondent of the Sunday Telegraph in 1974 I first imagined that life,
after my county cricket days, would consist of a perambulation
of rugby and cricket grounds on Saturdays, and maybe a
business interest during the rest of the week. The only advice
offered me was by E. W. Swanton. He, who had just retired as
the Daily Telegraph's cricket correspondent, and I were travelling in a taxi along the Mall, when Jim, regally wearing black-
tie and Homburg hat, turned and said: 'Try not to put all of the
eggs in one basket. Don't forget broadcasting. Be an all-
rounder. Fleet Street is not what it was, nor is the Telegraph.'

Now, seventeen years later, the Telegraph has long left Fleet
Street but flourishes after that gloomy period, and Jim Swanton
is still contributing fine articles on cricket to its columns from
the sanctuary of his home in Sandwich.

I never got around to the business interest nor even, after
four delightful years reporting the Home International
Championships in winter, could I cope with the rugby football.
For Mr Kerry Packer then started his battle for the rights to
televise home Test matches on his own Channel 9 in Australia.
It was thus that Test cricketers around the world found their
multi-millionaire, setting loose the force to shake the game and
its establishments, and unleashing a revolution which turned
cricket into a twelve-month-of-the-year profession. The
'Packer years' were such a turning-point in the history of
cricket that I make no apology for the number of pieces
reproduced in this book which cover that period.

We cricket correspondents suddenly made for the airports as
well as for the motorways, and the furrows which Jim Swanton
had ploughed on the A roads and B roads of Britain, as well as
on the slow boat to Australia, became white trails in the sky as

the men with typewriters and *Wisdens* became fast-moving, international travellers.

I have spent much time in many lands watching Test series, often not involving England. I have commentated for Rupavahini TV on a Pakistan–Bangladesh match in the Asia Cup competition while perched on a platform wedged up a tree in Moratuwa, Sri Lanka. I have been held at the Sharjah Post Office's pleasure in a small room while Arab officials tried to crack the code of a telex to the Sunday Telegraph which they said 'appears on the surface to be a sports report'. Cricket in Sharjah was set up for the great pleasure of the 750,000 exiled Asians, not for the Arabs who were more familiar with soccer and camel racing. Twice a year when a tournament is held in Sharjah the stadium, now holding 20,000 people, roars to life and the telephone wires buzz to the bookies in Bombay.

I have recorded sound pieces for the BBC from All-India Radio in Bombay with thirty-four spectators squeezed around me into a tiny studio. (We had a head count on the way out.) In 1988–89 Dev Enterprises of New Delhi employed me to commentate on the West Indies v. India Test for Durdeshan, India's national television corporation, the first time Test cricket had ever been televised in the Caribbean. It tested my health and my patience. Imagine commentating all day in Georgetown, Guyana, then retreating to an editing studio to do more commentary and then flying with the tape to Trinidad, the nearest satellite station, and back for the next day's play!

The word-processor has replaced the typewriter. Richie Benaud, my colleague in the BBCTV commentary box and correspondent for the News of the World and various Australian syndications, has what looks to the ignorant a complex system of plugging in and adapting his system in commentary boxes but by the time the first ball of a match is being bowled he is merrily collecting messages on to his screen from the offices of Benaud Associates in Sydney or London. Occasionally there are technical problems. At Edgbaston I once dictated my own copy to the Sunday Telegraph as Richie experimented, read manuals of instruction, spent an hour on his knees risking the future of a smart suit on the dirty floor. Eventually, as I ended my twenty-minute conversational stint he looked up grudgingly and squeezed out of the side of his mouth: 'So the human voice has triumphed yet again, has it?'

Test cricket itself has changed from the way it was in 1974. I have seen the West Indies dominate the world game by fast bowling, brilliant batting and consistently good fielding, but it is the fast bowling that has been the real destroyer of the opposition teams.

The greatest batsman of this period has been Vivian Richards; his talent was extravagant right from the start of his career when, in 1974, I recall playing one of my last games for Glamorgan at Bath and him one of his first for Somerset. His eye was fast, his mood at the crease always dominant and he played strokes which were his own personal expressions, passionately of African origin, arrogantly Caribbean, proudly Antiguan and devotedly Somerset, such a mixture, such a kaleidoscope of beauty and brutality.

Then there was the cultured jewel of India, Sunil Gavaskar. The little man, sideways in stance, an instinctive judge of length who reduced error by his attention to technique though he never sacrificed his scoring power. As a run-getter he could put himself on automatic pilot. He was the opposite of Javed Miandad, the Pakistani who fights at the crease like an alley cat, sweeping fours from dusty creases, letting the bottom hand steer the ball through the covers or hoik it over mid-on, improvising defence, scampering singles.

I watched Graeme Pollock's last first-class innings in South Africa when I was commentating on the Currie Cup final of 1988. His wide stance suggested a Farmer Giles style, but that changed as soon as the ball left the bowler's hand. He was elegant, left-handed of course, avaricious for runs in the way they say Don Bradman was: bowlers got no mercy, nor could he ever give away his wicket even in a charity match.

And if I was allowed a montage of batsmen to adorn my memory I would include as well Barry Richards, upright and regal, Gordon Greenidge, compact and punishing, and Greg Chappell, so civilised in style.

Only one England cricketer in my reporting days has got me

to the edge of my seat, determined not to miss a move: Ian Botham. Whether batting, bowling or fielding at slip he has been a talented entertainer who, like Viv Richards, expressed himself best with actions – mighty sixes off Dennis Lillee or lively swing bowling with the new ball.

The one disappointment in the West Indian domination of the Test scene has been that it appeared to be achieved by speed alone. The truth spread that fast bowlers, if sufficiently numerous, won matches. English county cricket teams became studded with an overseas signing, usually a fast bowler. The West Indians proved that it was blanket speed that gave the opposition little chance to be free from the physical intimidation involved.

This made the spectacle repetitive and boring. Over-rates dropped. The West Indies would calmly bowl 11 or 12 overs an hour and refuse to agree to a fine if the minimum number of overs for the day was not attained. There will, I suspect, have to be legislation to recover some of the game's skills, a regulation introduced into Test cricket compelling countries, for instance, to put into their teams at least two bowlers whose run-ups are not longer than seven yards. Otherwise spin and guile will become banished forever.

I would not have believed, in 1974, that the ICC would have to appoint referees to Test matches so that bad behaviour can be punished and therefore eradicated. 'Sledging' is the Australian description of the foul-mouthing of personal insults directed at an opposing player. Other countries join in but the Australians carry the responsibility and stigma perhaps unfairly. Dissent against an umpire's decision and the pressurising of umpires are current ailments. Pakistan above other countries led in the concerted chorus of appealing, acted out for a batsman's false dismissal.

The Pakistan players will feel aggrieved when I write this, but at least by travelling around the cricket world I have had the perfect opportunity to make such judgement. Part of their temptation has sprung from the magical deceptions of Abdul Qadir who had the ball ricocheting from bat to pad, pad to bat and hopping into the hands of close fielders so quickly that anything was possible and was so difficult for an umpire to see and hear accurately. Acting a dismissal by racing at umpires, hands in the air, or leaping to congratulate colleagues has been tantamount to cheating. If I highlight Pakistan it is not to say that others did not join in quickly. Of course false appealing is older than that: it has been in the game from the start, but sportsmanship has leaked out of the game and I doubt it can be formally restored by a referee.

Referee is the word of the moment because the International Cricket Council has adopted the idea of an independent observer at Tests. I presume the man will note slow over-rates, fine bad behaviour and generally monitor the conduct of the game. It is sad that it is thought necessary. It is rather like having a schoolteacher to supervise games in the school yard when what is needed has more to do with captaincy. A true leader would not allow gamesmanship, sledging or cheating and, as for the individuals involved, it shows how little respect they have for themselves.

Bad behaviour in the game is cricket's mirror on society but it particularly sheds light on the appalling condition of cricket in schools. The disappearance of competitive cricket matches in many parts of the United Kingdom has softened the lines of self-discipline and sportsmanship and in many instances has turned young people to more violent activities.

Only a determined effort by local authorities can restore the game. In 1990–91, when the South Glamorgan County Council allocated £30,000 to the redevelopment of youth cricket, it found that only six schools in the area played cricket at all and that they had no matches against each other. A year's hard work, supervised by the Glamorgan County Cricket Club, discovered tremendous enthusiasm just beneath the surface and schools willing to join in. There will be no magic wand to wave for the restoration of England as a leading force in the world of cricket. The National Cricket Association, the Schools Associations and many other bodies like the Lord's Taverners who raise funds work hard to re-establish the pillars of youthful enthusiasm for cricket; but only evangelism at the least spectacular leisure-end of young lives will achieve it.

Cricket has become visually less attractive. Batting helmets obscure the features of the heroes. Padding is strapped on to all parts of the body against the fast bowlers. Physical intimidation is outlawed by Law 42, Unfair Play, but umpires are reluctant to invoke it. They need instructing and supporting.

At the time of writing, the setting-up of an independent panel of umpires looks inevitable. This is because players do not accept the integrity of a decision or, to put it into what some think a more acceptable light, umpires from neutral countries can be seen by the players and crowds to be clearly honest: all their decisions are bound to be unbiased. Such mistrust shows a shocking decline in the behaviour of cricketers and will result in a lack of growth in good umpiring because the resident men will never get the chance to stand in a Test match at home.

My own impression of the change in cricketers' behaviour is to do with the increasing speed of life. Young players want to be stars the quick way. They can be stars in the one-day game and believe that they have matched the great players who toiled hour after hour, day after day at their skills. Few have had the sort of patience and determination that made Richie Benaud, Intikhab Alam and Abdul Qadir into international leg-spinners.

As I wrote in 1983, a change in playing regulations would help the problem of cheating near the wickets. Padding, and helmets worn by fielders, should be outlawed. In 1990, when India were touring England, we were subjected to the sight of Sanjay Manjrekar calling for shin guards so that he could field at short square-leg. The pads were little shorter than those worn by the wicket-keeper. I would remove all padding save a box protector for fielders, then only those who are brave and have the appropriate reflexes would advance close to the bat. Seeing an untalented fielder approach the crease area dressed as a Michelin man mocks the brilliance and bravery of the wonderful close fielders of the past. The enforced retreat of those very close fielders would reduce the opportunities for claiming catches off bat and pad and unsportingly pressurising both batsman and umpire.

Cricket as entertainment has changed. In some countries,

notably Pakistan, the one-day game attracts the paying spectator but the five-day Tests produce less and less income. Everyone talks about a balance between the two, preserving cricket in that awkward stance, one foot in entertainment, the other in the art of the game. The truth is that what suits one public does not suit another. Australia has taken to a high degree of sponsorship, coloured clothes, microphones in stumps and all sorts of innovation. England has made the great error of moving in that direction purely for marketing reasons even though, temperamentally and historically, few British people want to see their cricket jazzed up. The administrators of the game have been subjecting cricket's good to marketing gain.

Yet, the counties have to survive financially. They long for their players to win a one-day competition for the cash, but the players know that only the County Championship earns the respect of fellow professionals.

Marketing committees dictate to cricket committees. It will have to change. The game is being artificially sustained and is losing its character along the way. In South Africa there was an experiment of using substitute players whenever they wanted. So, when a fast bowler was required he went on the field but then came off in favour of a leg-spinner. It was just like American football coaches sending on a specialist kicker just for the minute. The idea was a disaster. Children were annoyed when their heroes were called off the field. The game was boring because it had lost the excitement of uncertainty. If you can bring on an expert at will, where is the fun?

South African cricketers, however, have got a lot right in the last ten years. Anyone who took the trouble to visit there could see how cricket was potentially a poisoner of apartheid. Once the South African Cricket Union developed its township cricket and had black schools playing against white, and the best black children playing games at the famous Wanderers Club, it was clear that the children conversed easily.

I recall watching a match at the traditional white St John's School. I was taken there by Ali Bacher, Director of the Cricket Union. The opposition was from the Alexandra township. The tall bowler for the township, Walter Mamesola, whom we all

[229]

knew as Wes, thundered in and delivered a bruising spell to a gutsy young white who eventually got out for 30. I sat alongside the lad as he took off his pads under a tree. 'I just hope that big, black boy likes to bat, because I'll knock his head off his shoulders when I get that ball in my hand.'

I took that to be a highly racial statement until I watched the battle between them in the next innings and later saw them, sitting together, laughing and gulping down lemonade after the match. Colour without prejudice is on the way and cricket lighting up the whole path towards a multi-racial life without social clap-trap.

Nowhere has progress been made through the medium of cricket more than in Cape Town. John Passmore is a legend and maybe should be a saint. He created in the Langa township a trust of white people by black within the game of cricket. Their ground is excellent, and the coaching good.

Cape Town and Durban were the most fertile grounds for the union on 29 June 1991 of all the cricketers of South Africa under one administration. Two years before I spoke at the banquet which celebrated the centenary-year birthday of South Africa's first Test match and said that, once cricket came out of the whole of South Africa with the approval of everyone who lived there, the world would welcome them back into Tests.

The very words 'South Africa' have been loaded with superstition and emotion. Say them in Barbados or Trinidad or Guyana and you will earn hatred. There is no reasoning, no inquiry, no curiosity about South Africa. Cricket's response to South Africa always came from the politicians, many of whom were keen to rake in the racial vote. The hope is now that international cricket will include Tests on beautiful grounds like Newlands between South Africa and West Indies. It will be an exciting new dimension of the cricket world and remove forever the niggle in the conscience that there is a sporting fraternity on whom we have turned our backs unless, of course, you believe that cricketers in South Africa – from the fine players who first walked off the pitch as a demonstration against apartheid to the current ones who coach in townships, or who lay artificial pitches in black schools and choose to play in poor clubs which include coloured and black players – have been playing out a wicked white man's charade.

This is not to say that England should have played against South Africa. The sporting isolation of South Africa served its serious purpose but few people realised in the 1980s that the time had come for encouragement, not chastisement.

It is important to realise why F. W. de Klerk's removal of apartheid from the statute book met general approval among white South Africans. Society had already moved ahead of change. I have sat in a Johannesburg cinema open to all races and yet failed to persuade Barbadian friends that that was possible. I have been on the beach in Durban opposite the Maharani Hotel and swum alongside black people. Two years later there was a considerable fuss when the beaches were legally open to all. It is over now, at least legally. The United Cricket Board of South Africa is born: 29 June 1991, I feel certain, will be an historic signpost.

Although I argue that cricket was a force for change in South Africa I never saw the game standing alone, apart from society. I did believe in the slogan 'no normal sport in an abnormal society'. I sat in the home of Mr Hassan Howa just outside Cape Town and this genial man, who led the coloured board of cricket control with such personal force, said that he lost faith many times in human beings, but never in cricket.

The appalling regime of apartheid which degraded those who lived according to its statutes, and which shocked and disgusted us who viewed it from outside, will live on until time takes its toll and it is finally throttled.

Cricket can be a civilising power. In the years which these writings cover, South Africa was the most bitter issue which burned its way into every cricket-playing country and separated friends. Perhaps the words we should take on into the new era are those of the late President Zia ul Haq of Pakistan when he abandoned warring words against India and simply flew to Jaipur to see a Test match between the countries.

'Cricket,' he said, 'is a bridge and a glue.'

So be it.

ENGLAND v WEST INDIES 1976 (Third Test)

Old Trafford, Manchester, 8, 9, 10, 12, 13 July
Toss: West Indies.   Result: WEST INDIES won by 425 runs

West Indies

Batsman	1st innings		2nd innings	
R.C. Fredericks	c Underwood b Selvey	0	hit wkt b Hendrick	50
C.G. Greenidge	b Underwood	134	b Selvey	101
I.V.A. Richards	b Selvey	4	lbw b Pocock	135
A.I. Kallicharran	b Selvey	0	(5) c Close b Pocock	20
C.H. Lloyd*	c Hayes b Hendrick	2	(4) c Underwood b Selvey	43
C.L. King	c Greig b Underwood	32	not out	14
D.L. Murray†	c Greig b Hendrick	1	not out	7
M.A. Holding	b Selvey	6		
A.M.E. Roberts	c Steele b Pocock	8		
A.L. Padmore	not out	10		
W.W. Daniel	lbw b Underwood	11		
Extras	(LB 8, NB 3)	11	(B 5, LB 30, W 1, NB 5)	41
		211	(5 wkt dec.)	**411**

1/1 2/15 3/19 4/26 5/137 6/154 7/167 8/193 9/193
1/116 2/224 3/356 4/385 5/388

Bowling: *First innings*—Hendrick 14-1-48-2; Selvey 17-4-41-4; Greig 8-1-24-0; Woolmer 3-0-22-0; Underwood 24.5-5-55-3; Pocock 4-2-10-1. *Second innings*—Hendrick 24-4-63-1; Selvey 26-3-111-2; Greig 2-0-8-0; Underwood 35-9-90-0; Pocock 27-4-98-2.

England

Batsman	1st innings		2nd innings	
J.H. Edrich	c Murray b Roberts	8	b Daniel	24
D.B. Close	lbw b Daniel	2	b Roberts	20
D.S. Steele	lbw b Roberts	20	c Roberts b Holding	15
P.I. Pocock	c Kallicharran b Holding	7	(10) c King b Daniel	3
R.A. Woolmer	c Murray b Holding	3	(4) lbw b Roberts	12
F.C. Hayes	c Lloyd b Roberts	18	(5) b Holding	1
A.W. Greig*	b Daniel	9	(6) b Holding	3
A.P.E. Knott†	c Greenidge b Holding	1	(7) c Fredericks b Roberts	14
D.L. Underwood	b Holding	0	(8) c King b Roberts	0
M.W.W. Selvey	not out	2	(9) c Greenidge b Roberts	4
M. Hendrick	b Holding	0	not out	0
Extras	(B 8, NB 11)	19	(B 4, LB 1, NB 20)	25
		71		**126**

1/9 2/36 3/46 4/48 5/48 6/65 7/66 8/67 9/71
1/54 2/60 3/60 4/80 5/94 6/112 7/112 8/118 9/124

Bowling: *First innings*—Roberts 12-4-22-3; Holding 14-5-17-5; Daniel 6-2-13-2. *Second innings*—Roberts 20.5-8-37-6; Holding 23-15-24-2; Daniel 17-8-39-2; Padmore 3-2-1-0.

Umpires: W.E. Alley and W.L. Budd

ENGLAND v AUSTRALIA 1977 (Second Test)

Old Trafford, Manchester, 7, 8, 9, 11, 12 July
Toss: Australia.   Result: ENGLAND won by nine wickets

Australia

Batsman	1st innings		2nd innings	
R.B. McCosker	c Old b Willis	2	c Underwood b Willis	0
I.C. Davis	c Knott b Old	34	c Lever b Willis	12
G.S. Chappell*	c Knott b Greig	44	b Underwood	112
C.S. Sergeant	lbw b Lever	14	c Woolmer b Underwood	8
K.D. Walters	c Greig b Miller	88	lbw b Greig	10
D.W. Hookes	c Knott b Lever	5	c Brearley b Miller	28
R.W. Marsh†	c Amiss b Miller	36	c Randall b Underwood	1
R.J. Bright	c Greig b Lever	12	c and b Underwood	0
K.J. O'Keeffe	c Knott b Willis	12	not out	24
M.H.N. Walker	b Underwood	9	c Greig b Underwood	6
J.R. Thomson	not out	1	c Randall b Underwood	1
Extras	(LB 15, NB 12)	27	(LB 1, W 1, NB 14)	16
		297		**218**

1/4 2/80 3/96 4/125 5/140 6/258 7/246 8/272 9/272
1/0 2/30 3/74 4/92 5/146 6/147 7/147 8/202 9/212

Bowling: *First innings*—Willis 21-8-45-2; Lever 25-8-60-3; Old 20-3-57-1; Underwood 20.2-7-53-1; Greig 13-4-37-1; Miller 10-3-18-2. *Second innings*—Willis 16-2-56-2; Lever 4-1-11-0; Old 8-1-26-0; Underwood 32.5-13-66-6; Greig 12-6-19-1; Miller 9-2-24-1.

England

Batsman	1st innings		2nd innings	
D.L. Amiss	c Chappell b Walker	11	not out	28
J.M. Brearley*	c Chappell b Thomson	6	b Walters b O'Keeffe	44
R.A. Woolmer	c Davis b O'Keeffe	137	not out	0
D.W. Randall	lbw b Bright	79		
A.W. Greig	c and b Walker	76		
A.P.E. Knott†	c O'Keeffe b Thomson	39		
G. Miller	c Marsh b Thomson	6		
C.M. Old	c Marsh b Walker	37		
J.K. Lever	b Bright	10		
D.L. Underwood	b Bright	10		
R.G.D. Willis	not out	1		
Extras	(B 9, LB 9, NB 7)	25	(LB 3, NB 7)	10
		437	(1 wkt)	**82**

1/19 2/23 3/165 4/335 5/348 6/366 7/377 8/404 9/435
1/75

Bowling: *First innings*—Thomson 38-11-73-3; Walker 54-15-131-3; Bright 35-11-12-69-3; O'Keeffe 36-11-114-1; Chappell 6-1-25-0. *Second innings*—Thomson 8-2-24-0; Walker 7-0-17-0; Bright 5-2-6-0; O'Keeffe 9.1-4-25-1.

Umpires: W.E. Alley and T.W. Spencer

ENGLAND v PAKISTAN 1978 (First Test)

Edgbaston, Birmingham, 1, 2, 3, 5 June

Toss: Pakistan.   Result: ENGLAND won by an innings and 57 runs

Pakistan

Batsman		1st		2nd
Mudassar Nazar c and b Botham	14		b Edmonds	30
Sadiq Mohammad c Radley b Old	23		b Old	79
Mohsin Khan b Willis	35	(4)	c Old b Miller	38
Javed Miandad c Taylor b Old	15	(5)	c Brearley b Edmonds	39
Haroon Rashid c Roope b Willis	3	(6)	b Willis	4
Wasim Raja c Taylor b Old	17	(7)	b Edmonds	9
Sarfraz Nawaz not out	32	(8)	not out	6
Wasim Bari*† b Old	0	(9)	c Miller b Edmonds	3
Iqbal Qasim c Taylor b Old	0	(3)	retired hurt	5
Sikander Bakht c Roope b Old	0		b Miller	2
Liaquat Ali c Brearley b Old	9		b Willis	3
Extras (LB 3, NB 13)	16		(B 4, LB 4, W 1, NB 4)	13
	164			**231**

1/20 2/56 3/91 4/94 5/103   1/94 2/125 3/175 4/94 5/214
6/125 7/125 8/126 9/126   6/220 7/224 8/227 9/231

Bowling: First innings—Willis 16-2-42-2; Old 22.4-6-50-7; Botham 15-4-52-; Wood 3-2-2-0; Edmonds 4-2-2-0. Second innings—Willis 23-4-3-70-2; Old 25-12-38-1; Botham 17-3-47-0; Edmonds 26-10-44-4; Miller 12-4-19-2.

England

J.M. Brearley* run out		38
B. Wood lbw b Sikander		14
C.T. Radley lbw b Sikander		106
D.I. Gower c Miandad b Sikander		58
G.R.J. Roope b Sikander		32
G. Miller c Wasim Bari b Mudassar		48
I.T. Botham c Qasim b Liaquat		100
C.M. Old c Mudassar b Qasim		5
P.H. Edmonds not out		4
R.W. Taylor†	did not bat	
R.G.D. Willis	did not bat	
Extras (LB 26, W 5, NB 16)		47
(8 wkt dec.)		**452**

1/36 2/101 3/190 4/275 5/276
6/399 7/448 8/452

Bowling: First innings—Sarfraz 6-1-12-0; Liaquat 42-9-114-1; Sikander 45-13-132-4; Mudassar 27-7-59-1; Qasim 14-2-56-1; Wasim Raja 10-1-32-0.

Umpires: H.D. Bird and K.E. Palmer

ENGLAND v AUSTRALIA 1978–79 (Fourth Test)

Sydney Cricket Ground, 6, 7, 8, 10, 11 January

Toss: England.   Result: ENGLAND won by 93 runs

England

Batsman	1st		2nd
G. Boycott c Border b Hurst	8	lbw b Hogg	0
J.M. Brearley* b Hogg	17	b Border	53
D.W. Randall c Wood b Hurst	0	lbw b Hogg	150
G.A. Gooch c Toohey b Higgs	18	c Wood b Higgs	22
D.I. Gower c Maclean b Hurst	7	c Maclean b Hogg	34
I.T. Botham c Yallop b Hogg	59	c Wood b Higgs	6
G. Miller c Maclean b Hurst	4	lbw b Hogg	17
R.W. Taylor† c Border b Higgs	10	not out	21
J.E. Emburey c Wood b Higgs	0	c Darling b Higgs	14
R.G.D. Willis not out	7	c Toohey b Higgs	0
M. Hendrick b Hirst	10	c Toohey b Higgs	7
Extras (B 1, LB 1, W 2, NB 8)	12	(B 5, LB 3, NB 14)	22
	152		**346**

1/18 2/18 3/35 4/51 5/66   1/0 2/111 3/169 4/237 5/267
6/70 7/94 8/98 9/141   6/292 7/307 8/334 9/334

Bowling: First innings—Hogg 11-3-36-2; Dymock 13-1-34-0; Hurst 10.6-2-28-5; Higgs 18-4-42-3; Border 23-11-31-1. Second innings—Hogg 28-10-67-4; Dymock 17-4-35-0; Hurst 19-3-43-0; Higgs 59.6-15-148-5; Border 23-11-31-1.

Australia

Batsman	1st		2nd
G.M. Wood b Willis	0	run out	27
W.M. Darling c Botham b Miller	91	c Gooch b Hendrick	13
K.J. Hughes c Emburey b Willis	48	c Emburey b Miller	15
G.N. Yallop* c Botham b Hendrick	44	c and b Hendrick	1
P.M. Toohey c Gooch b Botham	1	b Miller	5
A.R. Border not out	60	not out	45
J.A. Maclean† lbw b Emburey	12	c Botham b Miller	0
R.M. Hogg run out	6	(9) c Botham b Emburey	0
G. Dymock c Botham b Hendrick	5	(8) b Emburey	0
J.D. Higgs c Botham b Hendrick	11	lbw b Emburey	3
A.G. Hurst run out	0	b Emburey	0
Extras (B 2, LB 3, NB 11)	16	(LB 1, NB 1)	2
	294		**111**

1/1 2/126 3/178 4/179 5/210   1/38 2/44 3/45 4/59 5/74
6/235 7/245 8/276 9/290   6/76 7/85 8/85 9/105

Bowling: First innings—Willis 9-2-33-2; Botham 28-3-87-2; Hendrick 24-4-50-2; Miller 13-2-37-1; Emburey 29-10-57-1; Gooch 5-1-14-0. Second innings—Willis 2-0-8-0; Hendrick 10-3-17-2; Miller 20-7-38-3; Emburey 17.2-7-46-4.

Umpires: R.C. Bailhache and R.A. French

INDIA v ENGLAND 1979-80 (Jubilee Test)

Wankhede Stadium, Bombay, 15, 17, 18, 19 February
Toss: India.   Result: ENGLAND won by 10 wickets

India

Batsman	First innings		Second innings	
S.M. Gavaskar	c Taylor b Botham	49	c Taylor b Botham	24
R.M.H. Binny	run out	15	lbw b Botham	0
D.B. Vengsarkar	c Taylor b Stevenson	34	lbw b Lever	10
G.R. Viswanath*	b Lever	11	c Taylor b Botham	5
S.M. Patil	c Taylor b Botham	30	lbw b Botham	0
Yashpal Sharma	lbw b Botham	21	lbw b Botham	27
Kapil Dev	c Taylor b Botham	0	(8) not out	45
S.M.H. Kirmani†	not out	40	(7) c Gooch b Botham	0
K.D. Ghavri	c Taylor b Stevenson	11	c Brearley b Lever	5
N.S. Yadav	c Taylor b Botham	8	c Taylor b Botham	15
D.R. Doshi	c Taylor b Botham	6	c and b Lever	0
Extras	(B 5, LB 3, NB 9)	17	(B 4, LB 8, W 1, NB 5)	18
		242		**149**

1/56 2/102 3/108 4/135 5/160
6/160 7/181 8/197 9/223
1/4 2/22 3/31 4/31 5/56
6/58 7/102 8/115 9/148

Bowling: First innings—Lever 23-3-82-1; Botham 22.5-7-58-6; Stevenson 14-1-59-2; Underwood 6-1-23-0; Gooch 4-2-3-0. Second innings—Lever 20.1-2-65-3; Botham 26-7-48-7; Stevenson 5-1-13-0; Underwood 1-0-5-0.

England

Batsman	First innings		Second innings	
G.A. Gooch	c Kirmani b Ghavri	8	not out	49
G. Boycott	c Kirmani b Binny	22	not out	43
W. Larkins	lbw b Ghavri	0		
D.I. Gower	lbw b Kapil Dev	16		
J.M. Brearley*	lbw b Kapil Dev	5		
I.T. Botham	lbw b Ghavri	114		
R.W. Taylor†	lbw b Kapil Dev	43		
J.E. Emburey	c Binny b Ghavri	0		
J.K. Lever	b Doshi	21		
G.B. Stevenson	not out	27		
D.L. Underwood	b Ghavri	1		
Extras	(B 8, LB 9, NB 14)	31	(B 3, LB 1, NB 2)	6
		296	(0 wkt)	**98**

1/21 2/21 3/45 4/57 5/58
6/229 7/245 8/262 9/283

Bowling: First innings—Kapil Dev 29-8-64-3; Ghavri 20.1-5-52-5; Binny 19-3-70-1; Doshi 23-6-57-1; Yadav 6-2-22-0. Second innings—Kapil Dev 8-2-21-0; Ghavri 5-0-12-0; Doshi 6-1-12-0; Yadav 6-0-31-0; Patil 3-0-8-0; Gavaskar 1-0-4-0; Viswanath 0-3-0-4-0.

Umpires: J.D. Ghosh and S.N. Hanumantha Rao

WEST INDIES v ENGLAND 1980-81 (Third Test)

Kensington Oval, Bridgetown, Barbados, 13, 14, 15, 17, 18 March
Toss: England.   Result: WEST INDIES won by 298 runs

West Indies

Batsman	First innings		Second innings	
C.G. Greenidge	c Gooch b Jackman	14	lbw b Dilley	0
D.L. Haynes	c Bairstow b Jackman	25	lbw b Botham	25
I.V.A. Richards	c Botham b Dilley	16	not out	182
E.H. Mattis	lbw b Dilley	16	(4) c Butcher b Jackman	24
C.H. Lloyd*	c Gooch b Jackman	100	(5) lbw b Botham	66
H.A. Gomes	c Botham b Dilley	58	(7) lbw b Botham	34
D.A. Murray†	c Bairstow b Dilley	9	run out	5
A.M.E. Roberts	c Bairstow b Botham	14	(9) not out	0
J. Garner	c Bairstow b Botham	15	c Bairstow b Botham	
M.A. Holding	c Gatting b Botham	0		
C.E.H. Croft	not out	0	(3) c Boycott b Jackman	33
Extras	(B 4, LB 6, W 2, NB 2)	14	(B 3, LB 7)	10
		265	(7 wkt dec.)	**379**

1/24 2/25 3/47 4/65 5/219
6/224 7/236 8/258 9/258
1/0 2/57 3/71 4/130 5/212
6/365 7/365

Bowling: First innings—Dilley 23-7-51-3; Botham 25.1-5-77-4; Jackman 22.4-6-65-3; Emburey 18-4-45-0; Gooch 2-0-13-0. Second innings—Dilley 25-3-111-1; Botham 29-5-102-3; Jackman 25-5-76-2; Emburey 24-7-57-0; Willey 6-0-23-0.

England

Batsman	First innings		Second innings	
G.A. Gooch	b Garner	26	c Garner b Croft	116
G. Boycott	b Holding	0	c Garner b Holding	1
M.W. Gatting	c Greenidge b Roberts	2	b Holding	0
D.I. Gower	c Mattis b Croft	17	b Richards	54
R.O. Butcher	c Richards b Croft	17	lbw b Richards	2
I.T. Botham*	c Murray b Holding	26	c Lloyd b Roberts	1
P. Willey	not out	19	lbw b Croft	17
D.L. Bairstow†	c Mattis b Holding	0	c Murray b Croft	0
J.E. Emburey	c Lloyd b Roberts	0	b Garner	9
R.D. Jackman	b Croft	7	b Garner	7
G.R. Dilley	c Gomes b Croft	0	not out	7
Extras	(B 1, LB 1, NB 6)	8	(B 1, LB 3, NB 4)	8
		122		**224**

1/6 2/11 3/40 4/55 5/72
6/94 7/94 8/97 9/122
1/2 2/2 3/122 4/134 5/139
6/196 7/198 8/201 9/213

Bowling: First innings—Roberts 11-3-29-2; Holding 11-7-6-3; Croft 13.5-2-39-4; Garner 12-5-30-1. Second innings—Roberts 20-6-41-2; Holding 19-6-42-2; Croft 19-1-65-3; Garner 16.2-6-39-2; Richards 17-6-24-2.

Umpires: D.M. Archer and D. Sang Hue

ENGLAND v AUSTRALIA 1981 (Fifth Test)

Old Trafford, Manchester, 13, 14, 15, 16, 17 August

Toss: England.   Result: ENGLAND won by 103 runs

England

Batsman	1st innings		2nd innings	
G.A. Gooch c/lbw b Lillee	10		b Alderman	5
G. Boycott c Marsh b Alderman	10		lbw b Alderman	37
C.J. Tavaré c Alderman b Whitney	69		c Kent b Alderman	78
D.I. Gower c Yallop b Whitney	23		c Bright b Lillee	1
J.M. Brearley* lbw b Alderman	2		c Marsh b Alderman	3
M.W. Gatting c Border b Lillee	32	(6)	lbw b Alderman	11
I.T. Botham c Bright b Lillee	0		c Marsh b Whitney	118
A.P.E. Knott c Border b Alderman	13	(5)	c Dyson b Lillee	59
J.E. Emburey c Border b Alderman	1		c Kent b Whitney	57
P.J.W. Allott not out	52		c Hughes b Bright	14
R.G.D. Willis c Hughes b Lillee	11		not out	5
Extras (LB 6, W 2)	8		(B 1, LB 12, NB 3)	16
	231			**404**

1/19 2/25 3/57 4/62 5/109 6/109 7/131 8/137 9/175

1/7 2/79 3/80 4/98 5/104 6/253 7/282 8/356 9/396

Bowling: First innings—Lillee 24.1-8-55-4; Alderman 29.5-88-4; Whitney 17-3-50-2; Bright 16-6-30-0; Second innings—Lillee 46-13-137-2; Alderman 52-19-109-5; Whitney 27-6-74-2; Bright 26.4-12-68-1.

Australia

Batsman	1st innings		2nd innings	
G.M. Wood lbw b Allott	19		c Knott b Allott	6
J. Dyson c Botham b Willis	0		run out	5
K.J. Hughes* lbw b Willis	4		lbw b Botham	43
G.N. Yallop c Botham b Willis	0		c Botham b Willis	114
M.F. Kent c Knott b Emburey	52	(6)	c Brearley b Emburey	2
A.R. Border c Gower b Botham	11	(5)	not out	123
R.W. Marsh† c Botham b Willis	1		c Knott b Willis	47
R.J. Bright c Knott b Botham	22		c Knott b Willis	5
D.K. Lillee c Gooch b Botham	13		c Botham b Allott	28
M.R. Whitney b Allott	0	(11)	c Gatting b Willis	0
T.M. Alderman not out	2	(10)	lbw b Botham	0
Extras (NB 6)	6		(LB 9, W 2, NB 18)	29
	130			**402**

1/20 2/24 3/24 4/24 5/58 6/59 7/104 8/125 9/126

1/7 2/24 3/119 4/198 5/206 6/296 7/322 8/373 9/378

Bowling: First innings—Willis 14-0-63-4; Allott 6-1-17-2; Botham 6.2-1-2-3; Emburey 4-0-16-1. Second innings—Willis 30.5-2-96-3; Allott 17-3-71-2; Botham 36-16-86-5; Emburey 49-9-107-2; Gatting 3-1-13-0.

Umpires: D.J. Constant and K.E. Palmer

ENGLAND v SRI LANKA 1984 (only Test)

Lord's Cricket Ground, London, 23, 24, 25, 27, 28 August

Toss: England.   Result: Match drawn.

Sri Lanka

Batsman	1st innings		2nd innings	
S. Wettimuny c Downton b Allott	190		c Gower b Botham	13
S.A.R. Silva† lbw b Botham	8		not out	102
R.S. Madugalle b Ellison	5		b Botham	3
R.L. Dias c Lamb b Pocock	32		lbw b Botham	38
A. Ranatunga b Agnew	84		lbw b Botham	0
L.R.D. Mendis* c Fowler b Pocock	111		c Fowler b Botham	94
P.A. de Silva c Downton b Agnew	16	(7)	c Downton b Pocock	3
A.L.F. de Mel not out	20	(6)	c Ellison b Botham	14
J.R. Ratnayeke not out	5		not out	7
D.S. de Silva	did not bat		did not bat	
V.B. John	did not bat		did not bat	
Extras (B 2, LB 8, W 2, NB 8)	20		(B 5, LB 4, NB 11)	20
	(7 wkt dec.) **491**		(7 wkt dec.) **294**

1/17 2/43 3/144 4/292 5/442 6/456 7/464

1/19 2/27 3/111 4/115 5/118 6/256 7/276

Bowling: First innings—Agnew 32-3-123-2; Botham 29-6-114-1; Ellison 28-6-70-1; Pocock 41-17-75-2; Allott 37-7-89-1. Second innings—Agnew 11-3-54-0; Allott 1-0-2-0; Botham 27-6-90-6; Pocock 29-10-78-1; Ellison 7-0-36-0; Lamb 1-0-6-0; Tavaré 3-3-0-0, Fowler 1-0-8-0.

England

G. Fowler c Madugalle b John		25
B.C. Broad c Silva b de Mel		86
C.J. Tavaré c Ranatunga b D.S. de Silva		14
*D.I. Gower c Silva b de Mel		55
A.J. Lamb c Dias b John		107
I.T. Botham c sub b John		6
R.M. Ellison c Ratnayeke b D.S. de Silva		41
P.R. Downton† c Dias b de Mel		10
P.J.W. Allott b de Mel		0
P.I. Pocock c Silva b John		2
J.P. Agnew not out		1
Extras (B 5, LB 7, W 5, NB 6)		23
		370

1/49 2/105 3/190 4/220 5/218 6/305 7/354 8/354 9/360

Bowling: de Mel 37-10-110-4; John 39-12-98-4; Ratnayeke 22-5-50-0; D.S. de Silva 45-16-85-2; Ranatunga 1-1-0-0; Madugalle 3-0-4-0.

Umpires: H.D. Bird and D.G.L. Evans

ENGLAND v NEW ZEALAND, 1986 (First Test)

Lord's Cricket Ground, London, 24, 25, 26, 28, 29 July
Toss: England.   Result: Match drawn

England

G.A. Gooch c Smith b Hadlee	18		
M.D. Moxon lbw b Hadlee	74		
C.W.J. Athey c J.J. Crowe b Hadlee	44		
D.I. Gower c M.D. Crowe b Bracewell	62		
M.W. Gatting* b Hadlee	2		
P. Willey lbw b Watson	44		
P.H. Edmonds c M.D. Crowe b Hadlee	6		
B.N. French† retired hurt	0		
G.R. Dilley c Smith b Hadlee	17		
N.A. Foster b Hadlee	8		
N.V. Radford not out	12		
Extras (B 6, LB 7, NB 7)	20		
	(6 wkt dec.) 307		

1/27 2/102 3/196 4/198 5/237
6/258 7/271 8/285 9/307

Bowling: *First innings*—Hadlee 37.5-11-80-6; Watson 30-7-70-2; M.D. Crowe 8-1-38-0; Coney 4-0-12-0; Bracewell 26-8-65-1; Gray 13-9-29-0. *Second innings*—Hadlee 27-3-78-1; Watson 17-2-50-0; Gray 46-14-83-3; M.D. Crowe 4-0-13-0; Bracewell 23.4-7-57-2; Rutherford 3-0-8-0.

New Zealand

J.G. Wright b Dilley	0	c Gower b Dilley	0
B.A. Edgar c Gatting b Gooch	83	c Gower b Foster	0
K.R. Rutherford c Gooch b Dilley	0	not out	24
M.D. Crowe c and b Edmonds	106	not out	11
J.J. Crowe c Gatting b Edmonds	18		
J.V. Coney* c Gooch b Radford	51		
E.J. Gray c Gower b Edmonds	11		
R.J. Hadlee b Edmonds	19		
I.D.S. Smith† c Edmonds, b Dilley	18		
J.G. Bracewell not out	1		
W. Watson lbw b Dilley	0		
Extras (B 4, LB 9, W 6, NB 15)	34	(LB 4, NB 2)	6
	342		**(2 wkt) 41**

1/2 2/5 3/215 4/218 5/274   1/0 2/8
6/292 7/310 8/340 9/340

Bowling: *First innings*—Dilley 35.1-9-82-4; Foster 25-6-56-0; Radford 25-4-71-1; Edmonds 42-10-97-4; Gooch 13-6-23-1. *Second innings*—Dilley 6-3-5-1; Foster 3-1-13-1; Edmonds 5-0-18-0; Gower 1-0-1-0.

Umpires: H.D. Bird and A.G.T. Whitehead

AUSTRALIA v ENGLAND 1986–87 (First Test)

Woolloongabba, Brisbane, 14, 15, 16, 18, 19 November
Toss: Australia.   Result: ENGLAND won by 7 wickets

England

B.C. Broad c Zoehrer b Reid	8	not out	35
C.W.J. Athey c Zoehrer b C.D. Matthews	76	c Waugh b Hughes	16
M.W. Gatting* b Hughes	61	c G.R.J. Matthews b Hughes	12
A.J. Lamb lbw b Hughes	40	lbw b Reid	9
D.I. Gower c Ritchie b C.D. Matthews	51	not out	15
I.T. Botham c Hughes b Waugh	138		
C.J. Richards† b C.D. Matthews	8		
J.E. Emburey c Waugh b Hughes	8		
P.A.J. DeFreitas c C.D. Matthews b Waugh	40		
P.H. Edmonds not out	9		
G.R. Dilley c Boon b Waugh	0		
Extras (B 3, LB 19, NB 3)	25	(B 2, NB 3)	5
	456		**(3 wkt) 77**

1/15 2/116 3/198 4/198 5/316   1/6 2/25 3/40
6/324 7/351 8/443 9/451

Bowling: *First innings*—Reid 31-4-86-1; Hughes 36-7-134-3; C.D. Matthews 35-10-95-3; Waugh 21-3-76-3; G.R.J. Matthews 11-2-43-0. *Second innings*—Reid 6-1-20-1; Hughes 5.3-0-28-2; C.D. Matthews 4-0-11-0; G.R.J. Matthews 7-1-16-0.

Australia

G.R. Marsh c Richards b Dilley	56	(2) b DeFreitas	110
D.C. Boon c Broad b DeFreitas	10	(1) lbw b Botham	14
T.J. Zoehrer† lbw b Dilley	38	(8) not out	16
D.M. Jones lbw b DeFreitas	8	(3) st Richards b Emburey	18
A.R. Border* c DeFreitas b Edmonds	7	(4) c Lamb b Emburey	23
G.M. Ritchie c Edmonds b Dilley	41	(5) lbw b DeFreitas	45
G.R.J. Matthews not out	56	(6) c and b Dilley	13
S.R. Waugh c Richards b Dilley	0	(7) b Emburey	28
C.D. Matthews c Gatting b Botham	11	lbw b Emburey	0
M.G. Hughes b Botham	0	b DeFreitas	0
B.A. Reid c Richards b Dilley	3	c Broad b Emburey	2
Extras (B 2, LB 8, W 2, NB 6)	18	(B 5, LB 6, NB 2)	13
	248		**282**

1/27 2/97 3/114 4/126 5/159   1/24 2/44 3/92 4/205 5/224
6/198 7/204 8/239 9/239   6/262 7/266 8/282 9/275

Bowling: *First innings*—DeFreitas 16-5-32-2; Dilley 23.4-7-68-5; Emburey 34-11-66-0; Edmonds 12-6-12-1; Botham 16-1-58-2; Gatting 1-0-2-0. *Second innings*—DeFreitas 17-2-62-3; Dilley 19-6-47-1; Emburey 42.5-14-80-5; Edmonds 24-8-46-0; Botham 12-0-34-1; Gatting 2-0-2-0.

Umpires: A.R. Crafter and M.W. Johnson

MCC v REST OF THE WORLD, 1987
(The Bicentenary match)

Lord's Cricket Ground, London, 20, 21, 22, 24, 25 August
Toss: MCC. Result: Match drawn

MCC

C.G. Greenidge c Harper b Qadir	52	b Qadir	122
B.C. Broad lbw b Imran	10	c Dujon b Kapil Dev	2
G.A. Gooch run out	117	b Harper	70
D.I. Gower c Dujon b Harper	8	c Border b Imran	40
M.W. Gatting* b Walsh	179		
C.E.B. Rice not out	59	(8) not out	4
R.J. Hadlee did not bat		(5) c Imran b Walsh	36
R.J. Shastri		(6) not out	10
J.E. Emburey		(7) c Haynes b Qadir	7
Extras (B 11, LB 15, W 1, NB 3)	30	(B 15, LB 11, NB 1)	27
(5 wkt dec.)	455	(6 wkt dec.)	318

1/21 2/96 3/151 4/254 5/455
1/11 2/146 3/151 4/289 4/293 5/308

M.D. Marshall and B.N. French† did not bat.

Bowling: First innings—Imran 25-6-97-1; Walsh 28.1-6-97-1; Kapil Dev 24-8-54-0; Qadir 16.2-7-30-1; Harper 34-5-125-1; Miandad 5-4-0-21-0. Second innings—Imran 13-4-33-1; Kapil Dev 7-0-21-1; Walsh 12-3-54-1; Qadir 36-9-112-2; Harper 20-2-72-1.

Rest of the World

S.M. Gavaskar c and b Shastri	188		
D.L. Haynes c Rice b Marshall	23		
D.B. Vengsarkar c Gooch b Marshall	22		
A.R. Border* c Rice b Shastri	26		
P.J.L. Dujon† c Gooch b Marshall	9	b Marshall	0
Imran Khan b Shastri	82	not out	3
Kapil Dev c Marshall b Emburey	13		
R.A. Harper not out	17		
C.A. Walsh run out	21	(3) not out	9
Extras (B 3, LB 8, W 4, NB 5)	20	(LB 1)	1
(7 wkt dec.)	421	(1 wkt)	13

1/46 2/93 3/148 4/173 5/353 6/372 7/389
1/2

Javed Miandad and Abdul Qadir did not bat.

Bowling: First innings—Marshall 20-3-53-3; Hadlee 21-2-71-0; Rice 12-1-38-0; Shastri 42-4-130-3; Emburey 29-7-93-1. Second innings—Marshall 2·3-0-10-1; Hadlee 2-1-2-0.

Umpires: H.D. Bird and D.R. Shepherd

In addition to the above players, the following reserves were selected: MCC – P.H. Edmonds, M.A. Holding and C.J. Richards; Rest of the World – J.G. Bracewell, J. Garner, D. M. Jones, Maninder Singh, J. R. Ratnayeke and B. A. Reid.

WEST INDIES v ENGLAND 1989-90 (First Test)

Sabina Park, Kingston, Jamaica, 24, 25, 26, 28 February, 1 March
Toss: West Indies. Result: ENGLAND won by 9 wickets

West Indies

C.G. Greenidge run out	32	c Hussain b Malcolm	36
D.L. Haynes c and b Small	36	b Malcolm	14
R.B. Richardson c Small b Capel	10	lbw b Fraser	25
C.A. Best c Russell b Capel	4	c Gooch b Small	64
C.L. Hooper c Capel b Fraser	20	c Larkins b Small	8
I.V.A. Richards* lbw b Malcolm	21	b Malcolm	37
P.J.L. Dujon† not out	19	b Malcolm	15
M.D. Marshall b Fraser	0	not out	8
I.R. Bishop c Larkins b Fraser	0	c Larkins b Small	3
C.A. Walsh b Fraser	6	b Small	2
B.P. Patterson b Fraser	0	run out	2
Extras (B 9, LB 3, NB 4)	16	(B 14, LB 10, W 1, NB 1)	26
	164		240

1/62 2/81 3/92 4/92 5/124 6/144 7/144 8/159 9/164
1/26 2/69 3/87 4/112 5/192 6/222 7/222 8/227 9/237

Bowling: First innings—Small 15-6-44-1; Malcolm 16-4-49-1; Fraser 20-8-28-5; Capel 13-4-31-2. Second innings—Small 25-6-58-4; Malcolm 21-3-77-4; Capel 15-1-50-0; Fraser 14-5-31-1.

England

G.A. Gooch* c Dujon b Patterson	18	c Greenidge b Bishop	8
W. Larkins lbw b Walsh	46	not out	29
A.J. Lamb c Hooper b Walsh	132	not out	0
R.A. Smith c Best b Bishop	57		
N. Hussain c Dujon b Bishop	13		
D.J. Capel c Richardson b Walsh	5		
R.C. Russell† c Patterson b Walsh	26		
G.C. Small lbw b Marshall	4		
A.R.C. Fraser not out	2		
D.E. Malcolm lbw b Walsh	0		
Extras (B 23, LB 12, W 1, NB 12)	48	(LB 1, NB 3)	4
	364	(1 wkt)	41

1/40 2/60 3/116 4/228 5/315 6/315 7/325 8/339 9/364
1/35

Bowling: First innings—Patterson 18-2-74-1; Bishop 27-5-72-3; Marshall 18-3-46-1; Walsh 27.2-4-68-5; Richards 9-1-22-0; Best 4-0-19-0. Second innings—Patterson 3-1-11-0; Bishop 7.3-2-17-1; Walsh 6-0-12-0.

Umpires: L.H. Barker and S.N. Bucknor

ENGLAND v INDIA 1990 (First Test)

Lord's Cricket Ground, London, 26, 27, 28, 30, 31 July
Toss: India.   Result: ENGLAND won by 247 runs.

England

G.A. Gooch c Azharuddin b Sharma		123
M.A. Atherton b Kapil Dev		8
D.I. Gower c Manjrekar b Hirwani	c Vengsarkar b Sharma	72
A.J. Lamb c Manjrekar b Sharma	not out	32
R.A. Smith not out	c Tendulkar b Hirwani	19
J.E. Morris not out	b Prabhakar	15
Extras (B 2, LB 21, W 2, NB 4)	(LB 11)	29 / 11
(4 wkt dec.)	(4 wkt dec.)	653 / 272

1/14 2/141 3/449   1/204 2/207 3/250
4/641   4/272

R.C. Russell†, C.C. Lewis, E.E. Hemmings, A.R.C. Fraser and D. E. Malcolm did not bat.

Bowling: First innings— Kapil Dev 34-5-120-1; Prabhakar 43-6-187-1; Sharma 33-5-122-1; Shastri 22-0-99-0; Hirwani 30-1-102-1. Second innings— Kapil Dev 10-0-53-0; Prabhakar 11.2-2-45-1; Shastri 7-0-38-0; Sharma 15-0-75-2; Hirwani 11-0-50-1.

India

R.J. Shastri c Gooch b Hemmings	c Russell b Malcolm	100 / 12
N.S. Sidhu c Morris b Fraser	c Morris b Fraser	30 / 1
S.V. Manjrekar c Russell b Gooch	c Russell b Malcolm	18 / 33
D.B. Vengsarkar c Russell b Fraser	c Russell b Hemmings	52 / 35
M. Azharuddin* c Atherton b Hemmings	c Atherton b Lewis	121 / 37
S.R. Tendulkar b Lewis	c Gooch b Fraser	10 / 27
M. Prabhakar c Lewis b Malcolm	lbw b Lewis	25 / 8
Kapil Dev not out	lbw b Fraser	77 / 16
K.S. More† c Morris b Fraser	run out	8 /
S.K. Sharma c Russell b Fraser	not out	0 / 38
N.D. Hirwani lbw b Fraser	run out	13 / 0
Extras (LB 1, W 4, NB 8)	(B 3, LB 1, NB 6)	/ 10
		454 / 224

1/63 2/102 3/191 4/241   1/9 2/23 3/63 4/114 5/127
5/288 6/348 7/393 8/430 9/430   6/140 7/158 8/181 9/206

Bowling: First innings— Malcolm 25-1-106-1; Fraser 39-1-9-104-5; Lewis 24-3-108-1; Gooch 6-3-26-1; Hemmings 20-3-109-2. Second innings— Fraser 22-7-39-3; Malcolm 10-0-65-2; Hemmings 21-2-79-2; Atherton 1-0-11-0; Lewis 8-1-26-2.

Umpires: H.D. Bird and N.T. Plews

AUSTRALIA v WEST INDIES 1975
Prudential World Cup – Final (60 overs match)

Lord's, London, June 1975
Toss: Australia.   Result: WEST INDIES won by 17 runs

Man of the Match: C. H. Lloyd

West Indies

R.C. Fredericks hit wkt b Lillee	7
C.G. Greenidge c Marsh b Thomson	13
A.I. Kallicharran c Marsh b Gilmour	12
R.B. Kanhai b Gilmour	55
C.H. Lloyd* c Marsh b Gilmour	102
I.V.A. Richards b Gilmour	5
K.D. Boyce c G.S. Chappell b Thomson	34
B.D. Julien not out	26
D.L. Murray† c and b Gilmour	14
V.A. Holder not out	6
A.M.E. Roberts did not bat.	
Extras (LB 6, NB 11)	17
(60 overs, 8 wkt)	291

1/12 2/27 3/50 4/199 5/206
6/209 7/261 8/285

Bowling: Lillee 12-1-55-1; Gilmour 12-2-48-5; Thomson 12-2-44-2; Walker 12-1-71-0; G.S. Chappell 7-0-33-0; Walters 5-0-23-0.

Australia

R.B. McCosker c Kallicharran b Boyce	7
A. Turner run out	40
I.M. Chappell* run out	62
G.S. Chappell run out	15
K.D. Walters b Lloyd	35
R.W. Marsh† b Boyce	11
R. Edwards c Fredericks b Boyce	28
G.J. Gilmour c Kanhai b Boyce	14
M.H.N. Walker run out	7
J.R. Thomson run out	21
D.K. Lillee not out	16
Extras (B 2, LB 9, NB 7)	18
(58.4 overs)	274

1/25 2/81 3/115 4/162 5/170
6/195 7/221 8/231 9/233

Bowling: Julien 12-0-58-0; Roberts 11-1-45-0; Boyce 12-0-50-4; Holder 11.4-1-65-0; Lloyd 12-1-38-1.

Umpires: H.D. Bird and T.W. Spencer

AUSTRALIA v WEST INDIES 1979–80
Benson and Hedges World Series Cup (48 overs match)

Melbourne Cricket Ground, 9 December 1979
Toss: Australia.   Result: WEST INDIES won by 80 runs

Man of the Match: I.V.A. Richards

West Indies

C.G. Greenidge c Marsh b Lillee	11
D.L. Haynes c Marsh b Thomson	80
I.V.A. Richards not out	153
A.I. Kallicharran not out	16
L.G. Rowe	
C.L. King	
D.L. Murray*†	
D.R. Parry	
A.M.E. Roberts	
J. Garner	
M.A. Holding	
Extras (B 1, LB 10)	11
(48 overs, 2 wkt)	**271**

1/28 2/233
Bowling: Lillee 10-1-48-1; Hogg 10-1-50-0; Chappell 4-0-24-0; Thomson 8-0-43-1; Bright 6-0-29-0; Hookes 1-0-10-0; Border 7-0-40-0; Wiener 2-0-16-0.

Australia

B.M. Laird b Holding	7
J.M. Wiener c and b Parry	27
A.R. Border run out	44
G.S. Chappell* c Richards b King	31
K.J. Hughes b Holding	12
D.W. Hookes c Murray b Roberts	9
R.W. Marsh† c Rowe b Roberts	13
R.J. Bright not out	19
D.K. Lillee b King	19
R.M. Hogg not out	3
J.R. Thomson	
Extras (B 1, LB 6)	7
(48 overs, 8 wkt)	**191**

1/16 2/54 3/102 4/119 5/128
6/147 7/151 8/185
Bowling: Roberts 8-1-33-2; Holding 10-2-29-2; Garner 10-1-26-0; King 10-0-40-2; Parry 10-0-56-1.

Umpires: K. Carmody and R.V. Whitehead

AUSTRALIA v ENGLAND 1979–80
Benson and Hedges World Series Cup (49 overs match)

Sydney Cricket Ground, 11 December 1979
Toss: England.   Result: ENGLAND won by 72 runs

Man of the Match: G. Boycott

England

D.W. Randall run out	42
G. Boycott b Lillee	105
P. Willey c Walker b Chappell	64
D.I. Gower c Wiener b Lillee	7
G.A. Gooch b Thomson	11
I.T. Botham c Walters b Lillee	5
D.L. Bairstow† c sub b Lillee	18
J.M. Brearley* not out	2
G.R. Dilley	
D.L. Underwood	
R.G.D. Willis	
Extras (LB 6, W 1, NB 3)	10
(49 overs, 7 wkt)	**264**

1/78 2/196 3/220 4/236 5/242
6/245 7/264
Bowling: Lillee 10-0-56-c; Thomson 9-0-53-1; Walker 10-1-30-0; Laughlin 8-0-39-0; Border 4-0-24-0; Chappell 5-0-28-1; Walters 3-0-24-0

Australia

J.M. Wiener st Bairstow b Willey	14
W.M. Darling c Randall b Willis	20
A.R. Border b Willey	0
G.S. Chappell* run out	1
K.J. Hughes c Bairstow b Willis	1
K.D. Walters c Bairstow b Botham	34
R.W. Marsh† b Dilley	12
T.J. Laughlin c Gooch b Randall	74
D.K. Lillee b Botham	14
J.R. Thomson run out	0
M.H.N. Walker not out	9
Extras (LB 10, W 2, NB 1)	13
(47.2 overs)	**192**

1/33 2/36 3/36 4/38 5/39
6/63 7/115 8/146 9/147
Bowling: Dilley 9-0-29-1; Botham 10-1-36-2; Willis 10-1-32-2; Willey 5-0-18-2; Underwood 6-1-29-0; Gooch 7-0-33-0; Randall 0.2-0-2-1.

Umpires: J.R. Collins and L.J. Stevens

DERBYSHIRE v NORTHAMPTONSHIRE, 1981
NatWest Trophy – Final (60 overs match)

Lord's Cricket Ground, London, 5 September 1981
Toss: Derbyshire. Result: DERBYSHIRE won having lost fewer
wickets with scores level

Man of the Match: G. Cook

Northamptonshire

G. Cook* lbw b Tunnicliffe	....	111
W. Larkins c Miller b Wood	....	52
A.J. Lamb run out	....	9
R.G. Williams c Hill, b Miller	....	14
P. Willey run out	....	19
T.J. Yardley run out	....	4
G. Sharp† c Kirsten b Tunnicliffe	....	5
Sarfraz Nawaz not out	....	3
N.A. Mallender c Taylor b Newman	....	0
T.M. Lamb b Hendrick	....	4
B.J. Griffiths		
Extras (B 2, LB 9, W 1, NB 2)	....	14
	(60 overs, 9 wkt)	235

1/99 2/137 3/168 4/204 5/218
6/225 7/227 8/227 9/235

Bowling: Hendrick 12-3-50-1; Tunnicliffe 12-1-42-2; Wood 12-2-35-1; Newman 12-0-37-1; Steele
5-0-31-0; Miller 7-0-26-1

Derbyshire

A. Hill b Mallender	....	14
J.G. Wright lbw b Mallender	....	76
P.N. Kirsten lbw b Mallender	....	63
B. Wood* b Sarfraz	....	10
K.J. Barnett run out	....	19
D.S. Steele b Griffiths	....	0
G. Miller not out	....	22
C.J. Tunnicliffe not out	....	15
R.W. Taylor†		
P.G. Newman		
M. Hendrick		
Extras (B 5, LB 7, W 3, NB 1)	....	16
	(60 overs, 6 wkt)	235

1/41 2/164 3/165 4/189 5/191
6/213

Bowling: Sarfraz Nawaz 12-2-58-1; Griffiths 12-2-40-1; Mallender 10-1-35-3; Willey 12-0-33-0;
T.M. Lamb 12-0-43-0; Williams 2-0-10-0.

Umpires: D.J. Constant and K.E. Palmer

INDIA v WEST INDIES 1983
Prudential World Cup – Final (60 overs match)

At Lord's, London on 25 June 1983
Toss: West Indies. Result: INDIA won by 43 runs

Man of the Match: M. Amarnath

India

S.M. Gavaskar c Dujon b Roberts	....	2
K. Srikkanth lbw b Marshall	....	38
M. Amarnath b Holding	....	26
Yashpal Sharma c sub b Gomes	....	11
S.M. Patil c Gomes b Garner	....	27
Kapil Dev* c Holding b Gomes	....	15
K. Azad c Garner b Roberts	....	0
R.M.H. Binny c Garner b Roberts	....	2
Madan Lal b Marshall	....	17
S.M.H. Kirmani† b Holding	....	14
B.S. Sandhu not out	....	11
Extras (B 5, LB 5, W 9, NB 1)	....	20
	(54.4 overs)	183

1/2 2/59 3/90 4/92 5/110
6/111 7/130 8/153 9/161

Bowling: Roberts 10-3-32-3; Garner 12-4-24-1; Marshall 11-1-24-2; Holding 9.4-2-26-2; Gomes
11-1-49-2; Richards 1-0-8-0.

West Indies

C.G. Greenidge b Sandhu	....	1
D.L. Haynes c Binny b Madan Lal	....	13
I.V.A. Richards c Kapil Dev b Madan Lal	....	33
C.H. Lloyd* c Kapil Dev b Binny	....	8
H.A. Gomes c Gavaskar b Madan Lal	....	5
S.F.A.F. Bacchus c Kirmani b Sandhu	....	8
P.J.L. Dujon† b Amarnath	....	25
M.D. Marshall c Gavaskar b Amarnath	....	18
A.M.E. Roberts lbw b Kapil Dev	....	4
J. Garner not out	....	5
M.A. Holding lbw b Amarnath	....	6
Extras (LB 4, W 10)	....	14
	(52 overs)	140

1/5 2/50 3/57 4/66 5/66
6/76 7/119 8/124 9/126

Bowling: Kapil Dev 11-4-21-1; Sandhu 9-1-32-2; Madan Lal 12-2-31-3; Binny 10-1-23-1;
Amarnath 7-0-12-3; Azad 3-0-7-0.

Umpires: H.D. Bird and B.J. Meyer